BECOMING AN ENGAGED CAMPUS

A Practical Guide for Institutionalizing Public Engagement

Carole A. Beere

James C. Votruba

Gail W. Wells

JOSSEY-BASS
A Wiley Imprint
www.josseybass.com

Published by Jossey-Bass
A Wiley Imprint
989 Market Street, San Francisco, CA 94103-1741   www.josseybass.com

Library of Congress Cataloging-in-Publication Data
Beere, Carole A., 1944-
  Becoming an engaged campus : a practical guide for institutionalizing public engagement /
Carole A. Beere, James C. Votruba, Gail W. Wells ; foreword by Lee S. Shulman.
      Includes bibliographical references and index.
  ISBN 978-0-470-53226-3 (hardback)
ISBN 978-1-118-00996-3 (ebk)
ISBN 978-1-118-00997-0 (ebk)
ISBN 978-1-118-00998-7 (ebk)
  1. Community and college—United States. 2. Education, Higher—Social aspects—United States.
3. University cooperation—United States. I. Votruba, James C. II. Wells, Gail W.
    LC238.B44 2011
    378.1'03—dc22

                                                                            2010049431

FIRST EDITION
HB Printing 10 9 8 7 6 5 4 3 2 1

The Jossey-Bass
Higher and Adult Education Series

CONTENTS

This book is dedicated to the faculty, administrators, students, and community members who, through their public engagement commitment, and involvement, have helped ensure that Northern Kentucky University is deeply engaged in advancing regional and statewide progress.

FOREWORD

The term *engaged* carries many positive associations. We applaud students when they are deeply engaged in their studies. We take pride in professors who are engaged in serious scholarship. To engage is to be connected, committed, and invested. Yet, in the case of universities, engagement is sometimes an occasion for ambivalence. There are those who ask whether being engaged is a good idea for institutions of higher education. How could engagement engender anything but pride and satisfaction?

The source of academic ambivalence around institutional engagement derives from a long tradition that treats the special character of universities as a function of their *dis*engagement. Universities are special precisely because they are separated from the passions of the moment, the fads of the day, the flavor of the month, and those shifting political winds that so readily dominate the media. Although those outside the academy may view "the ivory tower" as an epithet, the tower's inhabitants view that very isolation as its greatest virtue. Tenure is valued in great measure because it protects faculty members from those inside and outside the academy who are so passionately engaged politically or intellectually that they would limit the academic freedom of others. A scholar can pursue basic research in mathematics, classics, or molecular biology without having to justify it with reference to its likely contribution to solving the problems of poverty, ignorance, or disease. If a university becomes too deeply engaged, some might worry, it may run the risk of trying to solve the short-term crises of a society instead of remaining focused on the longer-term mysteries of truth, beauty, and justice that are timeless rather than merely timely, enduring instead of immediate.

Nevertheless, in the face of that celebration of *dis*engagement, especially in the United States, a countercurrent developed.

Political and educational leaders began to realize how much
the talent within universities could contribute to the well-being
of ordinary people, without compromising their intellectual or
scholarly integrity. It had always been clear that some of the roles
for which universities prepared its students—in medicine, reli-
gion, law, engineering—were useful. But as the support of higher
education shifted rapidly from the private to the public sphere,
the expectation that the university itself might serve society more
directly became more compelling.

During the painful days of the Civil War, the Morrill Act
was passed by Congress setting aside federal land in each state
to be used to establish higher education institutions designed
to educate and conduct research in agriculture, mining, and
other applied fields. These land grants and the schools that were
created in their wake broadened the conception of the civic role
of universities even for institutions that were not technically land-
grant schools. Before long, the mission of universities and their
faculty members was defined as service in addition to teaching
and research. This triad of purposes was commonly articulated
in the formal statements of university missions. But did this set
of ostensible purposes yield a beautiful three-part harmony of
missions, or did it create a dissonance of competing purposes and
a competition for resources and prestige?

When I completed a PhD at the University of Chicago, I took
a faculty position at an institution that had been created a century
earlier as a prototype of the engaged university—Michigan State
University. The nation's first land-grant institution (as it proclaims
vigorously to this day), it exemplified the triad of commitments to
teaching, research, and service. I was unfamiliar with the notion
that a university's responsibilities were not only to teach and investigate, but also to serve. Michigan State took service to the state of
Michigan and to the larger world quite seriously, and, although it
also took considerable pride in its rapidly developing reputation
as a major research university, the core missions of service defined
the institution's identity. Faculty and student engagement lay at
the heart of Michigan State's narrative. It is no accident, I would
speculate, that I first met two of the three authors of this volume at Michigan State, where both Jim Votruba and Carole Beere
earned their doctorates and where Votruba later served as a faculty

member and administrator. For the authors of this book, service, engagement, and civic responsibility are more than activities; they are elements of both individual and organizational identity.

Many years later, when I began serving as president of The Carnegie Foundation for the Advancement of Teaching in 1997, one of its signature programs was the Carnegie Classification of Institutions of Higher Education. From the time when Clark Kerr and his Carnegie associates had invented it in the early 1970s, the classification rapidly became the arbiter of institutional purpose and prestige among America's universities and colleges. At the very top of the status hierarchy (though the creation of such a hierarchy was never Kerr's purpose) was the research university, especially those that attracted the most external financial support from government agencies. These institutions became known as R1 universities, the elite among those in the research category. Among liberal arts colleges, prestige was associated with selectivity, success in attracting the undergraduate equivalent of grants. Selectivity was the ability to attract the most academically elite high school graduates—as defined by SAT scores and grade-point averages. The quality or character of teaching, as well as the activities of engagement and outreach through service, were invisible as elements of the Carnegie Classification.

Thus, the wealth of dollars coming in from government to support research and the wealth of academic aptitude coming in to support the undergraduate teaching and learning were the significant indicators, and therefore the values that the university leadership, both academic and lay, attempted to raise via resource allocations, recruitment, and rewards. Nowhere to be found was teaching excellence of faculty, learning success of students, much less the amount and quality of community and social engagement of the faculty and its students—the evidence of its service and engagement.

Once we at Carnegie realized that what we chose to document was helping to drive what universities valued and where they invested their resources, we recognized that we were part of the problem. We had an obligation to create a broadened and more comprehensive form of classification that gave prominence to indicators of engagement and service, parallel to the indicators of research support and selectivity already in use. Unfortunately, no such indicators were routinely gathered and collected. In contrast to data on research support, student SAT scores, admission profiles by race and gender, or percentage of full-time faculty—all numbers that institutions were required to collect for the federal databases—the data that reflected patterns and amounts of outreach or engagement were not nationally available. If Carnegie intended to create a new classification around engagement, it would have to work with those institutions that elected to gather such information for themselves and were willing to transmit those data to a national database. To that end, Carnegie's elective classification of engagement and outreach was created, and institutions were invited to apply for membership in that classification to be included within it. When that first elective classification was published in 2008, 196 institutions were so classified. Northern Kentucky University was one of the institutions to which Carnegie turned for help in designing that classification.

I recount this story because it carries an important message for those of us who wish to see service emerge from the shadows of university life, no longer ignored by leaders and scorned by tenure committees. Not everything that counts can be readily measured, but what we do elect to measure invariably counts. Thus engaged universities will need to engage not only in the applications of understanding that their scholarship makes possible; they must also invest in a scholarship of engagement. This is a scholarship that will document how and where academic know-how contributes to the general good, how the resources of the university are employed through students and faculty to accomplish those goods, and what new knowledge and development occurs in our students and in our scholars as a function of outreach and engagement. We must learn how to create metrics of engagement that will be as vivid and comprehensible as those that currently describe the pursuit of research in labs, libraries, or in the field. We must invent indicators of the impact of engagement, rather than merely the fact that we are engaged. We must conduct studies that demonstrate over the long haul how being a student in an engaged university confers life benefits on students as citizens, scholars, professionals, and civic leaders. The practice of engagement by universities and colleges will not flourish absent the nurturing of a scholarship of engagement.

If service is at the heart of a university mission, then inquiry is its lifeblood. William Rainey Harper, the founding president of the University of Chicago, observed that in a university all topics, problems, and issues of the world should be legitimate objects of investigation. Universities survive and flourish by virtue of their commitments to raising questions and pursuing them in disciplined, scholarly, and responsible manners. If a topic is taught or thought about, it must also be investigated. And those investigations should not be limited to practices, artifacts, events, or processes outside the walls of the institution. The institution should always subject its own work to the same habits of questioning, research, evaluation, and testing that it demands from the world around it.

As the authors of this book observe forcefully, the engaged university carries a heavy responsibility for evaluation, documentation, and research on its efforts. Engagement is not only an occasion for service; when conducted by a university, it must become an opportunity for the development of knowledge and understanding. What kinds of engagement create short-term involvement and investment while others lead to long-term institutional transformation and commitment? What kinds of engagement create powerful learning opportunities for students who then matriculate as transformed citizens who will lead lives of service and responsibility? These and many other similar questions are prototypes for the kinds of inquiry that an engaged university must pursue if it truly melds its academic and its service identities.

Harper argued that universities must not only conduct experiments; they must be experiments themselves. They do not merely investigate innovation performed by others; they must innovate and then investigate the impact of their own experimentations. New and ambitious programs of university engagement are themselves critical experiments. As such the university will deploy its formidable capacity for research to study those experiments and learn how to maximize their positive impacts and limit their unintended negative consequences. We appreciate and value the benefits of disengagement for the dispassionate studies that have long characterized the life of the mind and the spirit. We now need the leadership of engaged universities to invent and sustain a scholarship of engagement so we can better comprehend the

parallel and interacting benefits of a university achieving a judi-
cious blend of reflection and outreach, of the work within and the
efforts without.

I do not believe that the authors of this superb and practical
guide to the development of an engaged university wish to see all
of university life shift from traditional academic pursuits to active
engagement. Not every course in Shakespeare or evolutionary
biology needs to become an occasion for service learning. They
are calling instead for a new and richer vision of the university in
which research, teaching, and service achieve a long-needed parity,
and where the fundamental identity of the institution should be as
rich and capacious as the identity of any wise, capable, and decent
individual human being. Universities too should be models of
conceptual, practical, and socially responsible ideas and actions.

I am reminded of a meeting I had with a group of senior
engineering students to whom I posed the question: What's an
engineer? They responded, "An engineer is someone who uses
math and the sciences to mess with the world by designing and
making useful and beautiful things ... . and once you mess with
the world, you are responsible for the mess you have made." I
love that definition of an engineer, and I see a version of it as
the definition of a good university: A university is an institution
where students and faculty develop deep understanding so they
can mess with the world ... and when they mess with the world,
they take responsibility for both the good and the problematic
consequences of what they have done. Moreover, by engaging
actively with the challenges of the society in which they live, they
create opportunities to learn and understand the world that would
not have arisen otherwise.

I know I join all this book's readers in acknowledging the
insight and inspiration that Carole Beere, James Votruba, and
Gail Wells have given to us in writing this volume. This work
will guide its readers in creating settings in which engagement
and disengagement are balanced and blended for the sake of
enhanced learning, greater institutional vigor, and the welfare of
society.

Lee S. Shulman
Stanford, California

ABOUT THE AUTHORS

Carole A. Beere retired in 2007 from her position as the first associate provost for outreach and dean of graduate studies at Northern Kentucky University, a post she held for six years. During that time, she began many of the public engagement initiatives that have become the hallmark of NKU. She has presented papers on public engagement at numerous state and national meetings, including meetings of the Coalition of Urban and Municipal Universities, the American Association of State Colleges and Universities (AASCU), and the Association of American Colleges and Universities, and she recently led workshops on public engagement for teams of faculty and administrators from more than a dozen universities. She is currently working with an AASCU task force on university-school partnerships. Dr. Beere previously chaired the boards of the Graduate Record Examination and the Council of Graduate Schools and was a member of the board of the Higher Learning Commission. She has a B.A. in business and an M.A. and Ph.D. in educational psychology, all from Michigan State University. Her career in higher education began at Central Michigan University, where she served for twenty-nine years, first as a faculty member in the Department of Psychology and later as dean of the College of Graduate Studies and associate vice president for research.

James C. Votruba has been president of Northern Kentucky University since 1997. Previously he served for eight years as vice provost for University Outreach and professor of higher education at Michigan State University, and prior to that as dean of the College of Education and Human Development at Binghamton University. Earlier in his career, he held faculty and administrative positions at the University of Illinois at Urbana-Champaign and Drake University. Much of his career has been focused on the role of colleges and universities in advancing public progress through the extension and application of knowledge. Dr. Votruba chaired the AASCU Task Force on Public Engagement, which published *Stepping Forward as Stewards of Place* in 2002. In 2004, he delivered the annual AASCU President-to-Presidents Lecture titled "Leading the Engaged University." He chaired the AASCU board of directors, served on the National Campus Compact board of directors, and was president of the Coalition of Urban and Metropolitan Universities. He is currently leading an AASCU task force on university-school partnerships. Dr. Votruba earned a B.A. in political science, an M.A. in political science and sociology, and a Ph.D. in higher education administration, all from Michigan State University.

Gail W. Wells is the vice president for academic affairs and provost at Northern Kentucky University. Her previous positions at NKU included dean of the College of Arts and Sciences, chair of the Department of Mathematics and Computer Science, and professor. Her commitment to public engagement has been manifest in each role. She received significant grants from NSF to support her work related to aligning the mathematics curriculum across the P–16 continuum and enhancing teacher preparation. She plays an active leadership role in the provosts' division of the AASCU and has presented papers on public engagement at conferences hosted by AASCU, the Coalition of Urban and Municipal Universities, and the Association of American Colleges and Universities. Dr. Wells was the 2010 recipient of the William M. Plater Award for Leadership in Civic Engagement, an award granted each year to one provost in the country who has shown outstanding campus leadership in support of civic engagement. She has a B.S. in mathematics and music from Eastern Kentucky University, and an M.S. and Ed.D. focused on mathematics education from the University of Cincinnati.

Becoming an Engaged Campus

INTRODUCTION

America's colleges and universities have a long and distinguished record of responding to the nation's call. Over the past 150 years, higher education institutions have helped increase agricultural production, contributed to intergenerational mobility, provided the workforce for economic expansion, supported national defense, promoted civic literacy, pioneered improved health care, and pushed back the frontiers of knowledge in nearly every dimension of our lives. In recent years, the public has reached out to its colleges and universities like never before. Confronted with a host of challenges that will define their future, states and local communities have called upon their higher education institutions to help advance progress related to such challenges as K–12 school improvement, economic growth, local and regional planning, urban renewal, environmental sustainability, and much more. In response, campus leaders have been thinking more deeply about the role their institutions can and should play in advancing public progress and how they can lead their campuses toward more robust and strategic public engagement.

Many books and articles have been written about public engagement: defining it, framing it, and extolling its benefits. These writings emphasize the importance of the work for the welfare of the communities, the campus, and the students. They discuss the value of public engagement and advocate various forms of institutional change in order to better support it. Yet little has been written on how to effect the necessary changes on the campus. How does the university institutionalize public engagement so it is no longer at the periphery and no longer so dependent on the support of specific individuals? How does the campus structure the elements that support public engagement? How can the institution weave public engagement into the fabric of the campus at every level? How can the institution encourage and support faculty to engage professionally with their communities? How does the institution prepare their various external constituencies for engaging in partnerships with the university? The primary purpose of this book is to help colleges and universities, regardless of their history, mission, or size, address these questions and institutionalize public engagement using proven strategies to strengthen both the quality and quantity of their work.

This is essentially a "how-to" book, showing the reader, step by step, how to institutionalize public engagement by aligning each of its organizational dimensions to promote and support public engagement. The book provides specific strategies on what one can do, how one should act, and what will make a difference. Although for simplicity sake the term *university* is frequently used throughout the book, its value is not limited to universities. The book is appropriate for all postsecondary institutions: community colleges, liberal arts colleges, comprehensive universities, and research universities; public and private; large and small.

The change strategy described in this book is called an *alignment process,* which relates to the work of Jim Collins and Jerry Porras, authors of *Built to Last* (1994). They found that companies successful over a prolonged period of time were fully *aligned* to support their vision—that is, all of the elements within the company were functioning in a way that promoted the company's goals. When correctly implemented, the alignment process described in this book will cause all of the elements within the college or university to function in a way that promotes public engagement.

INTENDED AUDIENCE

Change in higher education is rarely easy to accomplish. Significant, sustainable institutional change occurs only when there is commitment and buy-in across the campus. Thus, the intended audience for this book ranges from the president and vice presidents to various professionals in the academic, administrative, and support units of the institution. This includes deans, associate and assistant deans, department chairs, and faculty and professional staff, as well as unit directors and associate and assistant directors. The book will be an invaluable tool to guide the work of campus teams charged to institutionalize public engagement as well as a source of practical advice for individuals who seek to maximize their impact on public engagement. The advice in the book will prove very useful even on campuses that are not yet ready to fully embrace public engagement.

The book will also interest members of university governing boards and system offices, persons who need to understand how to support community engagement at their institutions, and it will interest faculty and graduate students studying higher education leadership, strategic planning, and organizational change. Those who have a professional interest in higher education, such as journalists, legislators, and researchers, will find the book to be a rich source of information for understanding public engagement: what it is and how it can be nurtured and supported on the campus, in the community, and through public policy.

THE AUTHORS' PERSPECTIVE

This book reflects three important perspectives: (a) that of a university president who has served in his position for 14 years; has a national reputation as an advocate for public engagement; has a regional reputation for engaging the university with the community; is very familiar with all aspects of the university; and thoroughly understands the critical role of the president in institutionalizing public engagement; (b) that of a chief academic officer who has served as provost for 6 years and, prior to that, as dean of arts and sciences for 5 years; is known both inside and outside the university for her commitment to public engagement; understands the rewards and challenges associated with its implementation; and has led the university's academic affairs division to increased public engagement and increased recognition for the work; and (c) that of a university's first chief public engagement officer who served in the position for 6 years; led the university's alignment process; created and implemented many of the university's initiatives to support and recognize public engagement; and fulfilled the chief public engagement officer's responsibilities as described later in this book. These three campus leaders worked closely together to institutionalize and expand public engagement at Northern Kentucky University. Together they see the big picture and the fine detail, both of which are reflected in the chapters that follow.

All three authors have spent the most recent part of their careers at Northern Kentucky University (NKU), a public, comprehensive university located in the Greater Cincinnati–Northern Kentucky metropolitan region. Opened in 1968, the university now enrolls about 15,500 students, of which about 85% are undergraduates. The balance are graduate and law students. Twelve percent of the students live on campus. The student-faculty ratio is 17:1. The median age of undergraduates is 21 and one quarter of the undergraduates are over age 25. In terms of degree programs, NKU offers 70 bachelor's degrees, 6 associate degrees, 19 master's degrees, 1 Juris Doctor, and 2 applied doctorates, education and nursing, as well as more than 30 graduate certificates. Public engagement is a significant aspect of the university's identity and reputation.

CONTENT OVERVIEW

After setting the context for expanding public engagement, the book explains in depth how to conduct an alignment analysis, examines in great detail each of the organizational dimensions that are part of the analysis, and describes how to complete the process by aligning and strengthening each of the dimensions. Although the book emphasizes the role of academic affairs, the student affairs, public affairs, and public relations departments all play key roles in expanding and ensuring the success of public engagement. The book treats NKU as a case study by sharing numerous examples from the university's alignment experiences.

Chapter 1 provides the context for the remainder of the book. It provides a brief history of higher education, with particular emphasis on outreach and public engagement. The chapter then looks at some fundamentals of public engagement: key terms, sectors that are commonly served, and possible services. The chapter continues with a description of the drivers of public engagement—both the issues and the organizations that are driving increased interest in public engagement. Finally, the chapter describes the benefits of public engagement: benefits to the institution, faculty, students, and community.

Chapter 2 provides a detailed discussion of the alignment analysis: what it is, how to design it, whom to involve, how to conduct the analysis, what to include in the report, and how to provide appropriate follow-up. The 16 organizational dimensions that make up the alignment process, along with the four levels of analysis, are explained in detail.

Chapters 3 through 11 each focus on a specific aspect of alignment. Chapter 3 deals with aligning the institution's foundational documents—that is, its vision, mission, and values—and aligning various aspects of the infrastructure and support systems, such as the institution's strategic planning; regional and statewide planning; internal and external financial support; academic and administrative policies and procedures; and other forms of support.

Chapter 4 focuses on leadership, a key factor in the institutionalization of public engagement. The chapter addresses the leadership roles and opportunities for those internal to the campus, including presidents, chief academic officers (CAOs), deans, chairs, faculty, governing boards, and unions, as well as those external to the campus, particularly statewide governing or coordinating boards and state legislatures.

Chapter 5 looks at aligning the organizational structure. It considers the importance of a *chief public engagement officer,* analogous to a chief research officer, and discusses the reporting line, qualifications, and responsibilities associated with such a position. The chapter also delineates the roles and responsibilities of offices that support service learning or community-based research (CBR); considers how centers and institutes can promote and support public engagement; and discusses standing and ad hoc committees.

Chapter 6 focuses on faculty and staff: obstacles that deter them from becoming engaged and the proactive steps that can be taken to overcome these obstacles. These steps relate to the recruiting, hiring, and orienting of faculty; methods of addressing workload issues; enhanced professional development; improved and expanded communication including the strategic use of campus conversations; the provision of appropriate support services; methods of fostering collaborations; and the use of various incentives and rewards. The chapter also looks at the roles of the department, the disciplines, staff, and graduate preparation.

Chapter 7 focuses on reappointment, promotion, and tenure (RPT) guidelines, because they so strongly influence how faculty allocate their time. The chapter suggests strategies for changing the RPT guidelines in order to strengthen the recognition of public engagement. The chapter defines engaged teaching, engaged service, and engaged scholarship; recommends criteria for evaluating them; provides appropriate methods for documenting them; and suggests processes for reviewing credentials.

Chapter 8 focuses on students, with particular emphasis on service learning and some discussion of student involvement in CBR. The chapter considers the curricular issues that relate to aligning for public engagement. It also considers the elements of a successful service learning program and discusses the issues and challenges that arise when students are engaged with the community.

Chapter 9 deals with aligning the accountability and reporting systems. The focus is primarily on addressing four questions: How can the institution document the *quantity* of public engagement they are doing? What is the *impact* of this work on faculty, students, and the community? How does a campus monitor the *quality and progress* of community partnerships? How effective are the various public engagement efforts—that is, are they *achieving their goals*? The chapter provides direction for addressing each of these questions, describes in detail a tool for assessing the quantity of public engagement, and explains how to most effectively use the data that are acquired from the various assessment activities.

Chapter 10 focuses on effective communication, which plays an important role in institutionalizing public engagement. After describing the various audiences and messages that might be addressed, the chapter provides a process for developing a strategic plan for communication related to public engagement. The chapter also provides examples of some effective communication techniques.

Chapter 11 focuses on partnerships between the campus and community. The chapter describes how to create and sustain successful partnerships and looks closely at their characteristics. The chapter emphasizes the importance of formal campus-community partnership agreements and identifies the important elements of such agreements.

While Chapters 3 through 11 looked at internal alignment, Chapter 12 looks at the public policy aspect of public engagement, with particular emphasis on state policy. The chapter talks about influencing state policy and describes the origins of Kentucky's Regional Stewardship Trust Fund, the country's first legislatively approved, state-supported public funding stream for public engagement.

Chapter 13 provides a broad summation of the book and includes advice as well as cautions for campuses that want to transform their institutions to promote extensive and effective public engagement programs.

USING THE BOOK

The book is meant to be read in its entirety; however, each chapter can stand alone, providing useful information and advice for those who have a special interest in the chapter's topic. For example, the president, CAO, and deans may be most interested in the chapters on leadership (Chapter 4) and communication (Chapter 10). Those on campus responsible for accountability will find Chapter 9 to be particularly valuable. Faculty may find the chapter on student engagement (Chapter 8) most useful. If there is a committee reviewing or revising RPT guidelines, its members will benefit from Chapter 7. The book is also useful as a reference for campus leaders confronting issues that relate to one of the chapters. Campus teams who are about to undertake an alignment analysis are urged to bring the book to their committee meetings, where it will be a good reference for dealing with various issues that will arise.

CONCLUDING COMMENTS

The alignment process is a powerful strategic tool for creating change—in this case, institutionalizing public engagement. By following the suggestions in this practical guide, colleges and universities can embed public engagement in the fiber of their institutions. Moreover, the process is adaptable for aligning the institution for any campus priority—for example, enhancing teaching and learning; improving retention and graduation rates; increasing emphasis on student research; expanding online classes; and so forth.

As will be pointed out throughout the book, the alignment process must be adapted for use on each individual campus. Campuses differ in their size, history, mission, and acceptance of public engagement as an important mission dimension. Some campuses may be ready to undertake the alignment analysis, to institutionalize public engagement; for others, as explained in Chapter 2, campus leaders will need first to lay the groundwork for a successful alignment process. Campus leaders can use the ideas and advice contained in this book to increase the campus's readiness before implementing the comprehensive alignment process. A campus that is somewhat ready might undertake the analysis and then pace implementing the recommendations to match its readiness level, which is likely to increase over time.

Finally, a cautionary note: because this book is focused on public engagement, it may suggest that public engagement should be the most important of the mission dimensions associated with higher education. That is not the intent: public engagement is only one of the important mission dimensions of the university. If this book were about research, then it could easily appear that research is more important than other mission dimensions. The authors do not intend for public engagement to replace teaching and learning or scholarly work. All are important. In fact, the authors believe that faculty are most effective when they integrate student learning, scholarship, and public engagement so that all three mission dimensions are the beneficiaries of their engaged work.

CHAPTER ONE

OUTREACH AND PUBLIC ENGAGEMENT

Understanding the Context

"The envy of the world!" (Yudof, 2008). "The crown jewels of America's human-capital economy!" (Farrell, 2009). "A ticket out of poverty!" (Clark, 2008). "The world's premier system" (Diamond & Adam, 2000, p. 151). These are among the many positive ways in which U.S. higher education has been described. In 2005, nearly 4,300 degree-granting institutions served approximately 17.5 million people in the United States (U.S. Census Bureau, 2009). Included in this mix are institutions that are public and private; for-profit and not-for-profit; urban and rural; large and small; brick-and-mortar and virtual; 2-year, 4-year, and graduate; hundreds of years old and relatively new. The accomplishments of these diverse institutions are striking. They educate the scientists and engineers; the teachers, doctors, dentists, and veterinarians; the lawyers, artists, social workers, and theologians; and the government, business, and community leaders who will serve our communities. In fact, almost every person who will play a significant role in the country's future will first acquire an education—and most likely a degree—from one of the colleges or universities in the United States. Although educating the future workforce and citizenry is the ultimate goal of higher education, these institutions do not stop with educating students. They also provide the research that drives the future, continuing education for those in the workforce, and a variety of benefits and services for their communities.

A BRIEF HISTORICAL OVERVIEW

History shows that U.S. higher education has, by and large, addressed public needs. Originally built on the British model of education, the early emphasis was on teaching, and for a period of more than 200 years, colleges focused on undergraduate education, the liberal arts, and the preparation of educated men to serve society, especially in the fields of education, law, medicine, and ministry (Chambers, 2005; Fisher, Fabricant, & Simmons, 2004; Kerr, 1991). In this way, they served the needs of their communities. Then, in the mid-1800s, the role of higher education expanded.

After the Civil War, U.S. institutions were influenced by the German model of higher education, which introduced the importance of research and emphasized the researcher whose work was supported by apprentices (Bok, 1982). In the late 1800s and early 1900s, passage of federal legislation led to significant changes in higher education. The Morrill Acts of 1862 and 1890 created the land-grant colleges that brought agricultural and "the mechanical arts" to large segments of the population. Along with training the professionals needed to support the developing nation, universities began conducting research to improve farming practices and domestic skills (Chambers, 2005). In addition, the Hatch Act of 1887 created the Agricultural Experiment Stations, which supported theoretical and applied research related primarily to agricultural production, and the Smith-Lever Act of 1914 created the Cooperative Extension Service, an outreach program that enabled land-grant universities to take research and apply it to local settings. The program also reached out to the farm population by taking instruction in agriculture and home economics to those not attending college.

The years following World War II were a period of significant change for the nation's higher education institutions. The Servicemen's Readjustment Act of 1944, better known as the GI Bill, led to enormous growth in enrollments. Universities served their communities and the nation by absorbing thousands of returning servicemen into their degree programs. In the ten years between 1940 and 1950, enrollments increased by 78% from 1.49 million to 2.65 million, and the number of degrees conferred more than doubled from 216,521 to 498,586 (U.S. Census Bureau, 2009). At the same time, the importance of research was escalating.

The commitment to research was propelled by the federal government's investment in scientific research, an investment that grew dramatically after World War II and continued to escalate after the Soviet Union launched *Sputnik* in 1957. As an example, in 1953 the federal government provided colleges and universities with $280 million to support R&D work; by 1970, that figure was up to $2.4 billion, more than an eightfold increase (National Science Foundation, 2008). Adding nonfederal support, by 1970 colleges and universities were spending more than $3 billion on R&D. With this investment, universities served society by providing the knowledge base underlying much of the country's scientific progress.

Securing federal grants became increasingly important. Faculty who were awarded grants added to a university's reputation as much as they added to its revenue stream. Graduate students— the future faculty—were most often trained at "research universities," where they were exposed to a culture that valued research productivity above all else. They took this value system with them to the diverse institutions that hired them, thereby spreading the commitment to research throughout higher education. These post–World War II changes had a profound impact on higher education. Research showed that, over time (1969, 1975, 1984, 1989), interest in teaching declined in *every type* of institution—research, doctoral, comprehensive, liberal arts, and two-year—and the importance of publication as a factor in granting tenure increased (Russell, 1992). Research and graduate education carried enhanced status. In many institutions, the concept of service moved away from service to society and was replaced with service to the institution or the profession. This shift demonstrates the profound impact of the government's significant, sustained funding for research.

Perhaps to counter the growing commitment to research, some higher education leaders began to call upon universities to pay more attention to their communities, especially the urban communities around them. Noted historian Henry Steele Commager (1960) appealed to universities to be more responsive to the needs of their cities: "[Faculty] should live in the city;

they should participate actively in the cultural life in the city.... They should be encouraged to take an active part in politics and public affairs. In all of those activities the university itself should cooperate, by making it convenient for its members to live in the city; by making the facilities available for civic purposes; by encouraging political or journalistic or even economic responsibility by members of its faculty" (pp. 88–89). Six years later, J. Martin Klotsche (1966), chancellor of the University of Wisconsin, Milwaukee, urged urban universities to apply research to address the problems of their cities, encouraged faculty from diverse disciplines to improve urban life, and even suggested that university resources should be committed to this task.

Although the calls for universities to be engaged with their communities increased over the years, public engagement was vying for attention with many other priorities. In 1992, the State Higher Education Executive Officers (SHEEO) distributed a survey to representatives of coordinating boards, governing boards, and community college boards. The survey included a list of 14 topics that respondents were to rate in terms of their importance in the coming years. The list included issues such as "Quality of undergraduate education," and "Minority student access and achievement" (Russell, 1992, p. 14). Not one of the 14 topics related to engagement! SHEEO also included an open-ended question asking respondents to list nonfinancial issues that were of concern to them. Engagement failed to attract any attention in that section either!

Change was on the way, however. Ernest Boyer published *Scholarship Reconsidered: Priorities of the Professoriate* in 1990, and his concept of four forms of scholarship—discovery, teaching, integration, and application (later called *engagement*)—began to influence campus conversations.

This brief overview shows clearly that U.S. higher education has traditionally served a public purpose, generally by preparing the graduates needed by the community and conducting the basic research upon which the nation and its communities could build. Over the past two decades, there has been a revival of interest in more directly serving the public through the extension and application of campus-based knowledge.

SELECTING AND DEFINING TERMS

Agreed-upon definitions are prerequisite for meaningful dialogue and debate, yet the fundamental terms that relate to the subject of this book are not clearly understood. Eavesdrop on a group of faculty talking about this work, and you are likely to find that they use different terms to refer to the same type of activity, and the same term to refer to different activities. In order for the campus to engage in rich and productive discussions—to avoid miscommunicating—the faculty, staff, and administrators must have a shared understanding of terms and definitions.

What should the work with outside groups be called? A review of the literature uncovers a variety of terms: *community engagement, civic engagement, public engagement, public service, community service, outreach,* and *regional stewardship*. What terms are used is not nearly as important as the need for everyone at the institution to ascribe the same meaning to the terms.

From experience, Northern Kentucky University (NKU) discovered that terms and their definitions must be broadly and repeatedly disseminated. Without this, there is a significant risk that intracampus communication will be impeded and arguing over terms will divert attention from issues more directly related to doing the work. NKU also found that definitions are most effectively communicated when accompanied by examples to highlight the scope of each term and the differences among terms.

Four important terms are defined here: outreach, public engagement, civic engagement, and community. Other terms, such as service learning, scholarship of engagement, and community-based research (CBR), are more specific to a particular type of work and will be explained in the later chapters.

OUTREACH AND PUBLIC ENGAGEMENT

Although *outreach* is an older term, dating back to the creation of the land-grant universities and their extension offices (Ramaley, 2005), NKU found it a useful term to describe work that involves reaching out to the community—work that is "one-way." At NKU, "outreach refers to the provision of programs, services, activities, and/or expertise to those outside the traditional university community of faculty, staff, and on-campus students. Outreach is one-way, with the university being the provider either on a gratis basis or with an associated charge" (Northern Kentucky University, 2006, p. 11).

After much discussion and debate, NKU adopted the term *public engagement* as the label for its partnership work with the community. NKU defined public engagement, saying: "[It] involves a partnership in which there is mutually beneficial, two-way interaction between the university and some entity within the metropolitan region [Cincinnati/Northern Kentucky] or the Commonwealth [of Kentucky]" (Northern Kentucky University, 2006, p. 11). Since originally defining the term, NKU has expanded the definition to include work irrespective of geographic location, which is consistent with how the term is used in the engagement literature.

Both outreach and public engagement are part of a continuum of activities that take resources and expertise to off-campus locations and bring the public or subsets of the public onto the campus. At one end of the continuum there is "outreach" in which the community is not involved in planning or implementation; the university has total control. Usually, the use of campus facilities, such as museums and athletic fields, and attendance at university events, such as theater and musical productions, fall at this end of the continuum. At the other end is public engagement at its purest—that is, there is complete reciprocity and total sharing of every step in planning and implementation. Most activities fall between these two extremes. This book focuses primarily on work that falls toward the public engagement end.

CIVIC ENGAGEMENT

The term *civic engagement* is sometimes used as an alternative to public engagement, but more often it is used in discussions about students' involvement in the community when a goal of that involvement is students' civic learning. That is, many student activities not only benefit the community but also develop the motivation, skills, and understanding students need to become active, contributing members of their communities. Although public engagement is the term used throughout most of this book, civic engagement is used in some instances to focus particularly on students' engagement and their civic learning.

Community

Since public engagement, by definition, involves the community, it is important to define the term *community*. This is not an easy task. In 1955, sociologist George Hillery identified 94 different definitions of community, and this was before the advent of online communities! Community is frequently defined geographically, such as a town, a county, or a state. It can also be defined by persons' identity or status, such as women or Muslims; by belief systems or interest areas, such as liberals, conservatives, or chess players; by age or occupation, such as preschoolers or mine workers; and by online connections, such as a Facebook community or a group of distance learners. Determining the community focus is an important part of institutional planning and will be discussed in Chapter 3.

Services: The Scope of the Work

Public engagement encompasses a variety of services. Although what follows describes services as being provided by one of three entities—the institution, the faculty and professional staff, and the students—it is generally the case that an activity is the combined effort of two or more of these groups.

From the Institution

The institution can serve the needs of the community in many ways, often sharing facilities or providing programs. Among the facilities that colleges and universities are most likely to share are libraries, athletic and wellness facilities, museums, art galleries, classrooms and meeting rooms, and expensive scientific equipment. Sometimes there is a charge, sometimes not.

Colleges and universities also offer programs on and off campus for the benefit of the public. These might include, for example, summer athletic or academic camps for children, health clinics, and mental health facilities. Programs might be cultural activities, such as musical programs, theater productions, or lectures, or they might be forums or debates on controversial topics. Programs may be open to the general public or serve specific audiences, such as government and business leaders. Colleges and universities also provide educational programs such as continuing education for various professional groups, noncredit adult education programs such as leadership training and English as a second language, and enrichment programs such as social networking and gardening.

The sharing of resources and programs is generally one-way rather than a partnership. Therefore, it is outreach by NKU's definition, and it is important to the university's relationship with its neighboring community. This is especially true in smaller communities where there may be limited opportunities and options. The college or university may be the major—or sole—provider of cultural and educational enrichment opportunities.

From the Faculty and Professional Staff

Faculty and professional staff apply their expertise to issues and challenges facing their community, however community is defined. They serve as board members of nonprofit organizations, speakers and panelists at community events, and jurors for competitions in various areas such as art, music, and creative writing. They conduct applied research, undertake policy analyses, and share best practices on issues confronting the community. Faculty and professional staff provide consulting help and technical assistance in program development and evaluation, data analysis, grant writing, technology assessment, and fundraising; in many instances, they actually assist community organizations with implementation in these areas. Faculty and professional staff create, implement, and evaluate demonstration programs to address particular challenges. They facilitate strategic planning activities and serve as experts to assist in planning or to enlighten controversial community discussions. They create works of art or music to support special events. They offer on-site training programs to businesses and nonprofit organizations. The list goes on and on, and the message is clear: faculty and professional staff have a great deal to offer to their communities.

From the Students

Students are engaged in the community in a myriad of ways. They volunteer, often through their sororities and fraternities, their religious groups, or their academic and nonacademic clubs. Their contributions range from one-day activities, such as painting a local nonprofit facility, to yearlong activities, such as tutoring in the local schools. During election years, they may undertake a "get-out-the-vote" campaign. Their various volunteer activities are often organized by the university's student affairs office.

In connection with credit-bearing activities, students assist with many of the faculty-directed public engagement activities, such as community-based research, program evaluation, strategic planning, specialized training programs, and a host of activities to improve P–12 education. These activities as well as service learning—a common form of student engagement—are generally tied to the students' academic courses; they are discussed in Chapter 8. Students are also involved in the community through internships, co-op experiences, and practica.

Sectors

In addressing university presidents at the American Association of State Colleges and Universities' (AASCU) 2004 annual meeting, James Votruba asked rhetorically: "What do our communities want from us?" He then explained: "Certainly they want well-educated graduates who can communicate clearly, think critically, possess a strong work ethic, and have skills that align with local employment needs. But this isn't all they want. They want us to be full partners in helping to strengthen K–12 education, expand economic development, enhance local government effectiveness, contribute to regional planning, nurture the nonprofit sector, expand the arts, improve the environment, and much more. In short, they want us to be fully engaged in helping to shape their future" (p. 4).

The sectors of the community with which a particular campus is most likely to engage are a function of the resources of the campus and the needs and nature of the community in which the campus is located. Commonly served sectors include

K–12 education, economic development, health care, agriculture, environment, nonprofits, and the government. The fact that there are so many sectors with which campuses might work highlights the importance of strategic planning, which is discussed in Chapter 3. Specifics on the selection of an appropriate partner are discussed in Chapter 11.

WHAT IS DRIVING ENGAGEMENT?

A variety of factors are driving universities to increase their engagement activities. The most significant are described here.

NEEDS OF THE COMMUNITY

Communities across the country are facing enormous problems: economic stagnation, underperforming schools, escalating costs and insufficient access to health care, increasing disparities between rich and poor, environmental threats, intolerance, and lack of civil discourse. Government, business, and education leaders are looking to their local colleges and universities to help address these problems. Although higher education should not own these problems, colleges and universities have a significant role to play. In partnership with their local community, they can apply the vast knowledge resources of their campuses as well as other campus resources such as human capital to help ameliorate community problems.

CONTEMPORARY VIEWS OF KNOWLEDGE

A powerful driver of this work centers on the concept of knowledge: both its creation and its dissemination. Traditional views suggest that knowledge is created by the objective, analytical, and experimental work of the scientist, one who is working away from the *real world*, detached from the application of his findings (Zlotkowski, 2002b). This is considered rigorous science. Donald Schön, however, argued that rigor and relevance are quite compatible and much knowledge is to be gained from what he calls *action research*. In 1983, Schön wrote: "The dilemma of rigor or relevance may be dissolved if we can develop an epistemology of practice which places technical problem solving within a broader context of reflective inquiry, shows how reflection-in-action may be rigorous in its own right, and *links the art of practice ... to the scientist's art of research"* [emphasis added] (p. 69). Twelve years later in proposing a new epistemology, Schön (1995) suggested: "We should think about practice as a setting not only for the application of knowledge but for its generation. We should ask not only how practitioners can better apply the results of academic research, but also what kinds of knowing are already embedded in competent practice" (p. 29). Schön's point is that knowledge is created not only in the laboratory but also in the real world, and in fact, he indicates that it already exists in the world of practice. Lee Shulman (1997), former president of The Carnegie Foundation for the Advancement of Teaching, supported the importance of the world of practice to the creation of knowledge, particularly for the professions: "Although a significant portion of the knowledge base of a profession is generated by scholars in the academy, it is not professional knowledge unless and until it is enacted in the crucible of 'the field.' The field of *practice* is the place where professions do their work, and claims for knowledge must pass the ultimate test of value in practice" (p. 154). Engagement work takes the faculty and the students into the real world where they create and test new knowledge in the process of applying existing knowledge.

Recent views of knowledge suggest that experts are not the only source of knowledge. In his book *The Wisdom of Crowds: Why the Many Are Smarter Than the Few and How Collective Wisdom Shapes Business, Economies, Societies, and Nations,* James Surowiecki (2004) talks about the wisdom that is found in groups of ordinary people, pointing out that their judgment and knowledge often exceed that of experts. The incredible success of Wikipedia shows that the general public believes that knowledge resides among many people, not just with the experts. And, at least some research—though not uncontested—has suggested that the error rate in Wikipedia is similar to that in sources prepared exclusively by experts (Anderson, 2006; Giles, 2005).

To keep new knowledge confined within the boundaries of academe makes little sense; it should be shared. Higher education has a strong history of sharing knowledge through publication in professional journals and presentations at professional meetings. But another way—and one with the potential for significant impact—is to share knowledge with the community by applying it to address community problems. As Ernest Lynton and Sandra Elman (1987) wrote: "As a group, [universities] need to involve themselves not only in the production of intellectual raw material through basic research but also in the synthesis, interpretation, distribution, and ingestion of knowledge so that it indeed becomes absorbed by society" (p. 14). At the same time, academics must be open to the knowledge and expertise that lies within the community. Knowledge transmission is, after all, not unidimensional.

CONTEMPORARY VIEWS OF SCHOLARSHIP

Traditionally, scholarship was equated with research, and engaging in scholarly activities meant working to create new knowledge. Boyer (1990) called this the *scholarship of discovery* and recognized its importance, but he recognized that other forms of scholarship were also important, specifically the scholarship of teaching, integration, and application, later called engagement. In interpreting and expanding upon Boyer's work, Eugene Rice (2005b) wrote about the importance of engagement. He indicated that one needs to do more than share results with the community; instead, he argued that the community should be involved from the very beginning in the planning and later implementation of a project. There needs to be *genuine collaboration*.

Although Boyer was not the first to talk about the importance of expanding the role of faculty, his book, with its four forms of scholarship, provided the tipping point that stimulated debate and discussion on many campuses. His conceptualization of these four forms of scholarship is congruent with the contemporary views of knowledge described earlier in this chapter.

CONCERN OVER EDUCATIONAL QUALITY

Both inside and outside the academy there is concern over the quality of education provided to college students today. Business leaders, for example, complain that today's college graduates lack the communication and analytical skills to be successful. Some in higher education have pointed out that lecture-based learning is of limited value. (See, for example, Howard, 1998.) Shulman (1997) pointed out: "Authentic and enduring learning occurs when the learner is an *active* agent in the process" (p. 164). As a result of these observations, there has been increasing interest in pedagogies that engage students in their learning inside and outside the classroom. Service learning and CBR are recommended as powerful forms of engaged learning. (See, for example, Antonio, Astin, & Cress, 2000; Eyler, Giles, Stenson, & Gray, 2001; Kuh, Kinzie, Schuh, Whitt, & Associates, 2005; and Pascarella & Terenzini, 2005.)

Another concern is the absence of civic learning. Although universities have historically been involved in preparing students for citizenship in a democratic society, many students and their families now seem more interested in ensuring that students acquire vocational skills. Yet, the future of a democratic society continues to rest on an informed and engaged citizenry. In the past 20 years, many have recognized the need to revive the teaching of civic skills and civic responsibility. Engagement with the community helps achieve this goal. (See, for example, Colby, Beaumont, Ehrlich, & Corngold, 2007; Jacoby, 2009.)

CRITICISMS OF HIGHER EDUCATION

In addition to concerns about its quality, the public has been critical of numerous other aspects of higher education. According to Alexander McCormick (2009), director of the National Survey of Student Engagement, the two most enduring criticisms are cost and slippage in international rankings. The public objects that tuition rises faster than inflation, especially since they often erroneously believe that faculty do not work very hard for their salaries and have advantages—such as tenure and "summers off"—that are not available to people working in other fields. Those aware of international rankings want to know why the United States is not number one in terms of the percentage of the population with college degrees and every other measure of academic achievement.

Over the past generation, the public has shifted from seeing higher education as a public good to seeing it as a private benefit.

As Boyer wrote in 1996: "What I find most disturbing... is a growing feeling in this country that higher education... [has] become a private benefit, not a public good. Increasingly, the campus is being viewed as a place where students get credentialed and faculty get tenured, while the overall work of the academy does not seem particularly relevant to the nation's most pressing civic, social, economic, and moral problems" (p. 14).

Beginning in the 1970s and continuing in many colleges and universities today, there has been a realignment of priorities away from teaching and service and toward research. The phrase *publish or perish* is recognized inside and outside of the academy, and the intense focus on research—especially basic research that does not appear to have any immediate applicability—has been the subject of stinging criticism from some higher education leaders. Zelda Gamson (1997) wrote: "We need to get over the traditional research culture that has sapped the vitality of most of our colleges and universities by drawing faculty away from commitment to their institutions and communities. The denigration of applied research and problem-solving has further eroded higher education's connection to the world" (p. 13). More recently, Richard Battistoni and his colleagues (2003) said: "Academic institutions have been engaged in what has been called 'mission creep'—the unending desire to improve the status of the institution by moving up the Carnegie ladder.... The path to excellence is obvious: get the big-ticket federal grants that will let you hire adjuncts and teaching assistants to take over undergraduate teaching, and leave the work of the university to those who can't do cutting-edge scholarship" (p. 14).

Implicit in these criticisms is the need for colleges and universities to be more involved in serving their local communities. Those quoted in the preceding paragraphs, as well as numerous other higher education leaders, have noted the importance of service to society. (See, for example, Boyte & Hollander, 1999; Kellogg Commission on the Future of State and Land-Grant Universities, 1999; and various articles in Kezar, Chambers, & Burkhardt, 2005.)

POLITICAL REALITIES

Legislators have made it clear that higher education must be accountable, and being accountable relates to holding costs down, providing quality education, producing more graduates, and serving the community. Legislators hear their constituents' complaints about the cost of higher education, and they frequently have little sympathy with the colleges' and universities' requests for more funds. As one legislator said at a statewide conference in 2008: "Universities have to pay more attention to what the policymakers want." His comment reflected his belief that universities are not responsive to community needs; they are not having a tangible impact on state and community problems.

Like the general public, an increasing number of legislators see higher education as a private more than a public benefit, and so they are willing to shift funding responsibility from the state to the individual students: between 1980 and 2008, the student's share of higher education funding increased from 20% to 36% (State Higher Education Executive Officers, 2008). When legislators see colleges and universities contributing to their communities—especially in the areas of economic development and the improvement of K–12 education—they might be more likely to support higher education.

With financial pressures on all levels of government, colleges and universities are sure to confront additional budgetary challenges. For example, local jurisdictions, such as Ann Arbor, Michigan; Durham, North Carolina; and Princeton, New Jersey, are asking their locally based, tax-exempt universities to make voluntary financial contributions to the community (Goodnough, 2009). Some communities are asking universities to pay for fire protection. In 2009, the mayors of Providence, Rhode Island, and Pittsburgh, Pennsylvania, both suggested that college students in their cities be taxed because they use city services (Marcelo, 2009; Moore, 2009). It may be possible to stem this tide if local jurisdictions find their colleges and universities bring significant benefits to the community.

WHO IS DRIVING ENGAGEMENT?

Throughout the past decade, a variety of organizations have been urging colleges and universities to respond to the needs of their communities and to strengthen undergraduate and graduate education by involving students with the community. Among the drivers of this movement is the growing number of university presidents who see engagement as serving the public interest as well as their institutional self-interest and the educational interests of their students. The presidents' promotion of engagement has been reinforced by many others.

HIGHER EDUCATION AND DISCIPLINARY ASSOCIATIONS

The Association of American Colleges and Universities (AAC&U—1,200 institutions), AASCU (430 institutions), the Association of Public and Land-Grant Universities (APLU, formerly the National Association of State Universities and Land-Grant Colleges—215 institutions), and Campus Compact (more than 1,100 college and university presidents) are among the higher education organizations actively working to encourage their members to become more engaged with their communities and to ensure that their students are developing the civic skills needed for active participation in a democratic society.

AAC&U's web page on "civic engagement" begins with the statement: "Civic engagement has become an essential learning goal for institutions throughout higher education" (www.aacu .org). AAC&U's focus is on developing "effective global and local citizens," and most of the approaches it suggests involve students directly in the community in activities that meet the definition of public engagement. AASCU encouraged institutional engagement with their communities in 2002 when it published *Stepping Forward as Stewards of Place*. AASCU's American Democracy Project, started in 2003, focuses on students' civic engagement, and now includes 230 colleges and universities (www.aascu.org). APLU's website includes a special tab for "university engagement," which links to several items related to public engagement (www.aplu.org). Campus Compact focuses on students' civic engagement: "Campus Compact promotes public and community service that develops students' citizenship skills, helps campuses forge effective community partnerships, and provides resources and training for faculty seeking to integrate civic and community-based learning into the curriculum" (www.compact.org). These are by no means the only higher education associations promoting engagement, but they are among the largest. Their websites contain information useful to those who wish to expand their students' civic engagement.

Given that faculty often feel a closer affiliation to their discipline than they do to their institution, the disciplinary associations that encourage public engagement can have a powerful impact on the behavior of faculty. Because public engagement is one of many priorities for the disciplines, it is not as prominent on disciplinary websites as it is on the websites of higher education associations.

THE CARNEGIE FOUNDATION FOR THE ADVANCEMENT OF TEACHING

In 2006, in an effort to recognize those institutions that were performing well and simultaneously encourage more public engagement on the part of all colleges and universities (Driscoll, 2008), The Carnegie Foundation added an elective classification system focused on "curricular engagement," and "outreach and partnerships." The creation of the elective classification sent a clear message that public engagement is neither a passing fad nor unique to a particular college or university. Rather it is highly valued and worthy of recognition in higher education.

ACCREDITING AGENCIES

Responsible for accrediting colleges and universities in 19 states, the Higher Learning Commission is the largest of the regional accrediting associations, making it a very powerful influence on higher education. Its revised accreditation criteria, effective in 2005, included a new standard, "Criterion 5: Engagement and Service." The criterion states: "As called for by its mission, the organization identifies its constituencies and serves them in ways both value" (Higher Learning Commission, 2003, 3.1–6). The criterion is followed by four core components, each of which is accompanied by five to six examples that make it clear that the commission requires students, faculty, and staff at institutions it accredits to engage with their communities. As an example, Core Component 5b states: "The organization has the capacity and the commitment to engage with its identified constituencies and communities," and one of the examples is: "The organization's educational programs connect students with external communities" (Higher Learning Commission, 2003, 3.1–6).

Statewide Entities

Colleges and universities, particularly publicly supported institutions, are likely to be encouraged by their legislators and their higher education boards to increase their engagement with the region and help them with the major challenges they face. In Kentucky, there is actually a *public agenda* for higher education. The heart of the agenda is a set of five questions, one of which asks: "Are Kentucky's people, communities, and economy benefiting?" Encouragement may go even further to include a requirement for accountability measures or the allocation of special funding for engagement work. In 2006, the Kentucky legislature created a special fund—the Regional Stewardship Trust Fund—which provided significant funding for the state's comprehensive universities to work with their communities to ameliorate local problems and advance the public agenda. The matter of public policy support for engagement and details about Kentucky's Regional Stewardship Trust Fund are discussed in Chapter 12.

Engaged Faculty, Students, and Communities

Faculty and students who are involved with the community are often among the strongest advocates for expanding public engagement. They experience the benefits. For example, students value experiences that let them apply what they learn to the "real world," especially when they feel it will make them more competitive in the job market. Those who have a positive service learning experience or who have discovered the value of CBR will push for more such learning opportunities. Similarly, community leaders and community organizations that have positive experiences with their local colleges and universities encourage more of this work. Community needs are vast, and when colleges and universities help address those needs, communities will push for more and more linkages.

WHAT ARE THE BENEFITS?

Public engagement represents the convergence of public interest and institutional self-interest. Benefits clearly accrue to the communities that partner with their local colleges and universities, but benefits also accrue to the institution, the students, and the faculty.

INSTITUTIONAL BENEFITS

Strong and effective public engagement activities provide evidence that the university is fulfilling its commitment to the public good and to its own mission. Compelling stories emerge from the public engagement activities, and these fuel public relations efforts that can lead to improved alumni and community relations and significantly impact revenue streams. A positive image can lead to more contracts with public and private entities and more donors willing to invest in the institution. For public colleges and universities, a positive image can lead to greater legislative support and increased appropriations. David Weerts and Lorilee Sandmann (2008) reported that a commitment to increased public engagement "was associated with increased levels of state appropriations for public research universities during the 1990s" (p. 100). Even earmarks should be easier to obtain when the university is seen as strongly engaged with the region.

A reputation for extensive public engagement helps student recruitment. As the University of Pennsylvania discovered, its public engagement "became a competitive advantage in the recruitment of different types of students, those who were turned on by the ideas and passion this commitment represented" (Rodin, 2007, p. 18).

Urban universities have a vested interest in maintaining (or creating) a local quality of life that supports the institution. Yet many of those institutions are located in areas where there are boarded-up buildings, drug rings, high crime, gangs, dilapidated housing, and underperforming K–12 schools. Universities that successfully partner with their neighborhood community to remedy these problems benefit in multiple ways. Among other things, they create a safer, more attractive neighborhood, which helps to attract and retain high-performing faculty and students.

The university benefits in other ways. When an institution is contributing to the community, business and community leaders are likely to advocate on its behalf. The community and university are likely to work together to develop strategic plans that are aligned with each other. Local expertise will be available to advise the university on program development. New grant opportunities are possible. The university is modeling good citizenship. Overall, the benefits to the institution are extensive and the risks are minimal, as long as the public engagement activities are implemented with integrity and the cautions described in this book are heeded.

STUDENT BENEFITS

Students derive significant benefits from taking part in volunteerism, service learning, and CBR. Janet Eyler and Dwight Giles (1999) observed: "The learning we saw in our service learning students was deeper than merely acquiring and spitting back a series of facts about a subject; it engaged our students' hearts as well as their heads and helped them understand the complexity of what they were studying" (p. xiv). This alone provides ample reason to engage students in the community as part of their college experience.

A review of the literature by Anthony Antonio, Helen Astin, and Christine Cress (2000) revealed that student engagement is "positively associated with persistence in college, interest in graduate study, the development of leadership skills, and commitment to racial understanding . . . higher grades . . . greater knowledge of subject matter . . . greater ability to apply course concepts to new situations . . . strengthened critical thinking skills . . . civic responsibility (increased commitment to serving the community, interest in influencing the political structure, engaging in future volunteer work, and helping others in difficulty) . . . [and] positively associated with student assessments of the relevance of their coursework to everyday life" (pp. 374–375). Not all students benefit to the same degree, however, and not all impact studies report the same results, at least partially because the quality of the student's experience affects its impact on the student (Eyler & Giles, 1999). Other benefits that at least some students are likely to derive include an appreciation of ethical issues that affect the world of practice; a better sense of self, increased self-confidence, and a clearer understanding of how to make a difference in one's community; and improved career readiness as a result of applied experiences, a better understanding of what those in the field really do, a stronger resume, some good networking connections, and a better understanding of the community and the problems it faces.

FACULTY BENEFITS

Engagement with the community benefits teaching. It influences what faculty choose to emphasize in the classroom, helps faculty remain current and keep course content up to date, reminds faculty of the relationship between what they are teaching and the real world, provides powerful examples for use in the classroom, and generally energizes faculty and enriches their teaching.

Likewise, engagement benefits faculty research. It provides new ideas for research, encourages and values all four forms of scholarship advocated by Boyer, allows testing of theories, provides access to research sites and research data that would not otherwise be available, opens up new grant possibilities, and provides opportunities for multidisciplinary and multiuniversity research. Overall, engagement invigorates the research enterprise by providing the faculty with new challenges and new opportunities.

Engagement provides faculty with many new sources of satisfaction: confronting a new challenge, using their expertise to make a real difference in the world, and testing how their theories translate into action. The faculty reduce their intellectual isolation and acquire new colleagues from their own university, from other universities, and from the community at large. Working with the community may increase consulting opportunities. Interestingly, "studies show that faculty who engage in significant consultation also score higher in the number of funded research projects, in the number of professional peer-reviewed publications, and in student evaluations of their teaching, than those who do not" (Patton & Marver as reported in Checkoway, 2001, p. 136).

The extensive benefits to faculty can lead a complacent faculty member to become energized and enthusiastic, strengthening his teaching, scholarship, service, and overall performance.

COMMUNITY BENEFITS

A project or program implemented as part of a university-community partnership should produce direct benefits for the community. However, communities derive many additional, sometimes less obvious benefits from partnering with a university. These include access to faculty expertise that can be an unbiased, trusted voice (Fogelman, 2002); access to an expanded resource base including grant opportunities and the university's physical, financial, and human resources; added credibility for jointly produced work (for example, grants, evaluation reports, and project proposals); the satisfaction of working with students; new ideas and new learning as a result of working with faculty, students, and other members of the community (Leiderman, Furco, Zapf, & Goss, 2003); access to an organization that has the capacity to convene, to bring together groups that are in conflict; and often, an opportunity to influence the university's direction and programs.

CONCLUDING COMMENTS

Given the abundant opportunities for university-community partnerships and the diverse benefits that accrue to all involved, many colleges and universities have become at least somewhat engaged with their communities. However, much of this work is person-dependent rather than an integral part of the fabric of the institution (American Association of State Colleges and Universities, 2002). Unfortunately, this means that engagement holds a tenuous position in the institution; its future is anything but secure. The balance of this book shows how to embed this work deep into the fabric of institutions so that it becomes as much a part of higher education as teaching and research.

CHAPTER TWO

THE ALIGNMENT PROCESS

There is little doubt that colleges and universities across the country have increased both their interest and their activities regarding outreach and public engagement. The drivers described in Chapter 1 have clearly been effective, but as Mary Jane Brukardt and her colleagues pointed out in their report of the 2004 Wingspread engagement conference: "Creating sustainable engagement will not be easy for it faces considerable resistance [from] institutional inertia, traditional definitions of scholarship and pressures from a market-based economy" (Brukardt, Holland, Percy, & Zimpher, 2004, p. 18). The evidence suggests they were absolutely correct.

To move forward, colleges and universities need to deeply embed public engagement in the fabric of their institutions. In too many places, it is dependent on specific individuals, marginalized, or an add-on disconnected from the institution's educational mission. In contrast, think about the research enterprise: presidents, chief academic officers (CAOs), and deans come and go, but the commitment to research and research productivity remains strong. Why? Because research is deeply embedded in the fabric of higher education, tied to the educational mission, and supported by public funding. Universities are aligned to support research. So too are the disciplinary associations. In contrast, an AASCU study of 205 institutions showed that "public engagement often has a weak link with the core academic mission, receives little or no public policy support, and is very person dependent" (Votruba, 2004, p. 6). The AASCU report observed: "There are countless stories of public engagement flourishing under the leadership of a particular president, provost, or dean, only to find that the commitment diminishes when the leader departs" (p. 6). If higher education is to sustain a commitment to engagement, then something has to change: public engagement has to be institutionalized.

UNDERSTANDING THE ALIGNMENT PROCESS

In their 1994 book *Built to Last*, Jim Collins and Jerry Porras share their findings from a 6-year, in-depth study of 18 companies that achieved and maintained high levels of performance over many years. They discovered that a major factor in the success of those companies was not that they had a clear vision but that they were fully aligned to support their vision. Collins and Porras described "alignment" this way: "All the elements of a company work together in concert within the context of the company's core ideology and the type of progress it aims to achieve" (p. 202). If alignment is key to business success, might it not also be a useful concept in higher education? NKU's experience suggests that it can be exceedingly helpful.

The alignment process—the underlying organizer for this book—looks at a broad range of organizational dimensions, some of which may, on the surface, appear irrelevant. The alignment process removes barriers, adds support, and ensures that each organizational dimension is designed to support the work. As a result, the work is no longer marginalized; rather, it is deeply embedded in the institution, and support and commitment for public engagement permeate the organization.

The alignment process is broad-based and inclusive and can lead to institutional transformation. "Transformation (1) alters the culture of the institution by changing select underlying assumptions and institutional behaviors, processes, and products; (2) is deep and pervasive, affecting the whole institution; (3) is intentional; and (4) occurs over time" (Eckel, Hill, & Green, 1998, p. 3). All four statements apply to the alignment process. The alignment process is recommended here as a way to institutionalize public engagement, but it can be used to institutionalize any change. Most recently, NKU initiated an alignment process focused on increasing retention and graduation rates.

THE ALIGNMENT ANALYSIS

The alignment process begins by taking a snapshot in time. It considers 16 organizational dimensions, determines the extent to which each is already aligned to support public engagement, and then identifies the changes needed to fully align each one. Thus, the alignment analysis is a diagnostic process that results in a road map for the future. The first phase of the alignment process contains four elements: the alignment grid, the alignment committee, the alignment analysis, and the final report.

THE ALIGNMENT GRID

As shown in Table 2.1, the alignment grid is a 16-row x 4-column grid in which rows are organizational dimensions and columns are organizational levels. The grid is a heuristic, providing a way of looking at organizational change from a systems perspective. The alignment process promotes both structural and ideological change, "the twin drivers of institutionalized change" (Hartley, Harkavy, & Benson, 2005, p. 212).

The first step in the alignment analysis is to respond to two questions for each cell in the grid: (a) "If our institution were completely aligned to support public engagement, what are the indicators that would be listed in this cell?" and (b) "Of those things just listed, which are in place today?" For example, the indicators listed in the cell that deals with "organizational structure" (row 7) at the "university" level (column 1) might include: (a) a high-level administrator who serves as the chief public engagement officer; (b) a centralized office to support service learning; (c) a centralized office to support faculty who are engaged with community partners in ways other than service learning; (d) support staff to assist faculty with the paperwork associated with community work; and (e) a process for monitoring whether faculty involved in public engagement feel that the organizational structures meet their needs. In response to the second question—which of these is in place today—there might be a service learning office, but the other indicators may be absent. A later stage in the process involves assigning priorities, as well as estimates of impact and cost, to each indicator that remains to be aligned.

TABLE 2.1. INSTITUTIONAL ALIGNMENT GRID

	University	College	Department or Academic Unit	Faculty and Staff
1. Vision, mission, and values				
2. Planning and goal setting				
3. Internal and external resources				
4. Facilities and environment				
5. Internal policies and procedures				
6. Leadership selection, evaluation, and development				
7. Organizational structure				
8. Faculty and staff: recruitment, selection, orientation, and professional development				
9. Individual incentives and rewards				
10. Unit-level incentives and rewards				
11. Rituals, awards, and ceremonies				
12. Curriculum and student educational opportunities				
13. Information and reporting systems				
14. Evaluation and accountability				
15. Communication				
16. Public policy				

Note: Not all cells are relevant; those cells deemed not relevant—which will vary by institution—should be shaded and ignored.

Source: A variation of the alignment grid was previously published as part of Northern Kentucky University's case study in *Tools and Insights for Universities Called to Regional Stewardship,* a publication of the Alliance for Regional Stewardship, the American Association of State Colleges and Universities, and the National Center for Higher Education Management Systems, 2006, p. 55.

Clearly, the answers to the two questions will be specific to each institution—that is, what one college or university lists as a component of alignment may be quite different from what another college or university lists. Furthermore, institutions will differ in the importance they attach to each item within the cell. The fact that the procedure is standardized but the cell entries are unique to each institution makes this a very flexible tool, useful for institutions of all types and sizes.

Organizational Levels

It is important to review each of the organizational dimensions at each of the organizational levels: (a) university, (b) college, (c) department or academic unit, and (d) faculty and staff. The extent to which there is alignment, and the indicators reflecting alignment, generally differ as a function of the organizational level. For example, the university may provide several different incentives and rewards for public engagement (row 9), but the colleges and departments may not provide any. Or perhaps colleges provide special incentives and rewards, but the university and departments do not. All permutations are possible, which is why it is important to review each cell of the grid, recognizing, of course, that some cells will not apply. Each college or university should decide which cells are not applicable on their campus and shade those cells to show they can be ignored.

Organizational Dimensions

Although some might believe their institution can be successful by aligning one or two of the organizational dimensions—for example, changing reappointment, promotion, and tenure (RPT) guidelines is seen as a powerful driver of faculty behavior—what is important is aligning all 16 dimensions. This process is what leads to organizational transformation and strong support for public engagement.

Consider the questions one might ask about the organizational dimensions at the university level:

1. Vision, mission, and values Do the institution's foundational documents—the vision, mission, and values statements—reflect the importance of public engagement? Are members of the campus community familiar with the documents? Do they understand how the documents relate to planning and budgeting?

2. *Planning and goal setting* Does the institution's strategic plan address how the institution will fulfill its commitment to public engagement? Does the plan identify where the institution will focus its public engagement efforts? Does the university set specific goals for each area of public engagement that is important to the university? Does the university's planning team include persons with strong interests in public engagement? Does the university's planning process include significant input from community members? Are public engagement goals repeatedly communicated across the campus?

3. *Internal and external resources* Do budget requests address whether and how the requests relate to public engagement? Do budgeting decisions consider the implications for public engagement? Are funds provided specifically to support public engagement? Given the overall budget picture, is the allocation for public engagement appropriate? Is there seed money to stimulate more public engagement? Is there strong support for seeking external grants in support of public engagement? Are there fundraising efforts in support of public engagement? Are the necessary nonfinancial resources adequate?

4. *Facilities and environment* Are appropriate facilities available to host public engagement activities on the campus? Is the campus welcoming to visitors from off-campus? Is there adequate parking for visitors? Do faculty have the space and equipment necessary for projects that address the institution's public engagement goals?

5. *Internal policies and procedures* Are the necessary internal policies and procedures in place to support public engagement? Has the institution revised its policies and procedures that created barriers to public engagement? Does the institution have a mechanism for periodically reviewing policies and procedures for their impact on public engagement?

6. *Leadership selection, evaluation, and development* Do advertisements for key leadership positions, such as president, vice

presidents, deans, and chairs, reflect the institution's commitment to public engagement? Are applicants asked to address the issue in their cover letter and during interviews? Is commitment to, and experience with, public engagement a factor in hiring? Do evaluations of leaders at every level consider public engagement? Does the institution provide leaders with professional development that relates to public engagement?

7. *Organizational structure* Does the organizational structure give adequate visibility to public engagement? Does the organizational structure give adequate support to those involved in public engagement? Does the institution know whether those who are engaged feel adequately supported? Does the organizational structure provide a way for community members to easily connect with the campus?

8. *Faculty and staff: recruitment, selection, orientation, and professional development* Do all advertisements for faculty positions reflect the institution's commitment to public engagement? Are applicants for faculty positions required to address public engagement? Is commitment to, and experience with, public engagement a significant factor in the hiring of faculty? Is public engagement a component of new faculty orientation? Does the institution provide faculty with professional development that deepens their understanding and commitment to public engagement? Do professional development opportunities provide faculty with the skills that are important to public engagement? Are there campuswide conversations that relate to public engagement? Are all faculty aware of the institution's commitment to public engagement?

9. *Individual incentives and rewards* Does the annual evaluation of faculty and professional staff consider public engagement? Does public engagement influence merit-pay decisions? Is public engagement appropriately represented in the RPT guidelines? In reality, does public engagement weigh significantly in RPT decisions? Does the institution offer professional development programs to show faculty how to report their own public engagement and evaluate the work of colleagues? Do opportunities for special support, such as funding and reassigned time, recognize public engagement as valuable and worthy of support?

10. Unit-level incentives and rewards Are there unit-level incentives to encourage public engagement? Are there rewards for those units that are most active and successful in public engagement? Does funding for partnership projects compensate departments for their indirect costs?

11. Rituals, awards, and ceremonies Do the institution's rituals, awards, and ceremonies recognize the value and importance of public engagement? Is public engagement celebrated?

12. Curriculum and student educational opportunities Is public engagement a part of students' educational experience? Do public engagement and service learning cut across the curriculum so that students can have experiences in many different disciplines at different points in their education? Does the course registration procedure allow students to identify and select those courses that include public engagement? Do students' service learning or volunteer experiences or both get transcripted? Does student affairs promote engagement in the community through various volunteer opportunities? Is there a way for students to earn special honors for completing a public engagement protocol? Are awards given for outstanding engagement work?

13. Information and reporting systems Does the university track and report how publicly engaged its faculty and staff are? Does the university track and report student engagement? Are reports of public engagement and service learning broadly shared?

14. Evaluation and accountability Do public engagement projects include clearly stated, measurable outcomes? Is there an evaluation of each project? Is there an office to assist with evaluating these projects? Does the university have a library of measures that can be used in evaluating public engagement? Are those who receive funds held accountable for achieving the promised outcomes? Do community members contribute to the evaluation of public engagement projects? Does the university consider public engagement's impact on students, faculty, the community, and the university? Does the university provide professional development regarding program evaluation?

15. *Communication* Is information about public engagement communicated internally? Are there annual reports of public engagement? Is information about public engagement effectively communicated to the external community? Does the university take advantage of the opportunity to use public engagement to boost its image? Do university leaders talk about public engagement in their speeches to internal and external groups?

16. *Public policy* Does the state have a public agenda that, among other things, expects colleges and universities to be publicly engaged? Do university officials talk with state and federal legislators about the value of the work to the community? Is there a public funding stream to support public engagement?

Although these questions are phrased as yes or no questions, the real intent is to use them to stimulate discussion. For example, under "internal policies and procedures," one question asks: "Are the necessary internal policies and procedures in place to support public engagement?" The discussion question that is implied is: "What internal policies and procedures do we need to support public engagement?" After those are identified, the next question is: "Which of these do we have?" and the final question becomes: "What do we need to do in order to have in place those policies and procedures that we are now lacking?" An example of one answer to the first question might be: "We need standardized forms for students to use before going into the community on a service learning assignment." If the university has those forms available, then the item can be checked off; if not, then this remains to be done, and in the final report (described later in this chapter), a specific office should be identified to take responsibility for developing the forms.

The preceding questions are intended as suggestions. This is certainly not an exhaustive list, and there may be other questions that are more appropriate for a particular campus. Each campus must decide its own set of questions. And after deciding which questions are appropriate at the institutional level, questions must be written for each of the other organizational levels—that is, the other columns of the grid. When the alignment analysis is complete, there should be a list of indicators of alignment in each cell of the grid (except for those that were shaded at the start of the process).

The Alignment Committee

The alignment analysis—the task of filling in the grid—is conducted by a committee, and the committee's composition significantly affects the outcome and the extent to which its recommendations will be embraced by the campus.

Committee Size

The committee size is important. If too small, there is not enough representation from the campus, not enough diversity of opinion, not sufficient knowledge to do a thorough job of completing the alignment grid, and not enough advocates to promote the final product. If too large, committee members are less likely to feel invested in the analysis, less likely to attend meetings regularly, and less likely to feel ownership for the final product. NKU found that a committee of 15 to 20 members plus the chair and a note-taker worked very well.

Committee Chair

Ideally, the committee should be chaired by someone who is: (a) knowledgeable about public engagement in general, (b) familiar with the campus environment for public engagement, (c) respectful of the broad campus perspective, (d) respected by the faculty and administration, (e) capable of providing leadership for the group, (f) available to see the analysis through to completion, and (g) experienced with systems thinking and analysis. If a campus administrator has assigned responsibility for public engagement or if someone is treated by the campus as the de facto leader of public engagement, this person may be the ideal chair. The selection process should be mindful of the fact that the chair's job is extremely time-consuming.

Committee Composition

To be effective, the committee needs broad representation from internal stakeholder groups and must include key opinion leaders from across the campus. Those selected must be willing to attend regularly and participate actively, sharing their ideas, opinions, and perceptions during the discussions. In order to include the administrative perspective, a dean should be included on the committee. If the colleges are of disproportionate size, it is advisable to have the dean from the largest college, particularly if that college is arts and sciences.

Department chairs are very important to the work of the committee and to the impact the work will have. Department chairs usually are familiar with what is happening on campus, and they know what is working and what will work with their faculty. They have a good sense of campus politics, and they generally have significant influence over their faculty. It is recommended that the committee include several chairs from different colleges, representing diverse disciplines and various professional programs.

Faculty are also critical to the process. They have credibility with other faculty and access to information that may not otherwise be available to the committee. Faculty representation from across campus, perhaps one person from each college, will energize committee discussions. Faculty thought-leaders and official leaders, such as the head of the faculty senate, are good candidates for the committee. Among the faculty and chairs appointed to the committee there should be some who are critical of or at least skeptical about public engagement. They are likely to provide a good balance for the enthusiastic support voiced by other committee members. When a committee learns about opposing views while still deliberating, it is able to modify its final report to account for these divergent views or at least prepare for the counterarguments that will be voiced. Experience suggests that the skeptics may become strong supporters once they participate in the committee discussions. When that happens, it is important to find a new way to ascertain the views of the campus skeptics.

Many campuses have centers or institutes whose mission is public engagement or service learning. NKU, for example, has the Institute for Nonprofit Capacity, the Scripps Howard Center for Civic Engagement, the Center for Applied Ecology, the Kentucky Center for Mathematics, and so forth. Larger universities have even more centers. Center directors can bring a perspective to the committee that is different from that of the faculty, chairs, and dean. They should be represented on the committee.

Because of the important role that student affairs plays in regard to students, the committee should include one or two professionals from student affairs. Those who work with student volunteers or with student organizations are likely to be good contributors to the committee. Representatives from offices such as public affairs and public relations will also add to the richness of committee discussions.

The student perspective is also important to the committee, especially when "curriculum and student educational opportunities" are being discussed. Student members should be upper-division students who have a broad perspective on the campus, understand the need for the confidentiality of committee deliberations, and are comfortable sharing their views in the committee setting. If they have been publicly engaged, perhaps by participating in a service learning class, that is an added benefit. Student government can help identify student members for the committee. If student members are not on the committee, another approach must be found to get student input into those issues that directly relate to them.

Because the committee's focus is public engagement, it seems logical to include persons from the community, but NKU's experience suggests this is not a good idea. NKU learned that the internal workings of the campus are both boring and mysterious to those outside higher education. The community is interested in partnering with the university and contributing to the university, but community members are not interested in the process by which the university aligns itself for this work. As a result, having community members on the committee is discouraged. This is in contrast to staffing the strategic planning process (see Chapter 3), which should certainly include community representatives. If community input is needed for the alignment analysis, it can be obtained through surveys and focus groups, or by inviting community members to attend when specific topics—such as external communications—are scheduled for discussion.

Note-Taker

It is critical for the committee to have a note-taker, someone who will understand the discussions and recognize what is important to document. The note-taker works for the committee chair so that she can focus on leading the meeting, confident that all important points are being documented. This may be one of the most difficult positions to staff because it requires someone with a deep understanding of higher education, someone willing to attend the meetings knowing that he cannot participate in the discussions because he has to focus on note taking. Good candidates for the note-taker position are associate deans, former department chairs, and retired faculty.

THE ALIGNMENT ANALYSIS

The initial meeting is a time for introductions, both to one another and to the task that is facing the group. The president or the CAO should give the charge, explain the importance of the committee members' work, and assure them that their report will have a significant impact on the institution. This is also a time for people on the committee to ask questions, express concerns, and share preliminary thoughts. For the committee to be effective, committee members need to understand the alignment process and have a basic, shared understanding of public engagement, both of which can be acquired through assigned readings completed before the initial meeting.

The committee meetings will very quickly get bogged down if there are not agreed-upon definitions of critical terms. There are two ways to handle definitions: (a) distribute a set of definitions at the first meeting, or (b) set aside time, early in the process, for the group to agree upon definitions. The former approach is more efficient. If the latter approach is taken, it is best to provide sample definitions for terms so that the group can build on what is already in the literature.

Setting a Time Line

Although the alignment analysis can be completed in one semester, it is best to allow 20 to 24 weekly meetings allocated as follows: one or two meetings for introductions, definitions, and discussion of the readings; one meeting for each of the 16 organizational dimensions; two or three meetings for considering timing, impact, and cost of the recommendations; and a few meetings for finalizing the report. Ninety-minute meetings have been tried but were found to be too short; people were deep in discussion when the meeting time expired. Even with two-hour meetings it was often difficult to end; people wanted to continue talking.

Using the Grid

The task of the alignment committee is to complete the alignment grid: to determine for each organizational dimension and each organizational level how the campus is and is not aligned and what needs to be done to become fully aligned. The committee also makes specific recommendations about those things that need to be done, which means developing a time line for completing each item and providing an estimate of projected cost and impact.

Before discussing any of the cells on the grid, the committee needs to determine whether the set of organizational dimensions is the right set for their campus. There may be others that should be added (for example, public safety, human resources, grants office) and there may be some that should be combined for a particular campus (for example, individual and unit-level incentives and rewards), but it is strongly recommended that none of the existing dimensions be omitted. All impact public engagement.

The committee engages in discussion of each cell of the grid, focusing on one organizational dimension (row) at each meeting and looking at it in relation to each organizational level (column). Committee discussions tend to be rich, the result of deep thinking, and highly productive, though they may sometimes seem intense, unfocused, and redundant. Committee members are likely to speak freely, even when they know their comments are being written down, as long as their names are not recorded.

When conducting its alignment analysis, NKU found that faculty members on the committee raised issues about workload and RPT guidelines at every meeting, no matter which organizational dimension was under discussion. The committee chair's task was repeatedly to refocus the discussion on the organizational dimension under consideration, but it was important that the note-taker recorded key points even when irrelevant to the topic at hand. After the meeting, the committee chair filled in the grid with the indicators discussed at the meeting. NKU found it useful to color-code grid entries. Different codes were used for: (a) indicators already in effect; (b) desired indicators that could be implemented by administrative action; and (c) indicators the committee was recommending but needed to be discussed and decided campuswide or by specific groups on campus (for example, the academic policies committee). At each meeting, an updated grid was returned to the committee members. When the committee had finished reviewing all of the unshaded cells, the completed grid had expanded to 7 pages. Later, when it was expressed as a road map, it grew to 20 pages.

Campus Conversations

A carefully selected, broad-based committee will collectively have a relatively good understanding of how public engagement is perceived and supported on the campus, but conversations across campus are still vitally important to the process. They add credibility and improve the accuracy of the alignment analysis, and they increase acceptance of the final report. There can be campuswide conversations, open to everyone, and there can be others at the college and department levels. Conversations can take place before the alignment analysis is even started or in conjunction with the alignment process. At NKU, the president and CAO hosted a series of open forums before the alignment analysis began; together they attended every forum in the series.

The Final Report

The structure and content of the final report will influence its impact. A long narrative report is unlikely to be read. What is needed is a road map that provides a straightforward plan of action that can easily be adopted and implemented. It should begin with information on the ways in which the campus is already aligned, perhaps presented in the format of the grid. This part of the report is relatively simple to prepare and provides an opportunity to emphasize the existing support for public engagement.

The second part of the report lists what needs to be done. It should be a multiyear road map for the future. The road map is most effective when presented in the order in which things should be implemented. For each item, it is helpful to include the following information: (a) an estimate of its impact (low, medium, high); (b) an estimate of its cost (low, medium, high); (c) the title of the person(s) who should be responsible for implementing the item or ensuring that it is implemented; and (d) a list of the strategies or tactics for implementing the item. Recommendations about timing and impact should be made collectively by the committee members who should be reminded that some simple, low-cost items that can be quickly implemented add to the perceived value of the road map. Timing and impact can be decided through discussion or a formal voting procedure.

Some indicators can be implemented simply as a result of actions by the president, CAO, deans, or chairs. Others need to be carefully shepherded through a review process involving various committees and councils, but someone must be responsible for taking the recommendations through the process. In many instances, the committee chair can suggest who should be responsible for each item, but these recommendations need the endorsement of the committee.

In recommending strategies and tactics, one needs to be sensitive to the institutional culture. There are differences between colleges even within a single university. For example, assume the committee recommends that colleges and departments establish public engagement goals. In some colleges, the departments will establish their goals first, submit them to the college, and the college will build its goals based on what the departments submit. In other colleges, the process may be reversed, with the college establishing its goals and the departments using the college's goals to guide their planning.

The final report should be endorsed by the committee and submitted to the university, either directly to the president or to the CAO. It is up to them to determine whether and how it will be shared with the campus. The committee, perhaps through its chair, will want to support the implementation of the report's recommendations. Exactly how that happens will be a function of the content of the report and the standard operating practices of the institution.

IMPLEMENTATION

In speaking about the British victory over the Germans at the Second Battle of El Alamein in 1942, Winston Churchill said: "This is not the end. It is not even the beginning of the end, but it is, perhaps, the end of the beginning" (www.quotationspage.com/quote/24921.html). The same can be said about the alignment analysis. Although the analysis is critically important, it is only the beginning of the process. The real challenge comes in implementing the committee's recommendations.

The president and CAO need to publicly endorse the report and indicate which recommendations they will support. To demonstrate their commitment, they will need to provide resources for at least some of the recommendations, and they will need to direct colleagues to implement recommendations in their spheres of influence. The committee's chair or a highly respected academic leader should be given responsibility to oversee the implementation of the alignment road map.

The committee should be convened at least quarterly to monitor progress on implementing the recommendations. If the alignment analysis fails to lead to change, it will have been a relatively useless, time-consuming exercise. Because committee members are broadly representative of the campus, they can help nudge people to implement recommendations that might have gotten stuck in bureaucratic red tape or faculty deliberations. The road map that emerges from the committee's deliberations will serve as a guide, but flexibility is a necessity. Some recommendations may prove more difficult to implement than anticipated; others may move forward more quickly than expected. As the campus gains experience in public engagement, the committee may suggest modifying the road map. They may add recommendations or conclude that some existing ones have become obsolete.

ADAPTING ALIGNMENT TO THE CAMPUS

The alignment process is a powerful vehicle for change, but how and when it is used will vary by institution. The process must be adapted to fit the university. Is the campus ready to accept public engagement as an important priority? Campuses will differ in their degree of readiness and their willingness to accept public engagement as an important mission dimension. Even on a single campus, departments will differ in their readiness. Some disciplines such as social work and education may feel they have been doing this work for decades while others, such as physics and literature, may wonder how the work relates to their fields. The president or CAO must judge the campus readiness for the alignment process. When the campus is ready, they can move forward with the complete alignment process. Before that, the leadership may decide to postpone the analysis, opting instead to prepare the campus and ensure that faculty and staff understand public engagement and the resulting benefits that accrue to the university, its students and faculty, and the community. They can address this topic using various communication techniques discussed in this book, such as speeches to various campus groups and informal communication with individuals and small groups. (See Chapter 10 for more ideas on communication.) Alternatively the leadership may opt to undertake the alignment analysis and develop a strategy for incrementally implementing the recommendations in the alignment analysis report. Whichever route they take, they are likely to find the suggestions in the following chapters to be very helpful.

The governing board's role will also vary by institution. At the very least, the board should share the institutional commitment to public engagement. Its members should be aware that the alignment process is taking place, and depending on what is customary at the institution, they might endorse the process at the outset. The results of the analysis—the final report or an executive summary of the report—might be shared with the board. At NKU, the governing board had endorsed the university's public engagement mission long before the alignment process was undertaken. The final report of the alignment analysis went from the CAO to the president, who shared it with the Board of Regents.

Each institution that embarks on the alignment process has to customize the process to fit its campus. In addition to the possible changes already mentioned in this chapter, the institution might modify the size and composition of the alignment analysis committee, the list of organizational dimensions and organizational levels, the timing of campus conversations, and the form and detail of the final report. The institution might even modify the process, having the campuswide alignment committee look only at one organizational level: the university. The analysis of the 16 organizational dimensions at the college level could then be done by the colleges, and either the colleges or the departments could handle the analysis for the departments and academic units and the faculty and staff.

CONCLUDING COMMENTS

Aligning the organizational dimensions for public engagement will embed public engagement deep in the fabric of the university. Public engagement will be institutionalized, but accomplishing this is a lengthy process. Creating alignment requires creating change, and change does not occur quickly, especially on a college or university campus. So although the grid can be filled in and the road map prepared in a matter of months, implementation of the recommendations will take years. One study looked only at service learning—not all of public engagement—at 43 institutions and found that full institutionalization "requires a five- to seven-year concerted effort" (Furco & Holland, 2004, p. 30).

Alignment is a process, a journey, not a place. Working toward alignment is iterative, a spiral, continually moving toward the goal but not in a smooth, linear fashion. Aligning everything in the way the committee deems important is an ongoing, ever-changing process that will never be fully "done." As circumstances change, the environment changes, the university gains experience, and the needs of the community change, the process of alignment will evolve. An oft-quoted maxim states that every organization is perfectly designed to achieve the results it achieves. Align the university for public engagement and the campus will achieve impressive results.

CHAPTER THREE

ALIGNING THE FOUNDATIONAL ELEMENTS

The institution's foundation and core infrastructure should be aligned to promote and support public engagement. This chapter looks at four elements: (1) vision, mission, and values; (2) planning; (3) resource support, which encompasses both financial and nonfinancial support; and (4) policies and procedures.

FOUNDATIONAL DOCUMENTS

Ensuring that public engagement is deeply embedded in the vision, mission, and values of the campus is critical to the alignment process. Taken together, these elements form the intellectual foundation of the campus from which all else flows.

VISION

At NKU, the vision is a one-sentence aspirational statement expressing what the university will be at some indeterminate future time. The importance of public engagement and the university's commitment to its region and state are clearly evident in the statement: "Northern Kentucky University will be nationally recognized as the premier comprehensive, metropolitan university that prepares students for life and work in a global society and provides leadership to advance the intellectual, social, economic, cultural, and civic vitality of its region and of the commonwealth" (Northern Kentucky University, 2009, p. 3).

Many other universities also include engagement in their vision statements. For example, North Carolina State University's vision statement includes the following sentence: "As an engaged research university, NC State will be a leader in collaborating with community, business, and government partners to develop informed policies and pursue bold strategies" (http://www2.acs.ncsu.edu/UPA/strategicplan/Final%2006_08_06.pdf). The University of Alaska at Anchorage's *Vision 2017* indicates that the university will be known for nine characteristics, one of which is: "Its role as public square: the extent and quality of its community engagement, its partnerships with public and private institutions, and its support for critical inquiry, public debate, and creative expression" (http://www.uaa.alaska.edu/strategicplan/upload/StrategicPlan_8pg.pdf).

MISSION

As Charles Dominick (1990) pointed out: "Mission is purpose. A statement of mission is a statement of intent, of direction. It serves as a guide for institutional decision making. A college or university that is clear about its mission can more easily choose among competing goals and can more readily establish its priorities than can one that is uncertain about its mission" (p. 30). Institutions that wish to make significant progress in public engagement will need to ensure their mission statement reflects this priority. After looking at 23 case studies completed between 1994 and 1998, Barbara Holland (1999) concluded: "No cases were found where institutions had been successful in adopting significant academic or organizational changes in the absence of a clear consensus on mission" (p. 62).

An institution is most likely to be successful in changing its mission statement if the following conditions are met: strong leadership from the president who has the support of the governing board to change the mission statement; input from diverse stakeholder groups including faculty, staff, current students, alumni, administrators, community members, the local governing board, and where it exists, the system board; and an approval process that results in buy-in from key stakeholders as well as from the governing board that has official authority over mission. The process of changing the mission provides an excellent opportunity to engage faculty and staff in deliberative discussions about public engagement and its role in the university's future.

A university's mission statement should be "realistic, operational, and sensitive to the unique characteristics and strengths of the institution" (Diamond, 1999, p. 3). It should be specific enough to provide clear guidance for goal setting (Holland, 1999). All too often, mission statements are not specific, and a mission statement for one university could apply equally well to hundreds of other institutions. Although it is true that for all universities the "fundamental mission is to promote learning" (Votruba, 1996, p. 28), an institution can differentiate itself by expressing how and where it promotes learning. For example, promoting learning through its application in the community is public engagement: if that is a priority, it should be reflected in the mission statement.

NKU's mission statement is several paragraphs long, with more than 25 percent focused on public engagement. The following excerpts differentiate NKU from many other universities and leave no doubt that public engagement is a very high priority: "The university supports multidimensional excellence across the full breadth of its work: teaching and learning, research and creative activity, and outreach and public engagement"; "The university embraces its regional stewardship role as reflected in its significant contribution to the intellectual, social, economic, cultural and civic vitality of the region and the commonwealth"; "emphasis on active learning, including student research, internships, co-op programs and service learning"; and "the university values its role as an integral part of the metropolitan region and recognizes the region as a powerful source of knowledge and experience that can strengthen, enhance and enrich every aspect of the university. Regional stewardship informs every dimension of the university's mission" (Northern Kentucky University, 2009, p. 3).

Many other universities include public engagement, directly or indirectly, in their mission statement. For example, LaGuardia Community College of the City University of New York includes the following as part of its mission statement: "Preparing students to become full participants in the economic and civic life of the city, the nation, and the world" and "Cultivating partnerships with business, community groups, government, and public schools to enhance the economic, social, cultural, and educational development of Western Queens and New York City" (http://www.lagcc.cuny.edu/about/mission.aspx); the University of Denver's mission statement includes this: "Our active partnerships with local and global communities contribute to a sustainable common good" (http://www.du.edu/chancellor/vision/); and Penn State's mission includes: "As Pennsylvania's land-grant university, we provide unparalleled access and public service to support the citizens of the Commonwealth. We engage in collaborative activities with industrial, educational, and agricultural partners here and abroad to generate, disseminate, integrate, and apply knowledge that is valuable to society" (http://www.psu.edu/ur/about/mission.html).

Developing a mission statement with a clear commitment to public engagement is important but not sufficient to advance the work. It is equally important that the university *lives* its mission. That is, its enacted mission, what it actually does, has to match its espoused mission, what it says is important (Kuh, Kinzie, Schuh, Whitt, & Associates, 2005).

The mission statement is the glue that connects the work of the university. It provides the rationale, the direction, the motivation, and the commitment. Given its pivotal role, the mission must be broadly and repeatedly communicated to all constituent groups through a variety of outlets such as presidential speeches, university publications (for example, annual reports, alumni magazines, college newsletters), and posters on campus bulletin boards. This increases the chance that there will be congruency between the espoused and enacted missions and provides a solid backdrop for strategic planning and decision making.

VALUES

It is not unusual for a university to have a stated set of core values: overarching, enduring principles that change little over time. The statement of values provides an additional opportunity to articulate the institution's commitment to public engagement. For example, NKU has agreed to eight core values, one of which is: "Public engagement that advances the progress of the region and commonwealth" (Northern Kentucky University, 2009, p. 3). In order to ensure that the values are known by the entire NKU community, they are printed, framed, and posted in all campus buildings. In addition, an abbreviated version of each value is printed on the back of all business cards.

Virginia Commonwealth University is another university that includes public engagement among its core values: "VCU is *one* university with a common future, that is engaged with and committed to the community of which it is a part" (http://www.vcu.edu/cie/pdfs/VCU_2020_final2.pdf).

STRATEGIC PLANNING FOR THE CAMPUS

Because the needs and wishes of a community generally far exceed the local university's capacity to respond, a planning process is needed to identify the institution's public engagement priorities. Planning is generally conducted after the vision and mission have been established, but some recommend reversing the procedure (Rowley, Lujan, & Dolence, 1997). Regardless of the sequence in which they are created, there must be total consistency among them.

Planning for public engagement must be considered in conjunction with the institution's other priorities, such as supporting research, increasing enrollments, and involving students in study abroad. The planning process should focus the institution's public engagement by considering the community's needs, existing university strengths, the institution's willingness to build capacity, and the attendant benefits to the institution, its students, and the region. For example, in most communities, working to strengthen the local schools meets an important community need, provides opportunities for students and faculty in numerous disciplines, and has the added benefit of strengthening the academic preparation of students likely to be applying for college admission in the future. Moreover, it represents an issue that has high political saliency. Strengthening K–12 education could be one of a limited number of public engagement priorities. Absent specific priorities, there is a danger that the institution's work will be too scattered to have a significant impact.

The strategic plan can specify the sectors to be served, such as education in the example just given, or go a step further and identify the specific projects that will be supported. The plan should identify the "public" in public engagement—that is, will the focus be local, regional, statewide, national, international, or some combination of these?

The process for developing the plan affects the outcome and sends a powerful message to the various stakeholder groups. The process should have the enthusiastic support of the governing board and seek input from a broad array of stakeholders: campus stakeholders include faculty, staff, administrators, and students; regional stakeholders include community leaders, local educators, business leaders, legislators, system office leaders, alumni, and donors. This process enables the university to understand the needs, wishes, and expectations of the different groups and identify opportunities for collaboration between campus and community stakeholders.

VISION, VALUES, AND VOICES

NKU has successfully used a planning process that is built on broad input from the campus and community. Called *Vision, Values, and Voices* (VVV), the process is jointly led by the university president, the CAO, and the prior year's recipient of the outstanding faculty award. Their committee includes faculty, staff, students, alumni, and community representatives. To guarantee broad representation, persons are selected from different levels of the campus organizational structure. This ensures that what is learned is filtered through diverse perspectives, and when the process concludes, it lends credibility to the final plan and creates champions for the plan at different levels of the organization.

The process has been used effectively at NKU three times, each five years apart. For the first VVV, initiated soon after the president's arrival, the committee met with more than 550 people in groups of 10 to 30. There were 35 such meetings—called "conversations" by the president—about half held on campus, each targeting a different campus group, and half with community members, each at a different off-campus location (for example, the county courthouse of a rural community 60 miles from campus, the cooperative extension office of a nearby community, and a downtown meeting room in a facility frequented by business leaders). The university president chaired the meetings, which in itself sent a powerful message about the importance of campus and community input. The meetings were held during a 90-day period, with each meeting typically lasting two hours. Campus meetings focused on identifying what the university does well, where it must improve, and what new opportunities are anticipated. At the community meetings, the first hour was devoted to identifying the aspirations and needs of the community; the second sought community input on how the university could support regional progress. The president concluded each meeting with a summary of the major points he heard during the meeting, thereby demonstrating that he was carefully listening to what was said. A note-taker took detailed minutes at each meeting. When the VVV process was repeated five and ten years later, the university also sought an assessment of the progress made on the issues raised five years earlier.

The VVV committee acquired a solid understanding of the needs, priorities, and concerns of the different constituent groups. In a two-day retreat they reviewed the meeting minutes and discussed what they heard. Not surprisingly, the diverse makeup of the VVV committee led to different interpretations of what was said, which in turn led to rich conversations. By the end of the retreat, the committee had integrated and synthesized what they heard, and identified the elements that would make up the university's five-year strategic plan.

Although the VVV process is time intensive and may be seen as a burden by university presidents, it reaps enormous benefits for the institution and its president—especially if the president is new—because it offers rich insights into the community and campus. If the campus is to take the strategic plan seriously, the president must be personally involved in its development; he cannot delegate this responsibility. The VVV approach involves the president at a deep level while still ensuring broad campus and community input. The process institutionalizes campus-community interaction and builds rapport that is likely to benefit relations between the two. Campus stakeholders at all levels learn that the top leadership is interested in listening and responding to their concerns and ideas, and community stakeholders learn that the campus is interested in listening and responding to the needs of the public. At the same time, the community is reminded of the centrality of the campus to the region and the benefits that can accrue from having a college or university in its midst.

VVV creates lasting impressions. Ten years after NKU's first VVV, a local business leader was still commenting how impressed he was that the university president came to the community and focused on learning about their needs and aspirations, unlike events he had attended at other universities where the focus was on what the university needed.

USING THE PLAN

Once the strategic plan is developed, there has to be time for comment at various levels of the university, and the plan has to be formally approved; after that it must be widely distributed and then used to guide decision making and actions. As the president of a large, private-sector company told NKU's president: "Everyone has a strategic plan; success is a function of execution." All too often, much time and effort are invested in developing a plan, only to have it sit on a shelf. The president and vice presidents bear the responsibility for preventing this. At the same time, they must recognize that when conditions change, when unanticipated opportunities or obstacles arise, they may need to alter the plan.

After the strategic plan is approved, the CAO should ask the colleges and departments to submit written plans describing how they will contribute to meeting the institution's goals. The CAO should emphasize the importance of having every unit address the full breadth of the mission and require each unit to submit goals, strategies, and assessment plans for each of the major mission dimensions.

Departments and colleges must determine how they will fulfill their public engagement responsibilities. How will they integrate public engagement into the curriculum? Which classes will incorporate service learning? Will all faculty be involved with the community? Will a subset of the faculty be assigned the responsibility for the entire unit and will they get "credit" toward their workload? Does the department or college need to build additional capacity in some areas in order to address the public engagement goals of the institution? How will public engagement affect RPT (a critically important topic that will be discussed in detail in Chapter 7)? Recognizing that not all faculty have the talent for this work, NKU emphasizes that all units, rather than all individuals, must be publicly engaged in ways that are appropriate to their discipline.

To close the circle on the institution's strategic plan and the individual unit plans, the institution must monitor the extent to which plans are implemented and goals are achieved. Strategies for improvement should be integrated into revised plans. When it comes to public engagement goals, the monitoring process is a good task for a joint university-community advisory group.

OTHER PLANNING INITIATIVES

Although the campus will be affected most by its own strategic planning work, two other planning efforts should be considered. The first is regional planning. When the region in which the university resides has a plan, it should be shared with the campus and used to inform the university's priorities. Where no such plan exists, university leaders ought to encourage the community to develop a plan. A multiyear regional plan helps the university know how best to align with the needs of the region. If there is no plan and if priorities are continuously shifting, it is more difficult for the university to set a long-range course. As will be explained in Chapter 4, NKU derived numerous benefits from its involvement in the region's strategic planning process, especially because NKU's president co-chaired the process.

Statewide planning is also helpful and benefits the campus in several ways: the institution knows the state's priorities, has a rationale for requesting funding in support of the priorities, and can anticipate how to document its contribution to advancing the state's agenda. When public engagement is part of the statewide agenda for higher education, it follows that it should be part of the strategic plan for the university.

Financial Support

In the fall of 2008, AASCU conducted a survey of the campus coordinators for the American Democracy Projects, a national civic engagement initiative involving 230 colleges and universities. Responses were obtained from 61 coordinators, who were asked: "In terms of resources, what does your project need most?" (Bentley, Dunfee, & Olsen, 2009). The number one response was "funding." The second most popular response was "staff members and faculty positions," which is a function of funding. These results are not at all surprising. Most often public engagement does not generate revenue; it is a cost center. Furthermore, it lacks the state and federal revenue streams that support the other two major mission dimensions: teaching and research. If the institution is truly serious about increasing its public engagement, there must be appropriate funding for the work.

What are the funding needs for public engagement? Although this will vary by institution, some needs tend to be common across campuses:

- Funding for infrastructure including money for leadership positions, facilitative offices, and centers and institutes, all of which are discussed in Chapter 5
- Internal grants, including course development grants that may include reassigned time for the faculty, seed grants or project grants for faculty work with the community, and university-community partnership grants, all of which are time-limited commitments
- Direct support for major, often multidisciplinary, initiatives
- Matching funds for external grants
- Scholarship support for engaged students

The list of potential funding sources includes internal reallocation; existing internal grant programs whose guidelines allow support for public engagement; new base funding or special one-time money from the state or system office; gifts from individual or corporate donors; grants from the federal or state government or from private foundations; contributions or cost sharing from community partners; fee-based, contract work; income from licensing, royalties, memberships, or sale of materials; and overhead from grants and contracts (Walshok, 1999). Unfortunately, despite the relatively long list of options, funding for public engagement is generally in very short supply. Institutions must make a concerted effort to ensure there is adequate funding to achieve the university's public engagement goals.

INTERNAL FUNDING

It is often said that you can tell what an organization values by looking at its budget. In order to achieve institutional goals, the budget process and the budget itself should be aligned with the institution's mission and strategic plan. Does the process take account of the relationship between a budget request and the institution's strategic goals—in this case, public engagement? Does the budget process encourage or inhibit cross-unit collaboration, which is often essential to public engagement? Will people be reluctant to request funds for collaborative projects because they see it as competing with funds needed for their own unit?

The commitment of institutional funds for public engagement provides both symbolic and substantive support. Allocating base funding communicates that public engagement is not a passing fad but an enduring commitment on the part of the university. Reallocating funds for public engagement sends a particularly powerful message because it says that public engagement is more important than whatever was previously funded. Not surprisingly, this will please those committed to public engagement but may upset those who feel that funds were taken from them. However, as long as the administration uses the mission and strategic plan to guide its funding decisions, their decisions can be readily justified to the campus. This underscores the important role of mission and strategic plan in decision making.

New and existing internal grant programs can facilitate public engagement. These programs are particularly important because they serve as "'green carrots'—financial incentives" (Brukardt, Holland, Percy, & Zimpher, 2004, p. 16) to encourage faculty to undertake public engagement and build students' civic engagement into their courses.

Guidelines for existing faculty grants should not overlook public engagement. For example, if the university offers summer grants for faculty, the guidelines should allow the support to be used for public engagement. New grant programs can be tied to a specific sector (for example, grants to work with the local schools) or serve a more general use (for example, grants for new university-community partnership projects). NKU's university-community partnership grants exemplify an internally funded grant program. With a yearly budget of $200,000, this program annually supported four or five large projects, each lasting one to two years. For example, the program funded a history professor who partnered with a local city government to research, preserve, and open a Civil War site and accompanying museum, and a nursing professor who partnered with the local health department and several other organizations to implement community-based primary and secondary prevention strategies designed to reduce and ultimately eliminate the presence of lead in local areas designated as high risk for lead poisoning. The success of each of these was a direct result of the work of many university students who contributed much and benefited greatly from these community-based projects.

If a faculty committee determines which grant proposals to fund, it may enhance the stature of the award because the proposals are peer-reviewed. It may also create a core group of faculty—the committee members—who strongly support public engagement and understand its impact on faculty work. However, when administrators determine which proposals to fund, they can control the direction of the institution's public engagement, ensuring that it aligns with the institution's priorities, and it lets them directly influence the quality of the projects undertaken. The benefits of the two approaches can be achieved by combining them: have the faculty committee make recommendations to the CAO, who has final decision-making authority.

When faculty receive grants, whether they are internally or externally funded, there are at least incidental costs and inconveniences that accrue to the home department. As a result, department chairs may be ambivalent about supporting and encouraging public engagement grants. Their ambivalence is often overcome by adopting the federal practice of adding "overhead costs" to a funded grant. NKU's university-community partnership grant program provided 20 percent overhead to the home department of each funded faculty member.

Much can be learned about a university's priorities during times of declining resources. It is important that cuts to public engagement not exceed cuts to other priority areas. Otherwise, faculty are likely to become cynical about the extent to which the work is really valued. If it is necessary to cut budgets, the university should consider narrowing the focus of its public engagement, concentrating on fewer areas or fewer initiatives. Both the internal and external communities are generally aware when university budgets must be reduced, and they are likely to understand the need to scale back. Above all, the institution should not eliminate public engagement or the infrastructure that supports it, because those actions undermine the community's trust in the university and the campus's belief that the work is an enduring priority.

External Funding

Whether the funding comes in the form of grants, gifts, or new allocations from the state, external funding can make the difference in whether an institution can achieve its public engagement goals. Though there are exceptions, external funds are most likely to support specific projects, leaving internal sources responsible to support the infrastructure. The type of external funding sought determines who at the university is responsible to pursue a particular opportunity.

Grants

Faculty and program directors are usually responsible for applying for federal, state, and foundation grants. The university's research office can help identify both governmental and private funders using free databases such as the federal government's *Grants.Gov* (http://www.grants.gov/applicants/find_grant_opportunities .jsp), and subscription-based databases such as AASCU's *GrantSearch* (http://www.aascu.org/grcinfo/) and InfoEd's *SPIN* (http://www1.infoed.org/modules/grantsAndContracts.cfm). Two federal agencies that have previously provided significant support for public engagement are the U.S. Department of Housing and Urban Development (HUD) (http://www.hud.gov/progdesc/copc.cfm) and the Corporation for National and Community Service (http://www.nationalservice.gov/). However, when the occupant of the White House changes or there are changes in the nation's priorities, there tend to be changes in federal funding opportunities: existing ones may be eliminated and new ones added. Similarly, over time, there are changes in the priorities of private foundations. Among the largest foundations that have supported public engagement in the past are the Pew Charitable Trusts, Ford Foundation, Kettering Foundation, Lilly Foundation, and the W. K. Kellogg Foundation (Zlotkowski, 2002a). It is important to monitor the funding opportunities to know which funding programs will be available when the campus is ready to seek funds.

Grant funds, whether internal or external, are valuable for starting a project or supporting a project of finite length. For an ongoing project, however, one must consider what will happen when the funding is gone. Promises that the project will be self-supporting should be viewed with great skepticism, and a business plan should be required to show exactly how that will occur.

Gifts

Unless public engagement is a fundraising priority for the institution, it is difficult to argue that the work itself is a priority. Prospective donors may be approached by the president, vice presidents, deans, directors, and chairs, always working in collaboration with the staff of the university office charged to coordinate fundraising. Because public engagement initiatives provide direct benefit to the community, gifts in support of public engagement may actually be easier to secure than gifts in support of other campus initiatives. Donors may feel they are getting "double mileage" from their gifts—supporting their local university and their local community. An excellent example is the Mayerson Student Philanthropy Project, which is supported by the Manuel D. and Rhoda Mayerson Foundation and has operated at NKU for more than a decade. In this program, each participating course section is given $4,000, which is often supplemented with money raised by students and their faculty. Students enrolled in the class identify a community need that relates to their course content, search for nonprofits that address the need, and then issue an RFP to those nonprofits. Once they receive the proposals, the students serve as the proposal review committee, determining what they will fund. The students award the money at a formal ceremony at the end of the semester. The Mayerson program benefits both the community agencies that receive the funds and the students involved in the program. These students learn about philanthropy, nonprofits, and the vast needs of the community, and they develop an understanding of the project's relationship to their program of study. The program has been effectively used with courses from more than a dozen disciplines, including art, nursing, English, sports management, and public administration.

State Funding

Although many people may provide assistance or support, securing additional funding from the state is primarily the responsibility of the president and the government relations officer. Their chance of success increases when they provide concrete evidence of the benefits that accrue to the community from public engagement, especially when community and business leaders assist in delivering the message. A coordinated effort involving several universities in the state may be more effective than one university acting alone. Moreover, if there is a system board, it can either coordinate the message or serve as the spokesperson for a message that is then echoed by the university presidents. Securing state funding is discussed in more detail in Chapter 12.

Federal Funding

The federal government's significant and long-standing support for research shows unequivocally that federal funding can have a profound effect on university priorities. At this time, the federal government provides limited support for public engagement, but college and university presidents, working with national higher education organizations, have the potential to sway federal decision makers in the direction of supporting more public engagement.

OTHER INFRASTRUCTURE SUPPORT

Although funding is most critical for public engagement, other resources are important to the success of the work. Space must be allocated for offices directly related to public engagement. Where these offices are placed sends an important message to the campus. Locating them centrally says the work is important; locating them on the periphery of the campus says it is not. Offices that deal with student engagement, such as a service learning center, should be convenient for students. In addition to providing office space, there should be a comfortable space for those involved in public engagement to interact and learn from each other (Walshok, 1999).

The availability of support staff can make a huge difference in a faculty member's willingness to become involved. Most faculty already feel overloaded, so they may be disinclined to take on projects that require them to spend time on administrative tasks they are ill-prepared to carry out or are a poor use of their time, such as filling out forms, managing budgets, and scheduling meetings. The availability of support staff to reduce this administrative burden positively affects faculty motivation.

Public engagement, especially that which involves students, also raises legal questions and risk management issues. Are faculty provided with forms for students to sign, showing they understand their risks and obligations? Is someone available to review contracts between the university and a community partner? Does the university have an orientation program for students going into the community, letting them know how to report something they perceive as questionable regarding the law, ethics, or standards of behavior, either on the part of their fellow students or on the part of those at the agency where they are placed? Do faculty have a place to take their legal questions about the work they are doing? Are they provided with insurance that covers them in the field? Do they assume any personal liability when taking students into the community? There must be infrastructure support to address these and other legal and risk management issues.

Transportation is unlikely to be a barrier for faculty, but it can be a major issue for students. How do students without cars get to the sites where they will be engaged? Is transportation available or should the sites be limited to those within walking distance from the campus? Are there vans or buses available for taking large groups into the community? For example, NKU takes performing arts students into rural communities to perform for K–12 students during the school day and for the community in the evening. The goal is to build greater awareness of higher education and to provide cultural events in communities where residents are unlikely to see high-quality, live musical or theater performances. To reach the rural communities, buses are needed to transport the students and their equipment.

A related issue is parking. If faculty leave campus to work with a community partner, will they find a place to park when they return? Is there sufficient visitor parking to allow community partners to meet on campus? Is there a charge for parking? If so, it may be offensive to some and a major obstacle for low-income persons who are part of a campus-community partnership project. Solving transportation problems is another way of providing infrastructure support.

Various other offices can make a difference to the quantity and success of public engagement. For example, depending on the particular project, services may be needed from information technology, accounting, human resources, career services, public safety (police), or the counseling and health centers. Writing proposals, developing contracts, and creating budgets are time-consuming and require special expertise that is generally available somewhere on campus. If the campus is aligned to support public engagement, these services must be readily available for those doing the public engagement work.

POLICIES AND PROCEDURES

As part of the alignment analysis, the alignment committee should review the institution's "internal policies and procedures" (row 5 in the alignment grid) to determine whether they facilitate or impede public engagement. However, considering the vast number of policies and procedures at a university, it is unlikely the committee will have time to thoroughly review all policies and procedures. It might be helpful to have a special ad hoc committee that reviews them after the alignment committee finishes its work.

They may find, for example, that policies work against providing some of the support discussed earlier. Perhaps the university does not provide the necessary insurance coverage for faculty to engage in this work; maybe public engagement is a low priority for reserving university vehicles; parking rules might prevent community partners from coming to campus; perhaps reimbursement policies are unnecessarily cumbersome; or maybe the institution charges for the use of its space when the community is involved. Obstructionist policies and practices need to be revised; new policies and practices may need to be written.

Besides considering administrative policies, the alignment committee should examine academic policies to determine their impact on students' public engagement, especially their participation in service learning classes. Are standards in place for designating courses as service learning courses, and do those standards make it likely that students will have a meaningful experience? Can students identify service learning courses before they register for classes? Do students get "credit" for service learning experiences? These issues will be explored more fully in Chapter 8 which deals with students' public engagement.

CONCLUDING COMMENTS

This chapter has considered the first five rows of the alignment grid: vision, mission, and values; planning and goal setting; internal and external resources; facilities and environment; and internal policies and procedures. For the campus to succeed in advancing public engagement, alignment of these organizational dimensions is critical. At the same time, numerous other campus priorities compete for their place in relation to these five dimensions. It falls to the campus leadership to weigh the needs, the importance, and the benefits associated with each of the priorities and ensure that the infrastructure supports each in ways that are appropriate for the campus.

CHAPTER FOUR

ALIGNING LEADERSHIP

Strong leadership is critical to a successful alignment process and to promoting an institutional commitment to public engagement. In addition to being good managers, leaders must establish the vision, align the players, and motivate and inspire, all of which leads to change (Kotter, 1996).

CAMPUS LEADERSHIP

When a campus is aligned as described in Chapter 2, public engagement is a factor in the hiring and evaluation of leaders in every division of the institution and at every level (president, vice presidents, college deans, unit directors, and department chairs). During the course of their tenure, campus leaders are provided with professional development experiences that deepen their understanding of public engagement and expand their knowledge of how best to support the work.

A vibrant campus has official leaders, such as the president, vice presidents, and deans, who are leaders by virtue of their positions; it has others who function as leaders because they are respected by the faculty and staff and serve as key opinion makers (Curry, 1992). Several authors imply that the most important leadership for creating change comes from the top, from presidents, vice presidents, and deans (Lynton & Elman, 1987; Percy, Zimpher, & Brukhardt, 2006). Peter Eckel and his colleagues (1999) noted: "Change directed from the top generally happens more quickly than that which percolates up from the bottom," but they also noted: "Change that comes from a group may elicit broader support because it takes place after wide-ranging participation by those affected" (p. 2).

Experience at NKU, as well as informal conversations with colleagues elsewhere, strongly suggests that change is most likely to occur when there is consistency and collaboration between the administrative views and the faculty and staff views. Little change will occur if the president and CAO are advocating engagement but the faculty and staff dismiss the message. Who then would be the implementers? Conversely, if the faculty and staff are interested in public engagement, little change will occur if the administration fails to fund, reward, and promote the work. Thus top-down or bottom-up is a false dichotomy: leadership and support are needed in both directions.

ROLE OF CAMPUS LEADERS

In order to achieve success, campus leaders at all levels must assume responsibility for promoting and supporting public engagement. They should cooperate in the alignment process, helping to implement the recommendations that emerge from the alignment analysis. They should serve as role models, working in partnership with the regional community. This effort not only demonstrates their commitment to public engagement but also improves their understanding of the local community. Campus leaders should support the public engagement of others, attending events and participating in celebrations of the work. They have a responsibility to foster discussion and debate about the university's proper role vis à vis public engagement.

Two significant but sometimes overlooked roles for campus leaders are those of translator and educator. Faculty tend to have very heavy workloads. They rarely interact with trustees, system boards, or legislators, and their academic reading generally focuses on their discipline. Acting as educators, campus leaders can help faculty appreciate the importance of public engagement and understand its intellectual underpinnings, familiarize them with external views and writings on public engagement, and help them understand the perspective of the various publics who have an investment in higher education. Faculty and community members often express themselves differently, have different priorities, and confront different demands. Acting as translators, campus leaders can help the two groups bridge their differences. To fulfill these dual roles, campus leaders need to be familiar with the literature on public engagement and understand the past and current state of campus-community relations.

Public engagement generally results in positive outcomes, but occasionally things can and do go awry. For example, a community-requested study of the economic impact of constructing a stadium downtown may show that there will be some negative consequences. This may inflame the supporters of the stadium as well as those requesting the study who were expecting a different outcome. Campus leaders should be prepared to guide and support faculty when their work creates problems with the community. They should also work with faculty to ensure they are not caught up in political agendas within the community. A faculty member in political science might have data showing that merging several local governments is a cost-effective move that would actually enhance local services. The merger issue, however, is likely to be highly controversial and highly politicized. The faculty member needs to be mindful of this when asked to share the data. He needs to be politically sensitive while still being intellectually honest.

Campus leaders also should make clear their support for the faculty's right to promote that which is scientifically supported. Activist groups on the Left and the Right, as well as special interest groups or those with a financial stake in an issue, might pressure the university to suppress information or terminate a particular project. Campus leaders must never compromise on intellectual integrity.

Presidential Leadership

Presidential commitment and leadership are critical for aligning an institution for public engagement. As the Pew Partnership for Civic Change (2004) noted: "Strong support on the part of the college or university president is almost a prerequisite for an engaged institution. While faculty and student buy-in are also critical, without a voice from the top articulating an institution-wide vision, engagement efforts are in danger of remaining episodic and incoherent" (p. 108). The president, more than any other person on the campus, is expected to see the total picture, ensure the institution's general welfare, and look beyond the benefits to any single department or unit (Kerr, 1991). The president's role is both internal and external to the campus.

Presidents bear the greatest responsibility for ensuring that the institution is aligned to support its priorities. As stated by AASCU, it is the president "who, when necessary, uses his or her 'bully pulpit' to challenge the status quo and overcome inertia in order to align all elements of the institution to support public engagement as a core campus mission" (American Association of State Colleges and Universities, 2002, p. 35). He is also responsible for creating the campus climate that will support this work, yet, as Frank Rhodes (2001), former president of Cornell University, pointed out: "Creating a campus climate is among the most challenging and most subtle of all presidential roles. . . . It means generating trust, encouraging initiative, building partnerships, promoting teamwork, rewarding achievement, [and] celebrating success" (p. 224). All campus units must understand that public engagement is a priority of the president so they will support it with both funding and appropriate services.

The president plays a primary role in creating and communicating the institution's vision and mission. He is their principal custodian and must ensure that they incorporate public engagement. He must also ensure that the vision and mission drive institutional planning and decision making. The president must repeatedly highlight the vision and mission as beacons guiding the university's future.

Presidents are responsible for institutional planning, the establishment of core values, and priority setting. These responsibilities cannot be delegated. How the president approaches the tasks as well as the product of the work will reflect the extent to which public engagement is an overarching institutional priority. For example, at NKU, the *Vision, Values, and Voices* (VVV) planning process (described in Chapter 3) ensured that the voice of the public was significantly represented in campus planning.

As chief executive officer of the institution, the president is responsible for establishing priorities (along with various stakeholders), aligning the institution to achieve intended outcomes, measuring progress, and holding others accountable. In all of these functions, the president has the opportunity to weave public engagement into the fabric of the campus.

The president is the prime institutional voice to the public and to the campus, and his messages must reflect the campus's most highly prized values and priorities. Public engagement should routinely be a part of the president's speeches both internally and externally, but how he contextualizes the message will differ depending on the audience. Language that connects with the hearts and minds of faculty and staff is different from that which connects with external community members.

Presidents must describe reality to their campuses and to the community. Part of the modern-day reality is that the public, including policymakers, want to know how institutions are affecting public progress. Institutions committed to matters important to the public are more likely to gain public support. The president must ensure that the campus understands this reality. At the same time, the public must understand the constraints on the university: limited resources and a host of other priorities that compete with public engagement.

Presidents should educate the campus and its governing board about the value of public engagement for the university's future. Presidents should describe how public engagement combines both public interest and institutional self-interest. They should convey to the external stakeholders the potential of the institution to help advance a public agenda in significant ways, but they should also help the community understand that universities exist to promote learning: to create, preserve, transmit, and apply knowledge. At its best, higher education promotes learning essential for the public to make informed decisions. It is the president who must explain that the university cannot promote partisan ideas, become embroiled in political controversy, or assume sole responsibility to solve community problems.

Presidents serve as advocates for public engagement, both internally, by convincing the campus of its value, and externally, by convincing donors and legislators to provide funds to support public engagement that will strengthen the regional economy, improve local schools, and enhance the quality of life in the region. Presidents also advocate for changes in state and federal policy to support a public engagement agenda. This external advocacy also communicates to the campus the importance of the work, the extent to which the president truly values it, and the extent to which the work should be an institutional priority.

Presidents fulfill these diverse responsibilities through what they say, what they do, how they spend their time, and how they allocate resources. For example, at the request of community leaders, the president of NKU co-chaired a regional visioning process that included NKU faculty as advisors to the various community-staffed subcommittees that informed the process. This involvement placed the university and its faculty in a highly visible position supporting regional progress; underscored the importance of the university in advancing a public agenda; ensured university input into regional goals; provided a forum for educating the community about potential contributions from the university; enhanced the university's understanding of the needs and future direction of the community; and deepened the president's connection with donors, policymakers, and other external constituencies. This was a time-consuming task for the president, but it provided extensive benefits for the community, the university, and the university's relationship with the community.

Leadership from the Chief Academic Officer

When the CAO and the president form a high-performing and integrated leadership team, they are a powerful force in support of the alignment process. Together, they can effectively encourage and support the public engagement of the faculty and staff. At institutions where presidential support for public engagement is weak or altogether lacking, the role of the CAO is doubly important because she bears an even greater responsibility for promoting public engagement. In all cases, as the "first among equals," the CAO must partner with the other vice presidents to help them understand the role of their units in public engagement and motivate them to eliminate barriers to engagement work. She should encourage those outside academic affairs to become involved in public engagement, sometimes in primary roles, sometimes in supporting roles.

Although the president leads in setting the vision for the university, it is the CAO who translates the vision into action. She sets expectations for the academic division, generally the largest division on campus. The CAO can require colleges and departments to set specific public engagement goals and then hold them accountable for achieving those goals. The CAO controls a significant pool of resources and can use them to influence behavior, to provide seed money for new public engagement projects and ongoing support for established projects.

Communication should be a high priority for the CAO. She must ensure the campus is aware of public engagement priorities and progress by communicating with the president, governing board, system board, and public relations office of the university as well as the campus in general. CAOs work with deans, chairs, and faculty to communicate the importance of public engagement, to advocate for its role in the education of students and in the research and service responsibilities of faculty. As one who understands the faculty and can communicate in a language that resonates with faculty, the CAO can serve as translator between the faculty and the president, governing board, system office, and legislature.

CAOs, like presidents, have a responsibility to educate the faculty about public engagement. A CAO should connect the campus with best practices in public engagement. She should explain the intellectual foundations for public engagement, as described in Chapter 1, and show how public engagement can encompass teaching, research, and service in ways that multiply its impact while not multiplying the workload. She should help faculty understand how the institution's commitment to public engagement affects them and their students. She must insist that public engagement, like all work at the university, reflects the academic integrity standards of the institution.

The CAO at a research university has a particular challenge, because there may be considerable resistance to public engagement. It is incumbent upon the CAO—and at some institutions, the president—to show how research and public engagement can benefit each other as well as the institution, students, and community without reducing the institution's research productivity or reputation. Highly respected research institutions such as Michigan State University, the University of Minnesota, and the University of Pennsylvania have embraced public engagement. They can serve as powerful examples and models for the faculty.

The CAO must monitor the major public engagement commitments to ensure they are aligned with campus priorities, have sufficient human and financial resources, build on faculty strengths, and avoid promising beyond the campus's ability to deliver. The CAO must also advocate for public engagement by ensuring that those above her—the president and the board—and those in her reporting lines—deans, chairs, and faculty—retain a focus on public engagement. The CAO must ensure that all units serve the full breadth of the mission: teaching, research, and public engagement.

The CAO has the responsibility to provide leadership when it comes to recruiting and hiring the next generation of academic administrators, faculty members, and staff, which empowers her to require that those hired have a deep commitment to public engagement. For those already hired, the CAO must ensure that public engagement is appropriately recognized and rewarded in RPT reviews, annual performance reviews, salary increases, campus celebrations, and professional development opportunities. Although the RPT guidelines are normally under the purview of the faculty, the CAO has a responsibility to ensure that guidelines are fair and reward activity consistent with the mission and core values of the institution. The CAO can ask the appropriate faculty committee to revise the RPT guidelines to reflect the institution's commitment to public engagement, and she can ensure that, at each level of the review process, the implementation of the policy appropriately recognizes public engagement.

The work of the CAO is primarily internal, yet, like all university leaders, the CAO should be active in the community, modeling public engagement. She should identify opportunities for public engagement that will have a significant, positive impact on the community and the campus and serve as a catalyst for establishing partnerships with the community. She needs to help faculty understand that the community is not a laboratory but rather a source of mutually beneficial partnerships, and she should urge faculty to pursue public engagement that advances the institution's goals. Finally, the CAO should encourage academic programs to have external advisory committees so that the community is in the university just as the university is in the community.

Leadership from Deans and Chairs

Unless it has the support of deans and chairs, the alignment process is unlikely to succeed. Deans and chairs are closer to faculty in the organizational structure and have more frequent contact with individual faculty. This often means they have a powerful effect on the behavior of faculty and staff. At some institutions, their influence is greater than that of the president or CAO. Hence, it is important for deans and chairs to reinforce the president's and CAO's messages, communicating that it is the responsibility of the faculty and staff to turn the leadership's rhetoric into specific, actionable, public engagement.

Deans and chairs should use their roles in the university governance structure to promote and support public engagement. They should lead their units in discussing public engagement: what it is and what it means for their unit. Likewise, they should lead their units in setting specific public engagement goals and determining how the units will achieve each of their goals. They should celebrate the public engagement accomplishments of their units and ensure that individual faculty are appropriately recognized for their public engagement, especially in the RPT process as well as in annual performance reviews and merit-based salary increases. In addition, they should model public engagement and facilitate the development of mutually beneficial partnerships involving the university and the community.

Deans and chairs should help faculty obtain the resources to support public engagement. In some cases, this will mean providing internal resources, but it also means encouraging faculty to write grants for external support, assisting faculty in the preparation of grant proposals, and seeking grants and gifts on behalf of the department or college.

Chairs serve as models and mentors, particularly for junior faculty. They can influence faculty decisions on where to invest their time and energy. They should communicate to faculty the benefits of public engagement. Kevin Kecskes, Sherril Gelmon, and Amy Spring (2006) looked at Portland State University's academic units that participated in an "engaged department initiative" designed to increase faculty involvement in public engagement work. They found the chair significantly influenced the work of a faculty team. "The chair's commitment helped the department team tie the initiative to other department initiatives. They were also able to garner additional resources to support the initiative, mobilize increased faculty support and participation across the department, and use department meetings to discuss the Engaged Department Initiative" (p. 157).

Faculty Leadership

Faculty who are active in public engagement provide leadership both by serving as models for their colleagues and by sharing examples of how public engagement benefits their own teaching and research and their students' learning. Faculty who are actively engaged are often among the strongest and most respected advocates for this work.

University Governing Boards

The board can have a significant impact on institutional culture. One of the governing board's most important responsibilities is to hire the president. Commitment and experience with public engagement should be high on the list of hiring criteria. They approve the university's vision and mission statements, and they can ensure that public engagement plays a significant role in each. Governing boards must hold the institution in general and the president in particular accountable for fulfilling the public engagement aspect of the mission. This offers the president an additional rationale for persuading the campus to embrace public engagement: "The board is insisting upon it." In addition, the board is a link between the campus and the community, helping each understand the values and needs of the other; the board may even go a step further and help identify potential partnerships and potential projects (Novak & Johnston, 2005). If the board members are committed to public engagement, and if they are kept informed about how it unfolds on campus and in the region, they can be strong advocates for promoting public engagement.

Unions

Where they exist, faculty unions can be a source of leadership and support. More than 20 years ago, Lynton and Elman (1987) pointed out: "Faculty unions, both locally and nationally, constitute a key element, either as facilitators or as barriers, in bringing about [change]" (p. 166). The union can take an official stance in support of public engagement and ensure that the important role of public engagement is recognized in the union contract, especially in RPT guidelines.

GENERAL PRINCIPLES FOR CAMPUS LEADERS

Campus leaders do not have an easy task as they work to provide the motivation, inspiration, and direction for public engagement, particularly because it is likely to be only one of several agenda items they are promoting. They must convince faculty and staff who are already juggling heavy workloads that the work is important to the students, the campus, and the community. It cannot and should not trump teaching and research, nor should it be in competition with them. Those who are most successful are those who integrate teaching, research, and public engagement.

An effective campus leader understands what motivates people, the principles of change, and what leads to resistance. She is patient, knowing that institutional change is a slow process. Effective campus leaders recognize that they cannot accomplish anything without bringing faculty and staff along. They listen carefully to what both their supporters and critics say. They continuously monitor the pace of change they are advocating to ensure it does not exceed what the campus is able to handle. Effective leaders recognize that the pace may have to be slowed to strengthen the base. Likewise, they monitor their base to ensure they have followers who are supporting their message. One is not a leader if no one is following!

A campus leader must understand the culture of the institution before attempting to alter it, and if she is new to the campus, this can be a time-consuming process. It can take five to seven years for even experienced leaders to embed public engagement deeply into the fabric of the campus. This is not a task for someone who intends to be a "short-timer" at the institution.

Change, especially in higher education, does not occur through force or threat. Change occurs when faculty and staff are convinced that it will lead to benefits for them, their students, or both. *Push strategies*, which rely on force or threat, are not nearly as effective as *pull strategies*, in which there are incentives encouraging the desired behavior. The federal government's use of grants to strengthen the research enterprise is an excellent example of a highly successful pull strategy.

Resistance to change is often based on fear. If resistors can articulate their fears and then are shown, patiently and respectfully, why they are ill-founded, resistance can be significantly reduced. Resistance is also reduced when faculty and staff are involved in shaping the desired change (Rowley, Lujan, & Dolence, 1997). Although university leaders are not expected to be experts on change or resistance, they do need to be sensitive to what does and does not work. There are many good sources from which leaders can learn more about change in higher education. (See, for example, Alter & Book, 2001; Eckel, Green, Hill, & Mallon, 1999; Farmer, 1990; Levine, 1980; Ramaley, 1996; and Rowley, Lujan, Dolence, 1997.) Other references focus on the business world but offer valuable lessons that can be adapted for higher education. (See, for example, Kotter, 1995, 1996.)

While providing leadership for public engagement, campus leaders must also ensure that the campus itself is running smoothly. If they ignore the internal, they will lose the respect and support of the faculty and staff. Furthermore, campus leaders should never compromise the values of the academy. As James Duderstadt and Farris Womack (2003) pointed out: "University leadership and governance should always reflect the fundamental values of the academy—particularly freedom of inquiry, an openness to new ideas, a commitment to rigorous study, and a love of learning" (p. 172). To that list must be added academic integrity.

EXTERNAL SOURCES OF LEADERSHIP AND SUPPORT

Institutional leadership can obtain support from external entities that promote, support, and encourage public engagement. Several were described in Chapter 1 including disciplinary associations, accrediting bodies, and higher education associations. Others are discussed here.

All states except Michigan have statewide governing boards, coordinating boards, or system offices. These groups can strongly influence the public institutions in their states; collectively they have enormous power. To ensure that they are promoting and supporting this work, Votruba (2005) suggested that leaders of these boards and offices consider the following questions: "(1) Is public engagement prominent in systemwide planning and priority setting? Have we established statewide priorities for campus public engagement? (2) Have we created a clear expectation that our campuses should be involved in public engagement activities? (3) Have we made public engagement (as well as enrollment growth and research) a priority in our political advocacy at both the state and federal levels? (4) Have we established measures that can be used to assess campus productivity in public engagement?" (p. 268).

Governing boards, coordinating boards, and system offices can communicate the importance of public engagement through a statewide public agenda that assigns a high priority to public engagement. Kentucky's public agenda, established by the Kentucky Council on Postsecondary Education, is expressed as a set of five questions, one of which is: "Are Kentucky's people, communities, and economy benefiting?" In elaborating on this point, the agenda-setting document states: "Postsecondary institutions [in Kentucky] must do their part by being good 'stewards of place,' working with community leaders to advance economic, social, and environmental progress" (Kentucky Council on Postsecondary Education, n.d.). The "Illinois Public Agenda for College and Career Success" includes four goals, with the fourth being: "Better integrate Illinois' educational, research, and innovation assets to meet economic needs of the state and its regions" (http://www.ibhe.state.il.us/masterPlanning/materials/ExecutiveSummary.pdf). Gordon Davies's (2006) monograph— *Setting a Public Agenda for Higher Education in the States: Lessons Learned from the National Collaborative for Higher Education Policy*—is very helpful for states working to develop a public agenda for higher education.

Statewide boards and offices can set specific public engagement targets for each university, provide funding on a competitive or noncompetitive basis, require accountability, and standardize accountability measures used in the state. They can facilitate statewide, general or discipline-specific, in-person or online, professional development workshops; use the "bully pulpit" to tout the advantages of public engagement; and sponsor relevant celebrations and conferences. Kentucky, for example, holds an annual, statewide public engagement conference for administrators and faculty.

State legislatures can often play the same or a complementary role by setting targets for public engagement, appropriating the necessary funding, and requiring accountability for engagement work. Whether it is the legislature or the statewide board that sets expectations for public engagement, the campus leadership can then honestly say: "This is not only the right thing to do, but we have no choice. The state is requiring this work."

CONCLUDING COMMENTS

Clearly, leaders, especially inside the institution, play a primary role in determining if the campus will be aligned for public engagement, if public engagement will be deeply embedded in the fiber of the institution, and if the campus will be productive in its public engagement. Thus, hiring decisions should be made with great care. When an institution has established a clear vision and mission, those hired must be committed to advancing that vision and fulfilling that mission, not creating their own. All too often, newly hired leaders want their own vision to mold the units in their sphere of influence, but they must do this within the parameters of the established vision and mission. Just as a university would not hire—or tolerate—a leader who suggested that research be discarded as an institutional value, so too must the institution ensure that its leaders promote the value of public engagement.

CHAPTER FIVE

ALIGNING THE ORGANIZATIONAL STRUCTURE

An institution's organizational structure both reflects and influences its values. It affects almost every aspect of the institution's functioning, including how and with whom people communicate and collaborate and even what work is accomplished. The organizational structure sends a powerful message about the priorities assigned to different work, which means that if public engagement is a high priority it must be reflected in the organizational structure. Yet at some institutions, simply mentioning organizational change evokes immediate suspicion, especially when the change will result in more administrative or staff positions. At those institutions, leaders should proceed with great caution in order to avoid provoking strong resistance to organizational restructuring, resistance that might generalize to public engagement. Where resistance is anticipated, restructuring in support of public engagement might be tied to a broader restructuring of the institution, or it might proceed more slowly.

Different positions and units can provide the organizational infrastructure to support public engagement. This chapter considers the *chief public engagement officer*, analogous to a chief research officer; a unit charged to facilitate public engagement, often focused on service learning; centers and institutes that focus on service to specific sectors or provide specific services across sectors; and standing or ad hoc committees that can be used in a variety of ways.

CHIEF PUBLIC ENGAGEMENT OFFICER

To make rapid and significant progress in public engagement, an institution must have a person whose primary focus is public engagement, a high-level administrator who wakes up every day thinking about how to advance the public engagement mission of the campus. To be successful, this leader needs broad campus support and must be seen as reflecting the views of the president and CAO.

REPORTING LINE

Because public engagement is a core element of the university's academic mission, the leader of public engagement should logically report to the CAO. If the position title is vice provost or associate provost, it connects the position to the academic mission and communicates significant status. The title of director may or may not be appropriate. If it is a rarely used title, reserved for high-level administrators, then it is appropriate; if the institution has a large number of directors, then public engagement will not stand out from other functions of the university. No matter what the title, his ability to be successful requires that the campus know he has strong support from the president and CAO and is authorized to speak on their behalf.

NKU created an associate provost position that reported to the CAO but also served with the vice presidents on the president's nine-person executive team and was a member of the Council of Deans. This balanced the need for status, visibility, and influence with the need to connect the position to the academic mission. In this book, the position is referred to as chief public engagement officer, reflecting its comparability to a chief research officer.

QUALIFICATIONS

The position of chief public engagement officer requires a full-time, highly regarded, academically qualified person who will command the respect of faculty, staff, and community leaders and who is strongly committed to the public engagement mission. He must believe in the capacity of the university to impact the public in significant ways through the public engagement mission. The person must be both a visionary and pragmatic, effective at driving an agenda and sensitive to pace—neither too slow nor too fast in promoting change—and base—ensuring that the leader maintains sufficient support among the various stakeholder groups upon which change depends. The chief public engagement officer must be a "boundary spanner" who can connect across diverse constituent groups, a systems thinker who understands the relationship between public engagement and other mission dimensions, and a collaborator who can work effectively both inside and outside the university.

RESPONSIBILITIES

The responsibilities assigned to the chief public engagement officer will differ by campus, but they will likely include the following:

- Advocating on behalf of the public engagement mission throughout the campus community
- Serving as a spokesperson for public engagement, on and off campus
- Providing an institutional front door for community organizations seeking to partner with the university
- Promoting accountability and tracking public engagement

To fulfill these responsibilities, the individual will need to focus attention both on and off campus. Potential tasks with a campus focus include these:

- Implementing the recommendations of the alignment committee
- Ensuring that public engagement is a focus of campus attention
- Educating the president and the CAO about the work, its importance in general and the progress being made on campus, both in terms of quantity and impact
- Ensuring that those involved in public engagement have the support they need and the cooperation of other offices
- Identifying and eliminating barriers to public engagement

- Assisting those seeking resources for public engagement
- Overseeing internal grant programs that support public engagement
- Connecting faculty and staff with colleagues working on similar projects or with similar interests or working with the same groups in the community
- Ensuring that public engagement is recognized and rewarded
- Requiring and facilitating assessment of public engagement
- Monitoring the quality and integrity of public engagement
- Promoting curricular change that increases public and civic engagement
- Ensuring that appropriate faculty development opportunities are provided
- Tracking and reporting public engagement
- Assisting faculty and staff to connect with community organizations.

Potential tasks with a community focus include these:

- Learning about and understanding the needs of the community
- Mapping the community's needs onto the university's resources
- Educating the community about the university's expertise and capacity limits
- Serving as a conduit for community organizations and individuals to connect with the right office at the university
- Brokering connections between campus and community
- Helping to resolve problems that arise in campus-community partnerships
- Representing the campus on selected community initiatives
- Convening campus and community representatives to engage in conversation about working together

The position and the person are most likely to be acceptable to the campus if his primary role is to be a facilitator who supports those involved in public engagement and removes obstacles they encounter. The university should avoid having all public engagement initiatives report to the chief public engagement officer. After all, if public engagement is to permeate the campus, then it seems logical that it would not all be organized under one academic leader. Furthermore, when the units focused on public engagement report to a dean or other academic leader to which they are otherwise tied, it diffuses public engagement throughout the campus.

Advantages and Disadvantages

The benefits of this leadership position are readily apparent: the focus on public engagement is increased; someone has responsibility to ensure that the institution is aligned in support of public engagement; and someone assumes the multitude of responsibilities previously listed. As Weerts and Sandmann (2008) discovered: "Community partners had more positive perceptions of institutional engagement efforts on campuses that operate centralized offices of engagement compared to decentralized systems lacking a clearinghouse function for engagement activities" (p. 96).

If the creation and filling of the leadership position is handled properly, there are no disadvantages other than the costs associated with creating the office and the position. But if this process is not handled sensitively, it could lead to negative attitudes on the part of those already involved in public engagement; opposition from other offices, such as student affairs, public relations, and public affairs; and an increase rather than a reduction in the barriers to public engagement. In creating the position, care should be taken not to disrupt relationships that faculty and departments already have with the community. Faculty, chairs, and deans should be assured they will benefit from the work of the chief public engagement officer.

Alternatives

On those campuses that either cannot financially afford to hire a chief public engagement officer or where there is strong opposition to the creation of this high-level administrative position, it is possible to assign the work to an existing administrator, such as an associate provost. However, because the associate provost or other existing administrator is likely to have a full portfolio before the addition of this responsibility, engagement is unlikely to get the attention it needs, and the list of responsibilities given for the chief public engagement officer may be only minimally fulfilled.

Alternatively, it is possible to delegate this work to the deans. In order for this to be effective, the president and CAO must ensure that the deans fully support public engagement, are willing to provide the services and support necessary for it to flourish, and are prepared to move this mission dimension to a relatively high place on their priority list. Even with these assurances, public engagement will be only one of the many concerns that the deans must consider, and it will not get as much attention as it will from someone for whom it is the primary focus. Delegating the responsibility to deans is likely to be more effective in colleges where public engagement is part of their history (for example, social work) than in colleges where it is not (for example, science and technology).

The best alternative is the creation of the chief public engagement officer who is supported by the president, the CAO, and the deans. The deans still have a special role: in addition to reinforcing the importance of public engagement in their own colleges, they can provide their faculty with services and support for the work.

ADMINISTRATIVE OFFICES SUPPORTING PUBLIC ENGAGEMENT

Working in the community, whether doing community-based research (CBR) or involving students in service learning, is both time-consuming and labor-intensive, often making many extra demands on faculty compared to the demands associated with traditional research or teaching. To the extent a centralized office can facilitate the work and reduce the administrative burden, it will help increase the prevalence of the work. As a result, many institutions create an office that supports these activities. Edward Zlotkowski (2002b) reported: "In my numerous visits to campuses around the country, I have found no single instance of an effective, comprehensive, community-based teaching and learning effort that does not draw upon the assistance of some specially organized and designated office" (p. 14).

Offices that support service learning and other community-based work are more likely to increase faculty involvement if located in academic affairs. This is logical: service learning and CBR are tied to faculty, students, and courses. Placing these offices in academic affairs increases their credibility with the faculty and is most likely to win over faculty skeptics. If there is a chief public engagement officer, these offices should be in his portfolio. Otherwise, the offices can effectively report to an associate or vice provost or another high-ranking individual in the CAO's office.

Service Learning Office

A service learning office may be housed in an office that supports public engagement more broadly, or it may be a largely independent entity. Either way, the office is likely to benefit a large number of students and faculty. The responsibilities of the office will be described here, with the understanding that an office that encompasses more than service learning will have more responsibilities. The responsibilities of a service learning office are both campus-focused and community-focused. There are seven clusters of campus-focused responsibilities:

- *Promote service learning:* For example, conduct strategic planning for service learning; ensure the work is counted in the RPT and annual review processes; develop appropriate policies related to service learning; facilitate universitywide, department, and college discussions about service learning; meet with departments to encourage service learning; host events to recognize and celebrate the work; develop and implement celebrations to honor individual faculty who incorporate service learning in their classes; and maintain a service learning website.
- *Handle administrative functions:* For example, supply the documents needed for service learning classes, including policies, forms, contracts, legal documents, handbooks for students, and so forth; track that students have completed necessary requirements for serving in the community, such as background checks and TB testing; handle financial management of funded initiatives; maintain records on service learning participation; and design and implement the evaluation of service learning programs.
- *Focus on faculty development:* For example, provide workshops that help faculty incorporate service learning in their classes;

bring in relevant speakers; develop a mentoring program pairing new and experienced service learning faculty; encourage faculty to join faculty interest groups to discuss service learning; and provide support for faculty to attend regional, state, and national conferences on service learning, especially conferences related to their discipline.

• *Provide direct faculty support:* For example, develop a faculty handbook that contains the materials that faculty need for implementing a service learning course; provide grants and reassigned time for faculty to develop service learning courses; maintain a library of materials that relate to service learning; maintain a collection of sample syllabi for service learning courses and assist faculty with developing syllabi; provide descriptions of various options for student reflection, a critical piece of the service learning experience; advise faculty on working with the university bureaucracy; keep faculty apprised of relevant laws and policies; help faculty document their service learning work; inform faculty of publication and presentation outlets and grant opportunities; answer faculty questions; and educate the administration about the faculty workload associated with service learning classes.

• *Secure funding for service learning:* For example, advocate for more internal support for service learning, including an internal grant program to support course development and reassigned time for faculty; write grant proposals and assist faculty writing proposals for external funding to support the expansion of service learning; and work with the appropriate campus offices to secure gifts in support of service learning.

• *Serve student needs:* For example, develop a service learning handbook for students; serve as ombudsperson for students with related problems; and assist students with transportation issues.

• *Connect with the community:* For example, maintain information on agencies having, or interested in having, service learning students work with them; assist faculty in locating partners in the community; negotiate service learning partnerships and develop the necessary written agreements; and prevent, or when necessary help to resolve, problems with service learning partnerships.

This office could also be more directly involved with service learning by facilitating the placement of individual students, monitoring students' attendance at their placements, and providing an orientation for students going into the community.

The service learning office can also assume several important community-focused responsibilities, such as these:

- Educating community partners about service learning and how it differs from volunteerism
- Educating agencies about their roles and responsibilities when accepting service learning students
- Developing a service learning handbook for community agencies
- Linking the community with faculty who already have incorporated, or are willing to incorporate, service learning into their classes
- Monitoring community satisfaction with the service learning program

Preventing or helping to resolve conflicts between a community agency and the faculty and students in a service learning course serves the community as much as it does the campus.

Although one might assume that a service learning office should maintain a database of service learning sites from which students select a placement, this is not recommended. The model has been shown to produce problems because the faculty do not develop relationships with the agencies where their students are placed. As Robert Exley and Joshua Young (2004) pointed out: "This clearinghouse model failed to foster ongoing, sustained faculty-agency partnerships, which in turn often led to superficial experiences . . . . Agencies complained that there was insufficient ongoing commitment from the program; in some semesters they received numerous students, in others none at all, and the students who did come were often unprepared, resulting in more work for the agency supervisor and less commitment from the students" (p. 188).

Many universities have service learning offices that can serve as models. See, for example, the *Service Learning Center* at

Bentley University (http://www.bentley.edu/service-learning/index.cfm); *Service-Learning* at Boise State University (http://servicelearning.boisestate.edu/); and the *Steans Center for Community-based Service Learning* at DePaul University (http://steans.depaul.edu/). Examples of offices with a broader focus can be found at Michigan State University, which has an office called *University Outreach and Engagement* (http://outreach.msu.edu/), and Indiana State University, which has the *Center for Public Service and Community Engagement.*

COMMUNITY-BASED RESEARCH OFFICE

Many of the principles described here apply equally to centers that support CBR. "Higher education institutions can best sustain and advance the practice of CBR by creating CBR centers. Relying on individual faculty to undertake CBR projects without such institutional support virtually ensures that when the faculty member leaves, changes interests, or goes on sabbatical leave, the CBR partnerships will be disrupted or dissolved" (Strand, Marullo, Cutforth, Stoecker, & Donohue, 2003a, p. 197).

CENTERS AND INSTITUTES

Centers and institutes often house public engagement projects. They may either provide a service—for example, a program evaluation center—or they may focus on a particular sector—for example, K–12 education. They are often multidisciplinary and organized around a problem area. For example, the staff of a large center that focuses on water quality might include chemists who deal with analyzing water, biologists who look at the effect of pollutants on aquatic life, psychologists who survey attitudes and behavior relating to protecting water quality, and public relations experts who focus on educating the public. All of these experts can be assisted by students who will gain excellent experience from working on real-world problems.

When a campus has identified the public challenges it hopes to affect, creating a center to house and promote the work can offer several advantages. The center is likely to bring people with common interests together, foster multidisciplinary work, and persist over time. In addition, a center provides a link for the community to access services and a group with whom the community can develop enduring relations. Centers generally free faculty from the administrative tasks associated with individual projects. A center may also have an easier time attracting external funds, both because its very existence may convince potential funders of the institutional commitment to the work and because it may be able to attract successful grant-getters. A very large center may even have its own gifts officer.

Making important decisions when a new center is created will prevent many problems that might otherwise arise. Among the most important decisions are the following:

Where Will the Center Report?

If the disciplines involved in the center are all in one college, then the center can logically report to the relevant dean's office. If the center cuts across colleges, then one dean can be appointed as the "lead dean" for the center, working collaboratively with the other deans. Alternatively, a multidisciplinary center might report to the chief public engagement officer, or if that position does not exist, to the CAO.

How Will the Center Be Funded?

If the center is internally funded, those not involved may object when a public engagement initiative is given resources that could have funded other campus priorities. Even if *new* funds are allocated for the center, some will argue that the new funds should go elsewhere, to more traditional purposes. If the center will rely on external funds, there must be clear agreement on how long the center will have to obtain the needed external funding commitments and what will happen if the external funding is not forthcoming or is eliminated later on. The institution should be wary when claims are made that a center will be self-supporting. Except at large research institutions, that is rare. Although centers can often generate funds to pay for individual projects, they usually find it challenging to provide infrastructure support.

Who Will Implement the Center's Projects: Faculty or Professional Staff or a Combination?

If the center employs only professional staff, then it is less connected to the academic mission, less likely to involve students, more likely to be marginalized in academic affairs, and less likely to be protected in the event of budget cuts. Yet professional staff might be extremely qualified to handle the specialized work of the center, highly skilled and experienced working with community entities, cost less than faculty, and be less distracted by other campus responsibilities. If the center employs primarily faculty, it is more likely to be tied to the academic mission, more likely to involve students, and more likely to influence the curriculum, but faculty may be pulled in multiple directions, especially if they are not yet tenured. Sometimes it is difficult to attract existing faculty to a center because they feel it will take time away from their other priorities. Their home departments may resent their work with the center rather than value it. When faculty are employed by the center, there are other questions to consider: Will the faculty be permanently or temporarily assigned to the center? Will they serve the center part-time or full-time? Could some faculty be hired with joint appointments: half-time in an academic department and half-time in the center?

Centers are not without risk. A community-focused risk is that they may be seen as "unfair competition." That is, if the center offers services that compete with the private sector, elements in the community may object to its existence, especially if the university accepts public funds. For example, concerns might be raised about the water-testing service provided by the water quality center mentioned earlier. There are likely to be for-profit businesses that offer the same services to the community. Owners of those businesses may feel the university is competing with their private sector businesses and doing so, at least partially, with public funds. Their objections may go beyond complaining to the university administration; they may also complain to their legislators or the local media. Furthermore, public engagement centers that compete with the private sector may, in some states, produce legal problems for the university. In most cases, these are not insurmountable problems, but they require preemptive strategies to diminish the risk.

A campus-focused risk is creating the erroneous conclusion that public engagement is the responsibility of the institution's centers and institutes rather than a responsibility that pervades the academic division. Other risks relate to funding and staffing, both of which were discussed earlier, and to the proliferation of centers that are not integral to the institution.

COMMITTEES

Standing and ad hoc committees, composed of both campus and community members, can be an important part of the organizational structure supporting public engagement. An example is the chief public engagement officer's advisory committee. This committee can provide direction on public engagement planning, set quality standards and accountability requirements, and advise on the development of a communication strategy (see Chapter 10). In fact, the committee's input and involvement will benefit most of the topics covered in this book.

Advisory committees can also be of great assistance to the service learning and CBR centers and to other centers and institutes. These committees must have meaningful work to do, tackle real issues, and be involved in long-term planning and agenda setting. Otherwise, their interest and attendance will quickly wane. College and departmental external advisory boards can also make a significant contribution to the public engagement mission. They serve to institutionalize the voice of the public and help ensure that academic units stay grounded in the external world.

Ad hoc committees can be created for a vast array of tasks—for example, to advise on the creation of accountability systems for public engagement, review proposals for new centers or institutes, consider how to increase student involvement, and advise on large, multidisciplinary projects. The membership of an ad hoc committee—whether it should include faculty, students, community members, or a combination—depends on the nature of the assigned tasks.

CONCLUDING COMMENTS

Organizational structures can help align the campus for public engagement and strengthen both the quality and quantity of public engagement. For the structures suggested here to be successful, it is critically important that the *right* people are chosen for the various leadership positions. As Collins (2001) pointed out in *Good to Great*: "Get the right people on the bus AND the wrong people off the bus" (p. 199). Failing to get the right people will drastically slow progress. Those hired to lead these units must be committed to the public engagement mission, continue the direction that has been started or is planned, and provide a blend of community and campus experience. They must be able to earn the respect of the faculty and be capable of communicating with both on- and off-campus groups. The leaders must see themselves as part of a team, not there to shape things in their own image. These are not easy positions to fill, and once hired, the individuals will need the support of those above them in the organizational hierarchy.

These suggested structures, albeit strongly recommended, are not the only organizational models, and each institution has to determine what works best for its campus. Furthermore, the organizational structure that is most effective when public engagement is new to a campus may be different from what is needed after public engagement is well established.

CHAPTER SIX

ALIGNING FACULTY AND STAFF

Meaningful public engagement goals cannot be achieved without significant involvement from the faculty. They are the researchers, the advisors, the consultants, and the teachers who work with the community. They are also the link to the curriculum and the students. Yet there are many factors that discourage faculty from engaging in this work. Universities can bemoan the faculty's lack of commitment to public engagement or they can seek to understand their concerns and work to address them. This chapter focuses on understanding and addressing their concerns.

OBSTACLES

Any discussion of faculty involvement in public engagement inevitably leads to a discussion of promotion and tenure guidelines. For faculty who are not yet tenured or promoted to professor, the guidelines play a major role in how they invest their time and effort. Thus, guidelines that do not reward public engagement are a significant obstacle. This topic is so important that it is given its own chapter, Chapter 7. The second most commonly mentioned obstacle is workload.

WORKLOAD

Over the last 40 years, the diversity of demands on faculty has expanded. Although faculty have long been expected to stay current in their field, teach their courses, keep their courses up to date, ensure that students adhere to high academic standards, advise and mentor students, participate in department, college, and university governance, develop new academic programs and courses, and participate in their disciplinary associations—all of which are very time-consuming—in recent years, their roles have expanded. Faculty are expected to master rapidly changing technology-based tools and pedagogical techniques, and they are accountable for program assessment. Even on campuses with heavy teaching loads—those that historically did not expect extensive research output—faculty are called upon to write and administer grant proposals and are held to higher standards for research productivity than was previously the case. Faculty may be involved with student recruitment, fundraising, supervising undergraduate student research, and engaging students outside the classroom in order to increase retention and graduation rates. Given their already heavy workload, it is not surprising that many are reluctant to embrace another initiative known to require a significant investment of time.

A New Role for Faculty

Public engagement tends to be messier than traditional faculty work—messy in terms of methods because one cannot control all of the variables and messy in terms of the various project dimensions that have to be negotiated with partners. Public engagement differs from traditional faculty work, which allows faculty a great deal of control and autonomy. Control over a public engagement project is shared, and hence autonomy, at least in regards to that project, is largely lost. Faculty must be willing to forgo some degree of control in exchange for the benefits and satisfaction of public engagement.

Public engagement requires collaboration, a difficult undertaking for faculty who have been trained for and acculturated to solitary work. Internal collaboration is often needed because no one person—not even one department—has all the required expertise. Multidisciplinary collaboration is particularly challenging: faculty often do not know how to identify the "right" people in other departments—that is, people with the needed expertise—and different departments tend to use different jargon, employ different theoretical frameworks, and apply different methodologies. Collaborating across college lines can be especially challenging, and the larger the institution, the less faculty are likely to know about the interests and talents of colleagues in other departments and other colleges.

Collaborating with the community requires patience and a set of skills that may be totally alien to faculty—for example, sharing decision making, giving up control, respecting the views and ideas of those who are not as educated or knowledgeable, and devoting extensive time and energy to process issues and establishing trust and rapport. Faculty may experience a conflict between their training to seek "truth" and the community's political agenda. Collaboration with the corporate world may lead to tensions over the free flow of ideas and the need to protect proprietary information and patent rights. Collaboration may require altering the typical rhythm of faculty work because the calendars of higher education and the community are different.

With public engagement creating a new role and new challenges for faculty, it is not surprising that some faculty question whether they can successfully do this work. Their concern may be justified. Most lack the relevant training and expertise. They may not be prepared to deal with the real-world challenges that occur when working in the community. They may lack experience in supervising students in settings outside the campus. They may not know how to find a community partner or establish a relationship once they have identified the partner. They may not know how to deal with local politics or how to establish a contractual relationship with the community. As will be shown in Chapter 11, partnerships create logistical challenges different from the challenges faculty usually encounter in teaching and research. It is understandable that faculty are reluctant to undertake work for which they lack confidence. Moreover, it can be dangerous to the university's reputation to encourage faculty to work in the community without adequate preparation, and it can lead faculty who try—and fail—to feel defeated, avoid future public engagement, and discourage their colleagues from becoming engaged.

"IT'S NOT WHAT WE DO"

Some individuals and even some entire departments view public engagement negatively. In fact, some are outright hostile to public engagement, respecting neither the work nor those who do it. Engaged research tends to be applied research, which is "valued less than basic, theoretical research. This is reflected in the hierarchy of most journal rating systems as well as tacit working assumptions of faculty review systems" (Bringle, Games, & Malloy, 1999, p. 196). Engaged work is often multidisciplinary, which some academics value less highly than traditional, discipline-based work. Pedagogical approaches that incorporate public engagement, such as service learning courses, are also questioned. Some fear that these approaches lower academic standards, take valuable time away from critical course content, provide little real benefit to the students, and "[replace] rigorous intellectual analysis with affective, shallow opinion based on limited, idiosyncratic experience" (Morton, 1996, p. 279). The view of colleagues is critically important to all faculty, as Andrew Furco (2001) concluded from a study of faculty at 45 colleges and universities in the western United States: "Even when institutional rewards and incentives are in place for faculty to participate in service learning, faculty members agree to [implement service learning] only when they are convinced that engaging in service learning will not be viewed negatively by their peers or the campus administration" (p. 69).

These negative views pose problems, especially for the untenured. In all likelihood, their doctoral programs did not prepare them to do this work, and they face a particular challenge because the time limit for tenure decisions may not be long enough to develop and complete a partnership project and have demonstrable results. In addition, the untenured will find that some administrators and faculty advise them to avoid public engagement until they have achieved tenure (Duderstadt, 2001; Gelmon & Agre-Kippenhan, 2002b). Such a position cannot be justified at a campus aligned to support public engagement. If public engagement is to be part of a faculty member's workload, then the institution ought to determine, prior to tenure, whether the faculty member has the skills and interest required for this work. Furthermore, if faculty are hired because of their interest and potential for public engagement, which is recommended in the following paragraphs, then it makes no sense to have them wait six or seven years before undertaking this work.

Changing the mindset of those who believe that public engagement is only for the tenured is very important. The work should be part of the faculty members' responsibilities throughout their careers, because it is important work that fits with the mission of the institution, contributes to the public good, and benefits students. The notion that public engagement is only for tenured faculty is a significant obstacle for expanding an institution's engaged work, especially at a time when many tenured faculty will retire and be replaced with untenured faculty. New faculty must be encouraged and supported in their public engagement work, and although it is not necessary for all faculty to be publicly engaged, all departments should be engaged. This can happen only if at least some new faculty are prepared to do the work.

Institutional Disincentives

A variety of institutional factors may act as disincentives to faculty considering this work. These will vary by campus and may involve policies or practices, may be institutionwide or localized to a particular unit, and may even be relatively minor. However, issues that may appear minor to the administration may be perceived by participants as major obstacles or at least major nuisances that lead them to say, "Why bother?" Campuses will have to identify their own disincentives in order to overcome them.

Increasing Public Engagement

It is highly unlikely that all faculty will embrace public engagement. For those who are wedded to the image of the academic as someone who works alone, removed from the realities of day-to-day challenges and problems, unconcerned about whether their work has applied value, and judged by the number of articles they publish and the stature of the journals in which they are published, public engagement requires an enormous shift in thinking. An institution may find itself repeatedly frustrated in trying to redirect or modify the emphases of these faculty. However, by carefully selecting, nurturing, supporting, and rewarding faculty, the institution is likely to see a significant increase in public engagement.

Recruiting, Hiring, and Orienting Faculty

Hiring people who are predisposed toward public engagement simplifies the institution's work: these faculty will need support, but not convincing. When faculty lines become available, the CAO has an opportunity to allocate positions with the stipulation that departments hire people whose responsibilities include public engagement. To attract faculty with this commitment, position announcements should include the institution's commitment to public engagement; applicants should be asked to document their public engagement experience; and the faculty, department chair, and dean should discuss public engagement with applicants brought to campus. When the department selects the candidate it wishes to hire, the dean should ask how the recommended person will fit with the public engagement goals of the department, college, and university. Finally, appointment letters for new faculty should delineate their responsibilities regarding public engagement.

Orientation for new faculty should include information about public engagement. One creative approach includes a guided bus tour of the community (Plater, 2004). The tour itself creates a context for substantive conversations on the role of the university vis à vis the community. It can also lead to more multidisciplinary work because new faculty from different disciplines are jointly looking at community issues and problems. Because new faculty are inundated with information when they first arrive on campus, it may be preferable to delay extensive discussion of public engagement for a few weeks, giving them time to adjust to the institution.

Addressing Workload Issues

In response to workload issues, the institution's leadership has an obligation to let the faculty know where public engagement fits within the institution's priorities. It cannot be the "priority du jour" with a new priority identified every semester or every year. As already pointed out, public engagement is time-consuming, challenging work. For it to become deeply ingrained in the institution's culture, the administration will have to continue to make its visibility a high priority.

Many faculty will feel that public engagement competes with their other workload demands. However, if they can integrate it with teaching, research, and service, then rather than being an add-on, it can actually enhance all of their work. For example, a faculty member in mathematics who undertakes a project with the local school district to increase middle school students' interest in mathematics could integrate the project into his teaching, research, and service. If the faculty member involves his students in designing the middle school curriculum and delivering the program to the schools, then the project is part of the faculty member's teaching role. If he applies appropriate methods to document the impact of the program, shares the findings at a professional conference, and publishes his methods and findings in a teacher education journal, then the project contributes to his research productivity. Finally, if he works with school personnel to share information about the program with the parents of the participating students, then this is part of his service role.

There appears to be some bias against what faculty sometimes call "double dipping" or as in the preceding example, "triple dipping." This suggests there is something wrong with having one activity contribute to more than one of the major mission dimensions. To the contrary, integrating teaching, research, and service helps reduce the workload burden on faculty while simultaneously increasing their productivity and their contribution to achieving the institution's strategic goals. In the example just described, everyone benefits: the middle school children, their parents, the participating college students, the faculty member, and the discipline of mathematics education. Because this is, for many faculty, a new way of viewing their roles, the institution may need to help them understand the value of integrating responsibilities and show them how to do it effectively.

An effective approach to workload issues is to allow faculty to change their emphasis over time. This can be done by adopting an individualized "contract" for each faculty member; in other words, in consultation with the department chair, each faculty member develops an agreement specifying how he is going to spend his time during the contract period. These annual, biannual, or even triannual contracts can emphasize a different aspect of the faculty role in each of the contract periods. Faculty are then evaluated annually on what they accomplished based on the terms of their contract. The individual faculty members benefit because, as Rice (2005a) pointed out: "Over the length of a professional career, [one] would practice all four forms of scholarship, leading to an integrated wholeness unique to the person. Such a pattern would accommodate what we have discovered through recent studies of adult and career development—the need to grow and change throughout a lifetime" (pp. 308–309). The department benefits because it can look at the aggregation of faculty contracts and ensure that, in total, they fulfill the department's public engagement responsibilities.

Another approach to dealing with workload issues is to hire faculty specifically for the purpose of fulfilling public engagement responsibilities. NKU has found it effective to hire several faculty who are expected to spend 50 percent of their time in the traditional faculty role and the other 50 percent on specific public engagement projects aligned with the institution's strategic agenda.

Many of the ideas shared in the balance of this chapter also positively affect workload, especially the discussion of support services.

THE ROLE OF PROFESSIONAL DEVELOPMENT

Before working with the community, faculty members need to be appropriately prepared, not only because it will benefit them but also because it is important for the institution. As Votruba (2005) stated: "Sending forth faculty who are unprepared to engage the public is a slippery slope for all" (p. 270). Professional development is a major tool for preparing faculty for public engagement.

Whom to Teach

Considering the important role of department chairs, as described in Chapter 4, it is essential to provide them with their own professional development activities to prepare them to play a leadership role in advancing public engagement. Other programs should be provided for faculty and professional staff jointly or there can be separate programs for each. Programs can take place at the level of the department, the college, or the institution. Because different disciplines have different ways of approaching public engagement, their professional development needs will vary. It is advisable, therefore, to offer some professional development by discipline or by clusters of related disciplines.

What to Teach

What to teach—what professional development to offer—should be determined by the faculty. If they are not consulted in advance and asked to identify the topics of greatest interest to them, they will "vote" by their attendance, or lack thereof, at professional development activities.

The institution's faculty development programs are likely to change over time as the faculty become more experienced. Gelmon and Agre-Kippenhan (2002a) described "stages in skill acquisition, relevant to community engagement" (p. 164). These levels go from *explorer*, the one who basically knows nothing about the work, to *novice, manager,* and finally *mentor,* the person who is prepared to help others learn how to do this work. Professional development should match the skill level of the participants.

Professional development content falls into three general categories: foundational content, which refers to the intellectual foundations underpinning public engagement; skills and resource-focused content; and content relating to scholarship standards. The foundational content includes at least the following: how service learning and other community-based experiences affect students; how the faculty member's work with the community enhances the faculty's teaching and traditional research; and how public engagement contributes to knowledge creation. Faculty should be conversant with Boyer's (1996) four forms of scholarship—discovery, teaching, integration, and engagement—and his notion that: "Both the civic and academic health of any culture is vitally enriched as scholars and practitioners speak and listen carefully to each other" (p. 15). Faculty can be shown how engaging with the community will provide them with a broader perspective on their own discipline, which is especially valuable in the professions. They should understand contemporary views of knowledge, as described in Chapter 1, including the importance of the "real world" for the generation of new knowledge as well as its application; the recognition that the source of knowledge is not limited to experts; and the importance of sharing knowledge.

Professional development activities can help faculty refine the skills they need to function effectively in the community. They need to know about the community, both broadly and deeply. Where are the greatest needs? How do these fit with the institution's priorities? Where are the political land mines? Faculty need to learn the language of the community, how to listen effectively, be sensitive to the community's culture and values, share decision making, and deal with community politics. They need to know how people can do the "messy" research that takes place in the field, where the complexities of the real world make it impossible to apply the methods of the laboratory. They need to learn how to include students in community-based work and how best to supervise them in the field. They need to know how to document their work, assess its impact, and evaluate its effectiveness. They need to know about the legal liabilities and how to manage risk for themselves, their students, and the university. They will be very eager to learn about the resources that are available—internally and externally—to support public engagement.

Faculty are familiar with the scholarship of discovery. They know what it is, how to document it, and how to evaluate it. They are much less likely to understand what constitutes the scholarship of engagement, what constitutes quality scholarship, and what constitutes acceptable peer review. These issues are of great concern to the faculty and are discussed in the next chapter.

Faculty need to learn how to integrate teaching, research, and service, especially if the campus has traditionally insisted that any particular faculty activity falls into only one of those mission dimensions. Faculty who are dedicated, productive researchers should be shown how they can combine their passion for research with their potential for positively affecting the community and do it in a way that benefits themselves, their students, the university, and the community. Medical schools offer a good example; faculty there traditionally pursued basic research but failed to connect it to the community. Today, many medical schools have a center for translational research, which is intended to take basic medical research and use it to improve the health of the community. For more details on the work of translational researchers, see, for example, Ohio State (http://medicalcenter.osu.edu/research/translational research /Pages/index.aspx); Johns Hopkins (http://ictr.johnshopkins .edu/ictr/); and Vanderbilt University (http://www.mc.vanderbilt .edu/victr/pub/).

Faulty who are going to introduce service learning into their courses are likely to have particular professional development needs. They may need help generating ideas for legitimate service learning projects, particularly in disciplines not tied to the professions or social sciences. Among other things, they need to learn how to orient and supervise their students, design appropriate reflection activities, and prevent (or handle) problems that students either cause or encounter in the community. The article by Robert Bringle and Julie Hatcher (1995), titled "A Service-Learning Curriculum for Faculty," is an excellent resource for people designing a service learning professional development program. Also helpful is Zlotkowski's (multiple dates) 21-volume set of books titled *Service Learning in the Disciplines*. Each volume looks at service learning from the perspective of a different discipline. Many journals and numerous books contain examples of serving learning courses across a variety of disciplines. See, for example, Kelshaw, Lazarus, Minier, and Associates, 2009; Pew Partnership for Civic Change, 2004; Redlawsk, Rice, and Associates, 2009; and Zlotkowski, 1998.

What Programs to Offer

Faculty teaching faculty is probably the most powerful approach to professional development. As a result, consideration should be given to a variety of peer-to-peer approaches to preparing faculty for public engagement. These include mentoring programs in which an experienced faculty member serves as a mentor to one who is just beginning to do public engagement; observational programs in which a faculty member involved in public engagement allows other faculty to observe or shadow her as she does the work; pairing an experienced faculty member with one just learning about public engagement to team-teach a service learning course; faculty learning communities in which a group of faculty meet regularly to learn more about the subject, share their experiences, and provide mutual support; and breakfast meetings or brown bag lunches where faculty discuss issues in public engagement. If the administration provides readings about public engagement—by purchasing and distributing a relevant book or several articles—these can form the basis for faculty discussions in small groups or at the department or college level. A challenge with this approach is that faculty who already feel overloaded are unlikely to do the reading unless they are convinced that there is some clear benefit to them.

Other programs—ones that may or may not involve peer-to-peer teaching—include formal workshops, seminars, and lectures on some aspect or aspects of public engagement; summer institutes where faculty are paid to participate in an intensive, multiweek, summer learning experience that prepares them to integrate public engagement into their teaching and scholarly work; special training in service learning coupled with time to develop a service learning course critiqued by other program participants; and institutionwide or statewide conferences with speakers on various aspects of public engagement.

If the institution has an office with responsibility for public engagement or service learning, faculty can be rotated into administrative positions in that office, serving, for example, half-time for the academic year. This provides the faculty member with good administrative experience and a deeper understanding of public engagement, provides an ongoing faculty perspective to others working in the office, and adds person power to the office without permanently increasing the number of administrative staff.

Several universities have adopted a "faculty fellows" program to bolster involvement in public engagement. For example, Indiana University-Purdue University Indiana (IUPUI) offers a Faculty Fellows in Service Learning program to advance service learning on their campus (http://csl.iupui.edu/OSL/2b4.asp); the Jonathan M. Tisch College of Citizenship and Public Service at Tufts University offers a faculty fellows program described as "a two-year fellowship for Tufts faculty members who are peer leaders in building active citizenship as a defining strength of Tufts" (http://activecitizen.tufts.edu/Faculty/FacultyFellowsProgram);

and the North Carolina system offers the GlaxoSmithKline Faculty Fellows Program "for faculty to apply their expertise to current public policy issues" (http://ncsu.edu/iei/faculty/).

Who Should Teach?

A variety of offices and individuals can provide professional development. If the institution has a teaching-learning center for faculty, then this office is likely to provide or coordinate most of the professional development. In addition to faculty peers, students and community members can contribute to professional development by providing their perspective on service learning and other forms of public engagement. Professional staff in the service learning office can be strong contributors, and as described later in this chapter, there is potential for the president and CAO to contribute significantly too.

In considering "who teaches," campuses should look beyond their borders. Bringing in experts from other institutions helps faculty understand that the emphasis on public engagement is not unique to their campus: it is a national movement. Moreover, expert voices from outside often have greater credibility than those on campus. The campus should consider collaborating on professional development with neighboring institutions or with other colleges and universities in the state, thereby providing faculty with access to colleagues in their own discipline but located at other institutions. These linkages can then be supported with listservs, blogs, or webinars, and may later lead to productive collaborations.

Professional and disciplinary organizations can provide professional development through their annual conferences. Institutions should consider sending individuals or teams to these conferences, and after the conferences, have them share what they learned with their campus colleagues in both formal and informal ways. Some professional and disciplinary associations have developed materials that can inform professional development programs.

THE ROLE OF COMMUNICATION

Internal communication primarily with the faculty and professional staff is closely related to professional development, which, after all, is basically communicating the why and how of public engagement. As a result, it is important for those doing the communicating described here to coordinate with the office responsible for professional development. Their messages should be consistent and complementary.

Who Communicates?

The administrative leaders—president, CAO, deans, chief public engagement officer—have the potential to profoundly influence the thinking and behavior of everyone at the institution. They need to communicate the importance of public engagement in what they say and what they do, such as being personally involved with the community or providing financial support for the work. As an NKU faculty member stated: "In the past, faculty doing engagement often kept quiet because they knew there was no recognition for doing it and it was better not to draw attention to it; now that the president and provost are talking about [public engagement], many of these people are delighted; others, who've never done it, are left feeling the earth is shifting beneath their feet."

Faculty, who are key opinion leaders and believers in the value of public engagement, can convince their colleagues of the benefits of engaging in this work, especially if the faculty doing the convincing already have a strong record of academic achievement. Their message can be oral, and their work and their views can be featured in publications shared with the campus. (See Chapter 10 for examples of publications.)

Just as there are advantages to having experts from outside the institution involved in professional development, so too it is beneficial to have "outsiders" carry the message of the importance of this work. When a group of NKU faculty were asked about having someone serve as the speaker at an internal celebration of public engagement, they indicated that hearing from someone from outside the institution would go a long way toward influencing faculty views. They recommended identifying a speaker from a national association, someone with a national reputation for public engagement success, or someone from an institution that NKU aspires to be like.

What Is Communicated?

There are several major strands in what is to be communicated. One is the role of public engagement nationally: it should be clear that it is a national phenomenon, not something unique to a particular institution. Closely related is the need to show how this work fits with the institution's strategic agenda and future. Faculty should hear what the institution is trying to accomplish through its public engagement and what benefits accrue to the students and their learning, the participating faculty, the institution as a whole, and the external community. They should see how the work ties to the institution's mission and how public engagement can be thought of as a form of teaching, scholarship, service, or some combination of the three. Examples of how the work has positively affected student learning and faculty research makes the message come alive. Faculty will be particularly interested to know that "Studies show that faculty members who consult with community agencies are more likely to have funded research projects, publications in peer-reviewed journals, and positive student evaluations of their teaching, than those who do not" (Checkoway, 2003, p. 43).

Another important communication strand is providing reassurance in some key areas. Faculty want to know that the emphasis on public engagement will not dilute the value placed on traditional research. They need to be reassured that the administration is not trying to further increase faculty workloads. They need to be confident that public engagement is not a "back door" to tenure, lowering the institution's standards. Public engagement is scholarly work tied to the faculty member's discipline and should meet the standards of all scholarship. (See Chapter 7 for more on the scholarship of engagement.) They need to know that they can take risks and get involved with the community, and they will not be penalized if things do not work out as planned. What is important is to assess the work and learn from the assessment.

Public engagement should be related to things that are intrinsically motivating for faculty and professional staff. "Over and over again, the research on faculty and motivation has found that those of us who enjoy a vital faculty life are driven by a relatively small number of motives: autonomy, community, recognition, [and] efficacy" (Wergin, 2003, p. 15). This means administrators should encourage faculty to try new ideas without fear of negative consequences, foster the development of a sense of community, provide recognition for faculty work, and encourage faculty to have a significant impact on their students and the community. The potential to benefit student learning can be a powerful motivator for faculty.

A message that is often best communicated by experienced faculty is that public engagement can be very satisfying. Some faculty will find that involvement in engagement—with or without the involvement of students—stretches them in new ways, and they will like that. Some will find it intellectually stimulating to work with colleagues from different disciplines. Some will derive great satisfaction from making a difference in their community or watching their students grow in ways that are unlikely to occur in a traditional classroom.

To weigh what messages to emphasize, consider the findings of Kerry Ann O'Meara (2008), who looked at faculty motivation for this work. She analyzed the essays from 68 nominees for the Thomas Ehrlich Faculty Award for Service-Learning. From these essays, submitted between 2001 and 2006, she identified seven types of motivation and calculated the percentage of respondents who cited each:

- To facilitate student learning and growth—94%
- To achieve disciplinary goals—53%
- Personal commitments to specific social issues, places, and people—50%
- Personal/professional identity—60%
- Pursuit of rigorous scholarship and learning—44%
- A desire for collaboration, relationships, partners, and public-making—47%
- Institutional type and mission, appointment type, and/or an enabling reward system and culture for community engagement—50% [p. 14]

O'Meara explains each of the motivators and provides connections to the extant literature. Although service learning was the focus of her analysis, one can reasonably assume that these identified motivators would apply in some degree to all of public engagement.

How to Communicate

Both written and oral communications are effective. NKU held a major event focusing on public engagement that included both forms of communication: a talk by a nationally known figure and a specially prepared booklet—*Aligning for Public Engagement: Laying the Foundation* (2006)—that included "position papers" on public engagement, one written by the president and one by the CAO. The booklet also featured articles about the work of ten different faculty, along with statements, in their own words, about why they do the work.

Public engagement should be included in internally directed speeches given by the president, CAO, and deans. It is not sufficient to do this once; it must be repeated during a given academic year and over many years. Breakfast meetings, lunch meetings, receptions, and regular department and college meetings all provide opportunities to promote public engagement.

Public engagement should be showcased on the campus website, which is good external public relations, and web postings also have an impact on the campus. The use of the web is discussed in Chapter 10.

Campus Conversations: A Special Form of Communication

Campus conversations in which the communication is a dialogue rather than a lecture or formal talk are valuable aids for advancing public engagement. These conversations can be organized at the department, college, or university level, but administrative leaders must be present. The goal is to share perspectives, raise questions, discuss issues, stimulate attendees to think deeply about public engagement—its value and its challenges—and create shared understandings between administrators and faculty. In order to have productive conversations, there has to be agreement on terminology. As one NKU faculty member stated: "We shouldn't be discussing how to count 'it' if we haven't even talked about what 'it' is." The term *scholarship of engagement*, in particular, leads to much confusion if it is not carefully defined. The term is discussed at length in Chapter 7.

It can be challenging to get faculty to attend campus conversations. Those who should attend—those not convinced of the value of public engagement—are least likely to want to attend. The following approaches can help increase attendance:

- Include food and drink at the event and allow time for social interaction.
- Send out repeated reminders, using both hard-copy flyers and e-mails.
- Schedule a conversation far in advance so faculty will not have already committed their time to another activity.
- Enlist the support of deans and chairs, asking them to urge their faculty to attend.

NKU has also found that faculty are more likely to attend when they know that the president and CAO will be present, but even then numerous reminders yield a larger turnout.

Campus conversations should be part of an overall institutional plan for expanding public engagement. Without some follow-up to the campus conversation, some faculty will believe that the conversation was part of a passing fad.

Support Services and Resources

Public engagement requires as much support as other university priorities. In fact, when engagement is in its infancy, it probably needs even more support. Elisa Abes, Golden Jackson, and Susan Jones (2002) conducted a study using survey responses from 518 Ohio faculty: "The results indicated that no matter the strategy employed, many non-service-learning faculty will not use service-learning without logistical support. . . . Anticipated logistical and time difficulties were not only the most frequently cited actual deterrents to service-learning use, but also the most frequently cited potential deterrents to service-learning faculty's continued use" (p. 14). The lack of logistical support is important to all forms of public engagement.

Anything that facilitates faculty work with the community is a form of support. So too is anything that reduces the administrative burden on faculty or removes disincentives identified by the institution. Special support offices, as described in Chapter 5, are an excellent source of support, as are professional development opportunities. Other forms of support include:

- Clerical support to handle the myriad forms and details related to specific projects
- Resources such as supplies and office space with computers, copy machines, and fax capability
- Readily available library materials covering various aspects of public engagement
- Technical assistance with grant writing and statistical analysis
- Legal assistance including, for example, help in developing contracts for community projects or drafting release forms for participants
- Tech support, such as creating listservs or websites for specific projects
- Assistance with identifying community partners, either on a one-to-one basis or through campus-sponsored events that bring community leaders and faculty together
- Databases containing information about community agencies and businesses
- Help for faculty who wish to disseminate their work

To help faculty disseminate their work, one might provide information about journals that focus on this work, ensure that the campus library subscribes to those journals, arrange for internal readers to provide feedback that strengthens the articles, and link faculty with colleagues who have successfully published in the area. One might also keep faculty apprised of conferences at which they could present their work.

Obtaining funding for public engagement can be very challenging. As a result, financial support is particularly valued by faculty. Furthermore, financial commitments are a powerful way to demonstrate the institution's overall commitment to public engagement.

Productivity is likely to increase if grants are available for such things as travel (including travel to attend conferences where the focus is public engagement), service learning assistance, undergraduate and graduate assistants, summer stipends, reassigned time, project evaluation, dissemination, exploratory activities, and entire projects. Multiyear grants are important for projects that cannot be completed in a single year. Sabbatical leaves can provide strong support for public engagement. Summer stipends and reassigned time can be used to write external grant proposals, observe public engagement at other institutions, redesign a course to incorporate service learning or CBR, establish a partnership and lay the foundation for a joint initiative, or even carry out a partnership project. Reassigned time and summer stipends are particularly important for junior faculty because of their need to meet the benchmarks for tenure.

Partnership projects often require that teaching schedules be adjusted and are likely to create administrative burdens on the faculty member's home department. To compensate the department for these inconveniences—and to ensure that department chairs support public engagement—internal grants can allocate "overhead" monies to the home department, as described in Chapter 3.

FOSTERING COLLABORATION

Activities that bring groups of faculty together encourage internal collaboration. Some of the activities suggested earlier—such as holding brown bag lunches and sending faculty teams to relevant conferences—encourage faculty to interact with colleagues in other departments and colleges. The creative assignment of office space can encourage collaboration. For example, at NKU the chairs of the three science departments share an office suite and support personnel. By working in close proximity to each other, they develop strong working relationships and are comfortable collaborating. Multidisciplinary centers, as described in Chapter 5, and cross-disciplinary grant writing can also foster collaboration. Resource allocation must support, not impede, multidisciplinary work.

To encourage collaborative work with the community, the institution should provide professional development for faculty to develop the skills that will help them feel confident and be successful; help them connect with the community by introducing them to community partners and bringing potential partnership projects to the attention of the appropriate faculty; and provide support and eliminate barriers so that faculty can effectively and efficiently partner with the community. Many of these ideas have already been discussed in more detail.

INCENTIVES AND REWARDS

As mentioned earlier, *push* strategies that attempt to force faculty in a particular direction are much less effective than *pull* strategies that provide incentives to encourage desired behavior. Internal grant support, mentioned earlier, and recognizing public engagement in the RPT process, discussed in the next chapter, are examples of pull strategies. Several other pull strategies are described here.

Awards and Recognition

An internal awards program recognizing outstanding public engagement benefits the institution and the individual. It calls attention to the institution's public engagement initiatives; provides excellent material for internal and external publications, showcasing both the institution and the individual; identifies publicly engaged faculty to hold up as models for all faculty; and serves both to reward those doing the work and motivate those who are considering it. Awards can be at the department, college, or institutional level. They can be honorary, such as recognition in a university publication, a place for the winner's photograph on a wall of honorees, or a special title such as "engaged scholar." Awards can also include a gift, such as a book, or financial benefit such as a onetime stipend or an increase in base salary. The ultimate award is to appoint someone to an endowed chair in public engagement.

There are many less formal yet highly effective ways to recognize the public engagement of individuals or groups of faculty, including, for example, praise in the form of a note from the president or CAO, an invitation to lunch or dinner with either of them, or a reception at one of their homes. Similarly, faculty are rewarded when their work is publicly recognized: one can invite a few faculty to present their exemplary public engagement work at a meeting of the governing board; high-level academic leaders can mention specific public engagement projects in their speeches both inside and outside the academy; and the institution can highlight particular public engagement projects on its website and in its publications. Several of these suggestions are discussed in more detail in Chapter 10, dealing with communication.

National awards are available to honor public engagement or service learning work. Examples include:

- Outreach Scholarship/W. K. Kellogg Foundation Engagement Award and the C. Peter Magrath University/Community Engagement Award, both of which recognize the outstanding outreach and engagement partnerships at four-year public universities (http://www.aplu.org/NetCommunity/ Page.aspx?pid=304)
- Ernest A. Lynton Award for the Scholarship of Engagement, which recognizes the work of individual faculty (http://www.nerche.org/Lynton_Award/lynton_award.html)
- Thomas Ehrlich Civically Engaged Faculty Award (http://www.compact.org/resources/ehrlich-faculty-award-for-service-learning/1077/)
- William M. Plater Award for Leadership in Civic Engagement, which recognizes the work of CAOs (http://www.aascu.org/programs/adp/pdf/PlaterAward.pdf)

Simply nominating people for these external awards recognizes their contribution, and the campus can celebrate the nomination itself.

Celebrations

Annual celebrations can create excitement and enthusiasm for public engagement. Celebrations may include poster presentations documenting public engagement. These posters help other faculty learn more about the work of their colleagues, inspire new ideas among those reading the posters, and encourage collaborations among those discussing the posters. The selection of posters can be a peer-reviewed, competitive process or an honor bestowed "by invitation."

Those receiving awards for outstanding work may be recognized at these celebrations. They may be asked to describe their projects, perhaps explaining why they are drawn to public engagement. Community partners and potential partners may be invited to share in the celebration, and the local media should be invited to the event. For universities that offer competitive, public engagement grants, the grant recipients can be announced at the celebration. Celebrations can become an annual tradition that brings together faculty and administrators from throughout the campus—often with community members or students—to celebrate and promote public engagement.

Celebrations on a smaller scale can also be effective—for example, a luncheon to celebrate the successful conclusion of a project, a dinner to honor recipients of internal grants, or a reception to celebrate a single public engagement project. Such celebrations may be limited to those involved in the project or extend to other members of the campus or broader community. A celebration can bring positive closure to a project and allow participants to enjoy the feeling of "a job well done." The presence of high-level administrators at these events communicates the importance the institution attaches to public engagement.

Unit-Level Incentives and Rewards

Departmental support is essential for expanding public engagement. The ideas suggested in the preceding paragraph can be adapted for recognition of a department or a group of faculty rather than individuals. For example, an award can be created for the department that contributes the most to public engagement or shows the greatest improvement in service learning courses; there can be an award for the outstanding multidisciplinary project; and a special luncheon can be provided for the department that best epitomizes the engaged department. Awards might carry a financial benefit that provides the department with discretionary funds to support their public engagement or other departmental priorities. Any funds awarded should carry forward to the next fiscal year or the intent to reward will backfire

(B. Burch, personal communication with the author, November 20, 2009).

Two national programs recognize the work of the institution as a whole. One is from The Carnegie Foundation for the Advancement for Teaching, the other from the Corporation for National and Community Service. As mentioned in Chapter 1, in 2006 The Carnegie Foundation for the Advancement of Teaching introduced an elective classification system that recognizes universities for two aspects of public engagement: curricular engagement, and outreach and partnerships. In 2006 and 2008, universities could apply for either or both designations; in 2010, they were required to submit evidence of both. The next opportunity to apply for the elective classification will be in 2015. The application process is extensive, requiring the institution to document "through indicators of institutional identity and culture and institutional commitment" (Driscoll, 2009, p. 7) that they have institutionalized community engagement, and to then document examples of their engagement work. For information on applying for the Carnegie designation, see http://classifications .carnegiefoundation.org/descriptions/community_engagement .php.

The Corporation for National and Community Service, in collaboration with the Department of Education, Department of Housing and Urban Development, Campus Compact, and the American Council on Education, annually invites colleges and universities to apply for the President's Higher Education Community Service Honor Roll. Selection for this award is "based on a series of selection factors including scope and innovation of service projects, percentage of student participation in service activities, incentives for service, and the extent to which the school offers academic service-learning courses" (http://www.learnandserve.gov/ about/programs/higher_ed_honorroll.asp).

THE ROLE OF THE DEPARTMENT

Although much of what has been written here and elsewhere about engaging faculty focuses on the individual, the importance of the department cannot be overstated. "The department is arguably the definitive locus of faculty culture . . . [yet] departments prove to be unusually effective points of resistance; their faculties have little turnover and substantial autonomy from higher levels of administration, so they develop a deep consciousness of themselves as 'we' versus the 'they' of the rest of the institution" (Edwards, 1999, pp. 18, 21). Thus it becomes important to think in terms of engaged departments. "In an engaged department, the emphasis shifts from individual faculty, courses, and curricular redesign to collective faculty culture—changing the culture from one of 'my work' to one of 'our work'" (Battistoni, Gelmon, Saltmarsh, Wergin, & Zlotkowski, 2003, p. 3). To assist in creating engaged departments, Battistoni and his colleagues developed the Engaged Department Toolkit, which is available from Campus Compact (http://www.compact.org/resources/engaged-department-toolkit/1195/). For more information on engaged departments, see Kecskes, 2006.

As part of the alignment process or as part of the institution's planning process, departments should develop public engagement goals and determine how, collectively, they will achieve those goals. Ideally they will develop a plan that encourages faculty members to contribute in ways that best match their strengths and contribute the most to the growth and development of their students. This approach underscores that all departments, but not all individual faculty, must be publicly engaged.

The department chair should be strongly committed to the institution's public engagement mission. A chair influences her faculty's views on what is important, where faculty should put their efforts, and how they will be judged. Chairs allocate departmental resources and make teaching assignments. Faculty, particularly untenured faculty, recognize that chairs have significant power that can affect the working life of each faculty member. Because of the important role of chairs, CAOs and deans should ensure that the selection and evaluation of department chairs consider their ability to lead across the full breadth of the mission, including public engagement.

THE ROLE OF THE DISCIPLINE

Public engagement opportunities vary by discipline. Furthermore, faculty often consider their closest colleagues to be faculty in their discipline at other universities, especially now that computers enable visual and auditory communication independent of geography. As a result, disciplinary associations can play an important role in legitimizing public engagement and demonstrating its relationship to the discipline. Many disciplinary associations have accepted this role and actively promote public engagement. Sending faculty to their conferences and otherwise helping to promote the ideas of these associations can help advance public engagement on individual campuses. It is beyond the scope of this book to provide suggestions for getting disciplinary associations more involved, but a good source for exploring this issue is Sherwyn Morreale and James Applegate's (2006) chapter titled "Engaged Disciplines: How National Disciplinary Societies Support the Scholarship of Engagement."

THE ROLE OF STAFF

Although this chapter has focused primarily on faculty, much of what is discussed here applies equally to professional staff, who can be very instrumental in advancing the campus's goals. In fact, some professional staff are assigned totally to public engagement. Others are involved in smaller ways. Examples of staff involvement include these: information technology staff assisting a nonprofit with installing a local computer network; student affairs staff working with student organizations to train their members as volunteers for local nonprofits; and athletic staff helping the community to develop a youth soccer program. The institution must be clear on the extent to which staff should be publicly engaged, and there must be clear goals and appropriate recognition for the work. Those who are expected to be involved may need professional development to help them meet the institution's expectations.

THE ROLE OF GRADUATE PROGRAMS

Professional development begins when one is in graduate school, but unfortunately "interviews with graduate students and early career faculty disclose a serious mismatch between the doctoral preparation that most receive and the needs of the universities and colleges in which they are likely to be employed" (Rice, 2005a,

p. 311). Chris Golde and Timothy Dore (2004) surveyed doctoral students at 27 universities. Responses were obtained from 4,114 students who had been in their programs for at least two years. More than half were interested in providing service to the community, but "this positive news was offset by very low proportions of respondents reporting that their programs had prepared them for service roles. Indeed, this aspect of preparation is nearly absent"(p. 27). The implications are clear: those who offer doctoral programs should take every opportunity to engage their students in the acquisition of skills and perspectives essential for public engagement. The students need opportunities to observe and participate in service learning, CBR, and other public engagement work. They should learn how to integrate public engagement with teaching, research, and service. When possible, they should engage in multidisciplinary, collaborative work with the community, and the doctoral faculty should support their students in this work by participating, modeling, or supervising. A further implication of Golde and Dore's research is that newly hired faculty are unlikely to have acquired public engagement skills in their graduate programs. As a result, they will need help to be successfully engaged with the community.

Concluding Comments

This chapter focused on aligning the faculty and professional staff to be successfully involved and to involve their students in public engagement. Before an institution decides what approach to take, faculty and staff should be asked about the obstacles that create the biggest barriers and how they can best be overcome. This does not need to be done with a large-scale survey; an advisory committee including key opinion leaders who are familiar with the campus culture and history will know what is likely to be effective.

Some faculty will be involved in public engagement even before the institution makes it a priority. The institution should provide them the support they need to be successful and the recognition they deserve for their work. Some faculty will simply not be interested in public engagement, and from a cost-benefit perspective it is probably best to focus attention elsewhere. There will be a large group in the middle: not yet engaged but willing to consider it. Focusing on this group is likely to be very productive, but it is important to realize that none of the approaches described here can be effective as single, isolated activities. Campus conversations, for example, need to take place again and again; administrators need to give public engagement a high profile year after year; celebrations and awards should be annual events. Ideally, all of this work should be driven by a strategic plan designed to increase the institution's public engagement.

CHAPTER SEVEN

ALIGNING REAPPOINTMENT, PROMOTION, AND TENURE

There is probably no issue as fundamental to institutionalizing public engagement as reappointment, promotion, and tenure (RPT). In every campus conversation that even touched on increasing public engagement, NKU faculty mentioned these issues. They were unequivocal in their views: RPT policies must support public engagement in order for them and their colleagues—especially junior faculty—to invest significant time and energy in the work.

THE CHANGE PROCESS

Changing the RPT guidelines is not a simple matter, nor should it be. RPT guidelines reflect enduring values of the institution and of higher education in general, so it is not surprising that change is resisted. Moreover, change creates uncertainty, and uncertainty creates anxiety. When RPT changes are contemplated, the faculty are concerned about what will "count," how the changes will affect them personally, and how they will affect the institution's reputation.

- *Will those seeking tenure or promotion be evaluated in terms of a new set of expectations?* This concern can be addressed by phasing in changes, giving those already at the institution a fixed number of years (for example, four years) during which they can choose to apply for RPT under the original or revised guidelines.
- *Will all faculty be expected to do this work?* This fear creates a significant hurdle and is overcome only by repeatedly

reassuring the campus that all departments, but not all individuals, must be publicly engaged. Although some campuses may want all faculty to be involved, it is unrealistic and probably unwise to apply this expectation to all faculty already at the institution.

• *Will the institution be perceived as having lower standards than similar institutions?* Demonstrating that highly respected institutions have modified their RPT guidelines to accommodate public engagement, and emphasizing quality and rigor in the new guidelines will help address this concern.

Aligning RPT guidelines requires as much attention to process as to end product. That is, one could design a set of RPT guidelines that dovetail perfectly with the institution's public engagement mission, but if the process by which the guidelines were developed is not acceptable to the campus, the new guidelines are likely to be rejected outright or simply ignored. It is, therefore, critically important to pay attention to process issues while attempting to revise RPT guidelines. The campus should take whatever time is necessary to ensure that institutional history and culture are respected during the revision process; it is not unusual for it to take one or two years to change RPT guidelines. This does not mean that those wanting change have to be passive bystanders, but they do have to proceed carefully and wisely. An important role for the administration is to remind the campus that promotion and tenure should be tied to institutional mission.

Different triggers can initiate the change process. The most effective is when faculty make clear their belief that the RPT process must be strengthened, clarified, and aligned. Absent this, if the administration carefully cultivates the faculty voice and enlists the support of key faculty, it can successfully request reconsideration of the RPT guidelines, explaining that the changing mission requires a change in the RPT guidelines. Requests from the administration can be bolstered by input—or even a mandate—from the governing board or the system office. Without a significant number of supportive faculty, however, this is not a process that can be easily achieved.

Promotion and tenure policies can also be affected by public policy. Consider, for example, the dramatic increase in federal research support that followed World War II and how it helped ensure that research is a priority on almost all campuses. Public policy could have the same effect on public engagement, but currently it lags behind many colleges' and universities' commitment to public engagement.

On most campuses, rewriting the RPT guidelines will be undertaken by a faculty committee, which should begin by establishing its goals and objectives. There will be some variability among institutions, but at least three goals are likely to apply to all institutions: (a) create a system that recognizes and rewards behavior that advances each institution's mission dimensions; (b) ensure that RPT guidelines are fair and promote quality work; and (c) develop guidelines that clarify what work is acceptable within each of the mission dimensions, the criteria by which it will be evaluated, what constitutes acceptable documentation, and the process by which the documentation will be evaluated.

The committee must allow sufficient time for debate and discussion, not just among the committee members but also at the department and college levels. They will need support from the president, CAO, and deans. NKU found it very effective to support the committee by providing a draft document, a revised RPT policy. This saved the committee time, provided a starting point for change, and modeled how to incorporate public engagement in the RPT guidelines without minimizing the importance of other faculty roles. If, given the campus culture, an administrator-written draft is not acceptable, then an alternative is to direct the committee to the policies of institutions that already incorporate public engagement in their RPT guidelines.

The committee may find it useful to evaluate the institution's existing RPT guidelines using the *Community-Engaged Scholarship for Health Collaborative: Review, Promotion and Tenure Analysis Protocol* (Mikkelsen, Gelmon, Seifer, & Kauper-Brown, 2005). The protocol lists nine elements that should be included in RPT policies at engaged institutions. For example: "Community-engaged scholarship is recognized and valued for all categories of appointments, regardless of tenure and/or clinical, teaching and/or practice emphasis." Each element is rated on a three-point scale: "absent, some activity, potential role model."

RPT guidelines must be consistent at all levels of review. Faculty should not be expected to satisfy one set of standards at the department level, another at the college level, and a third at the institutional level. Thus, after institutional policies are changed, colleges and departments must review—and in all likelihood revise—their guidelines for consistency with the new institutional guidelines.

RPT changes are likely to need approval at various levels of the institution: faculty, CAO, president, and governing board. It may not be possible to get all the changes that each stakeholder group would like; hence, compromise is important, especially if the proposed revisions address the major issues. At a later date, when faculty are comfortable with the revised policies, it may be relatively easy to make refinements.

SOME FUNDAMENTAL ISSUES

Several fundamental RPT issues warrant consideration at the outset of any change process. Some involve basic principles recommended for all institutions. Others must be resolved by each institution in a way that fits with its history, culture, and mission.

BASIC PRINCIPLES

The importance of "double" and "triple dipping"—allowing work to count in more than one category—was made clear in the previous chapter. The final set of RPT guidelines should make it equally clear that the institution not only allows counting work as contributing to more than one category, but in fact encourages work that fulfills more than one mission dimension. Orange Coast Community College, which collaborated with the Orange County Department of Education, provides a good example of how triple dipping can work. Geology students at the college undertook several projects to excite and educate children about science. This was engaged teaching because the undergraduate geology students worked in teams to develop interactive materials and posters that were shared at "family science nights" attended by elementary school students, who would be, it was hoped, accompanied by their parents. It was certainly engaged service to the community, and a highly reflective piece about this work was published in Kecskes' *Engaging Departments* (Yett, 2006), which qualifies it as engaged scholarship.

When discussing what can be included in a faculty request for RPT consideration, a question commonly arises about paid work. Again, the term "double dipping" is used, suggesting that there is something unseemly about being paid and counting the work toward promotion and tenure. However, whether someone is paid is irrelevant. What is important is the quality of the work and the benefits that the community derives. Lynton and Elman (1987) addressed this issue more than 20 years ago: "The basic academic reward system should judge the quality, the importance, and the appropriateness of a faculty member's professional activity. Whether it is done for additional compensation or pro bono, whether for a token honorarium or a substantial consulting fee usually depends on factors that have little relevance to the intrinsic merit of the activity" (p. 155).

A final issue relates to setting minimum parameters around what work will be evaluated for an RPT decision. Specifically, it is recommended that only work that relates to a faculty member's discipline or role at the institution be included.

For Committee Consideration

Two fundamental issues arise in relation to the categories of faculty work: How many will there be and what will they be called? Historically, there have been three categories: teaching, research, and service. An important and highly controversial question is whether to treat engagement as a fourth category or whether to consider it cross-cutting. Each campus must grapple with this issue. Adding public engagement as a fourth category raises its status so that public engagement is comparable to the other three mission dimensions; makes clear that public engagement is different from service; and communicates the importance attached to the work. But treating public engagement as a cross-cutting dimension is more acceptable to the faculty because it is a less radical change; encourages faculty to integrate public engagement into their teaching, research, and service; reduces the tendency to think of faculty work as falling into silos that are independent of each other;

and is more consistent with the idea that not all faculty have to be publicly engaged. After extensive discussions, NKU concluded that public engagement would be a cross-cutting dimension, not a fourth dimension. This conclusion was reinforced in workshops involving faculty and administrative teams from more than a dozen institutions, ranging from small private colleges to large research universities: all favored retaining three categories and treating public engagement as a cross-cutting dimension.

What labels should be attached to the dimensions of faculty work? Faculty and administrators have traditionally used the terms *teaching, research,* and *service.* Some have argued, however, that a different set of terms would suggest a more contemporary role for faculty. For example, in 2000 the Kellogg Commission on the Future of State and Land-Grant Universities suggested using the terms: "learning, discovery, and engagement in the public interest" (p. 14). Campus conversations focused on appropriate labeling can help the campus clarify the faculty role and the relationship between the various mission dimensions. At NKU, the terms used are *teaching, scholarship,* and *service,* and within the RPT guidelines, public engagement is clearly identified and integrated into each of the categories.

DEFINING ENGAGED FACULTY WORK

In discussing engaged faculty work, it is important to understand how "engaged" work differs from faculty work that is not labeled "engaged."

ENGAGED TEACHING

Teaching is appropriately labeled as engaged when course- or curriculum-related learning activities involve students with the community in mutually beneficial ways (Northern Kentucky University, n.d., p. 25). Common forms of engaged teaching are service learning and CBR, both discussed in Chapter 8. The learning associated with these pedagogical approaches has a strong experiential base, connects the classroom with the world of practice, and requires students to consciously reflect on the learning experience and share their reflections in some meaningful way.

Many would also classify internships, co-op experiences, and practica as engaged teaching.

ENGAGED SERVICE

Service is an extremely broad term, referring to work that serves three very different "masters": the institution, the profession or discipline, and the community. Although service to the institution and service to the discipline-profession are critically important and should not be undervalued, only service to the community is considered engaged service.

Major engaged service initiatives often meet the criteria for engaged scholarship, the subject of the next section, and faculty certainly want these initiatives recognized in the RPT process as both service and scholarship. However, faculty also want credit for work that is more routine, perhaps more repetitive. For example, when a faculty member in economics serves on the advisory board for the local economic development commission, the work is unlikely to qualify as engaged scholarship. It is, however, engaged service and worthy of recognition in the service category.

Colleges and universities provide many educational opportunities for persons who are not enrolled at their institution, such as continuing education for accountants, workshops on site at a local company, and lectures on state history offered at local libraries. Activities such as these might be classified as engaged teaching or engaged service, or both, depending on the institution's guidelines.

ENGAGED SCHOLARSHIP

In the engagement lexicon no term causes as much confusion or intense debate as *engaged scholarship*. *Engaged* is the easy part of the term: it refers to work done in partnership with the community. The challenge comes in determining what constitutes scholarship. As an example, assume that a faculty member, working with a community agency, designs a public relations campaign to reduce drunk driving and shares what is learned from the experience. Is that engaged scholarship? In all likelihood, conversations about this example would quickly reduce to the question, "Were the results published?" However, even if not published, it is quite possible that this work could satisfy the criteria for both engaged scholarship and engaged service.

After exploring faculty roles and rewards with faculty at many universities and with various disciplinary associations, Robert Diamond and Bronwyn Adam (2000) concluded: "There is no single definition or conceptualization of 'scholarship' that works easily across disciplines," and "Certain activities are more central to particular disciplines than to others" (p. 5). Thus, each campus must struggle with defining scholarship in a way that is acceptable to that institution. The adopted definition needs to be broad enough to encompass all of the disciplines, yet sufficiently restrictive to ensure rigor.

As a starting point for campus conversations, consider the following set of recommended criteria. They are based on criteria suggested by Robert Diamond (2004), Charles Glassick, Mary Huber, and Gene Maeroff (1997), Ernest Lynton (1996), and the National Review Board for the Scholarship of Engagement (www.scholarshipofengagement.org/evaluation/evaluation_criteria.html).

- The work relates to the faculty member's disciplinary expertise.
- The work reflects knowledge of the relevant professional literature, theory, and best practices.
- At the outset, there were clear goals and objectives for the work. If the goals and objectives were modified, there was a clear rationale for doing so.
- Appropriate methods were used. The scholar selected his methods as a function of the field in which he was working and the problem he was attempting to address. Although the ideal methods may have been modified to accommodate real-world challenges, the modification was made with care and full knowledge of the implications associated with the modification.
- The work makes a significant contribution to the community or the knowledge base in the discipline. Input from those affected by the work should help determine whether the work was significant for the community.
- The work and the results were documented, appropriately shared, and evaluated. This criterion addresses the question of whether something must be published to be considered

scholarship. The answer is "no." It must be appropriately shared and it must be reviewed, but that does not necessarily mean distribution through a scholarly publication or review by other academics. A study of the economic impact of creating a technology incubator for small businesses might result in a report that has significant impact on the community but the report may not be published. Those reviewing the report might be local investors who are qualified to assess the contributions of the report. If they review it positively and if it meets the other criteria for scholarly work, then it can justifiably be considered engaged scholarship as well as engaged service.

• The faculty member critically reflected on the process and product of the work, asking himself such questions as: What can be learned from this project? What worked? What did not? How should similar work be done in the future? How do the outcomes of this project add to the existing body of knowledge? What are the next logical steps?

It should be noted that research does not have to contribute directly to the faculty member's discipline in order to be considered scholarship; it could deal with improving, expanding, or otherwise enhancing engagement in relation to the discipline. For example, a psychology professor who conducts research on the impact of service learning on her introductory psychology students is involved in the scholarship of engagement, provided that the work satisfies the criteria for scholarly work. Although her work is not contributing to the science of psychology, it helps develop best practices and thus should be counted as scholarship.

MAKING REAPPOINTMENT, PROMOTION, AND TENURE DECISIONS

There are three aspects to making RPT decisions: criteria, documentation, and evaluation. Faculty need information about each of these before beginning their engagement work, long before they are ready to apply for promotion or tenure. The information helps guide the choices they make about the use of their time, the records they keep about their work, and the additional data they collect as evidence of their contributions.

CRITERIA

Public engagement work must meet the highest quality standards and reflect intellectual rigor. Emphasizing quality and rigor is reassuring to those who are concerned that public engagement lowers standards and provides a "backdoor" to promotion and tenure. Ideally, the work should also make a significant, positive difference in the community and achieve agreed-upon goals, but this is not always the case. There may be justifiable reasons why the project did not unfold as planned, and if the work meets the other criteria, it may still contribute positively toward RPT consideration.

Engaged Teaching

Evaluating engaged teaching means looking at its impact on the students and the community. Looking at how a course affects students is not very different in a course using engaged approaches than in a course that relies on traditional pedagogical approaches: Did the students achieve the academic goals? Did the students develop a deep appreciation for the course content? Are the students more interested in the subject matter? In an engaged course, one would also ask whether the students have a greater understanding of how what they learned in class is applied in a community setting. Community impact can be assessed through a variety of qualitative and quantitative approaches. Gelmon and her colleagues' (2001) book, *Assessing Service-Learning and Civic Engagement*, is discussed in Chapter 9; it describes a variety of measures that can be used for this assessment.

In evaluating teaching, reviewers should recognize that engaged teaching generally requires more time and is more complex than traditional teaching, and faculty who undertake this work should be given credit for doing it.

Engaged Service

Evaluating the quality of engaged service is similar to evaluating the quality of institutional or professional service. Consideration should be given to the role of the faculty member, the significance of the activity, the duration of the involvement, the complexity and scope of the work, the quality of the contribution as assessed by those who were involved, the number of people who were affected, and the amount of impact. Ongoing, complex, engaged service should contribute more to the overall assessment than brief involvements with the community. As with engaged teaching, information should be obtained from the community, either systematically or anecdotally.

Engaged Scholarship

Seven criteria for evaluating engaged scholarship—criteria that can also be used with more traditional scholarship—were suggested earlier. The sources from which the criteria were excerpted provide a more in-depth look at each one. For example, one of the listed criteria stated in part: "The work and the results were documented, appropriately shared, and evaluated." Although Glassick, Huber, and Maeroff (1997) use different wording—they talk about "effective presentation"—their detailed explication of the concept included the following three questions: "Does the scholar use a suitable style and effective organization to present his or her work? Does the scholar use appropriate forums for communicating work to its intended audiences? Does the scholar present his or her message with clarity and integrity?" (p. 32).

DOCUMENTATION

Applying for promotion or tenure is sufficiently stressful without the documentation process being a mystery. Whereas it may be a simple matter for a faculty member to collect the necessary documentation at the time she is doing the engaged work, it is often impossible to obtain the information years after the work is completed. Therefore, before faculty begin their engagement work they should know what constitutes appropriate and expected documentation, and how the documentation of engaged work compares with that of traditional work. The institution should offer workshops with sample dossiers to help faculty understand the documentation process. Faculty should be encouraged to work closely with their department chair and the department's RPT committee to ensure that while they are doing the work they are also gathering the needed documentation.

Some institutions encourage faculty to report all of their activities; others ask that faculty select examples showing their most important work. Whichever is the case, documentation should provide clear evidence that each reported activity satisfies each of the relevant evaluation criteria. Information and evaluations from partnering organizations, project participants and beneficiaries, and independent reviewers are all important components of the documentation of engaged work. At some institutions, these particular inputs are provided by the faculty member being reviewed; at others, they are obtained by the department chair or another administrator.

Revising the RPT guidelines provides an opportunity to rethink the manner in which documentation is presented. Glassick, Huber, and Maeroff (1997) recommend a professional profile with three principal sections. The profile begins with a statement of responsibilities that, if faculty have workload contracts (see Chapter 6), would reflect the responsibilities specified in the contract. The second section includes the faculty member's professional achievements as they relate to the statement of responsibilities. Finally, "for depth, *selected samples* of the scholar's best work would be documented to the standards by a reflective essay and by rich and varied materials" (p. 43).

Some institutions are adopting the concept of the academic portfolio, which has much in common with the professional profile. As described by Peter Seldin and Elizabeth Miller (2009): "An academic portfolio is a reflective, evidence-based collection of materials that documents teaching, research, and service performance. It brings together, in one place, information about a professor's most significant professional accomplishments. It includes documents and materials that collectively suggest the scope, quality, and significance of a professor's achievements" (p. 2). As Seldin and Miller pointed out, the portfolio approach provides information on the *how* and *why* of faculty work in contrast to traditional approaches that emphasize *what* a faculty member has done. Preparing a portfolio is time-consuming—it usually takes 15 to 20 hours to prepare—but Seldin and Miller (2009) reported that faculty they mentored found it well worth their time. Their book, *The Academic Portfolio,* is an excellent resource for those wanting to adopt the portfolio approach. With inputs from more than 200 faculty and chairs representing a variety of disciplines and types of institutions, the book offers practical advice on preparing an academic portfolio, describes the role of mentoring in the preparation and use of the portfolio, and provides examples from 16 different disciplines.

Another resource that may prove helpful to faculty is the 2002 article by Gelmon and Agre-Kippenhan (2002b): "Promotion, Tenure, and the Engaged Scholar: Keeping the Scholarship of Engagement in the Review Process." Both authors were promoted and tenured at Portland State University, and the credentials of each included engaged scholarship. Their article provides specific advice for faculty navigating the promotion and tenure process, especially when their work relates to public engagement.

Evaluation

Changing the RPT guidelines is only the first step, and as difficult as it might be, it is often easier than the next step, which is ensuring that those judging credentials implement the new criteria, particularly in the scholarship area. It is much easier to count publications than to evaluate whether work satisfies the criteria for scholarship and whether it achieves standards of quality and rigor. NKU faculty who were publicly engaged repeatedly expressed concern that their departmental colleagues would give lip service to the new criteria, but when judging credentials would revert to the standards with which they were most familiar: the number of publications and the prestige of the journals in which they appeared. The faculty concerns were not without merit: the potential is great for senior faculty—the ones most likely to be evaluating junior colleagues—to undermine the new RPT criteria by using traditional standards for judging credentials.

Careful selection of those who will review credentials using the new RPT guidelines can help ameliorate the concerns of junior faculty. Faculty selected for RPT committees should believe in the value of engaged teaching, scholarship, and service and recognize that it is often more time-consuming than traditional work. The institution should require and provide training for all persons serving on departmental or college RPT committees as well as for department chairs, deans, and the CAO. Even those who strongly support public engagement need the training so that their commitment to engagement does not override considerations of quality and rigor. The training should help people understand the complexities and importance of public engagement; accept that work can contribute to more than one mission dimension; ensure that interpretations of the revised guidelines are consistent with the intent of the policies; and ensure the policies are interpreted consistently at different levels of review. As part of the training, it is useful for small groups to review, evaluate, and discuss sample dossiers.

An important part of the evaluation process is an independent review, typically a peer review. However, with engaged work, the reviewer might more appropriately be someone other than an academic peer. For example, community members or nonprofit professionals who are not involved in the project may be well qualified to judge the value and impact of a particular project. There are at least three issues to consider here:

- *Who should be approached to provide the review of a particular project?* Faculty working on other campuses might be appropriate reviewers but only if they understand and appreciate engaged work; reviewers might be people working in the community who know what was required to complete the work and understand its value to the community; and professionals from outside the university who have a deep understanding of the subject matter can provide the independent review.
- *When should the reviewer or reviewers be identified?* If the department chair and faculty member agree on the reviewers before the work is undertaken, and if they document their agreement, future conflicts over the review process can be avoided. They might agree to persons by specific name or simply by position (for example, the director of the XYZ Community Agency or the local mayor).
- *Who will seek the review?* Evidence of an independent review might be included in the documentation submitted by the faculty member being reviewed or it might be obtained by the department chair or other academic administrator; the latter approach is often assumed to be more objective.

CONCLUDING COMMENTS

Changes in RPT policies will have significant implications, particularly for junior faculty. Prolonged discussions, which are probably inevitable when change is contemplated, are likely to create anxiety for the untenured. Although it is impossible to completely alleviate this anxiety, it can be reduced by keeping everyone apprised of the expected changes and letting junior faculty know how they will be affected. As mentioned earlier, an effective approach is to allow those hired under the old guidelines to have the option of being judged by either the old or new guidelines for a fixed number of years.

The implementation of RPT policies should be a blend of consistency and variability. It is important that there be consistency across the different levels that evaluate the faculty: department, college, institutionwide RPT committee, and CAO. Although there should also be fundamental consistency across the campus, there are differences among disciplines and differences in the work responsibilities of individual faculty. The system should be open to rewarding differences as long as quality and rigor are not sacrificed. Professional development, as described earlier, must be provided at every level to ensure that reviewers understand the new guidelines and the importance of applying the new criteria.

When engagement work lacks rigor or falls exclusively in the service category, or when teaching is substandard, a faculty member will not meet the criteria for RPT even if heavily engaged with the community. When the person is denied promotion or tenure, some faculty will erroneously conclude that one cannot be tenured or promoted on the basis of engaged work. Because administrators cannot discuss personnel issues, they are challenged to counter these erroneous conclusions. One effective approach is to share positive examples of persons who are doing engaged work and being tenured and promoted; it is most powerful if those people are on the campus, but until the institution has those examples, one can share hypothetical examples or examples from other campuses. The examples should make it clear that engagement work can weigh heavily in RPT decisions, providing the work meets the quality standards in each category where faculty are evaluated.

There is a significant risk that changing the RPT policies will result in little real change. Unless faculty are absolutely convinced that documented, engaged scholarship will truly count toward RPT, the admonition that public engagement is only for senior faculty will persist. Senior faculty will warn junior faculty that the rhetoric of the institution is not matched by the reward system, and junior faculty will likely conclude that the traditional route—the scholarship of discovery—is a safer route to building their careers. If the goal is to embed public engagement into the fabric of the campus, then both the wording of RPT policies and their implementation must make it clear that high-quality, effective public engagement will make a significant contribution to a positive RPT decision.

Although this chapter has focused on RPT, the ideas set forth also apply to the annual performance review of faculty and professional staff and to evaluations for merit-based salary increases. They, like RPT, are effective pull strategies to motivate greater involvement in public engagement.

CHAPTER EIGHT

ALIGNING FOR STUDENT ENGAGEMENT

A Chinese proverb says: "Tell me and I forget. Show me and I remember. Involve me and I understand." There are many variations on this proverb, but regardless of the wording, the message is always the same: one learns more by doing than by simply listening and looking. If students are going to *do*, it makes good sense for them to do something that is beneficial beyond the classroom, and serving the community meets this criterion. As an example, students in a graphic arts course could be asked to design promotional materials for an imaginary company, but if the materials are designed for a local nonprofit organization, both the students and the community will benefit.

PEDAGOGICAL APPROACHES TO PUBLIC ENGAGEMENT

The two most common public engagement pedagogies are service learning and community-based research (CBR).

SERVICE LEARNING

Bringle and Hatcher (2004) provided a frequently quoted definition of service learning: "Service-learning is ... a course-based, credit bearing educational experience in which students (a) participate in an organized service activity that meets identified community needs, and (b) reflect on the service activity in such a way as to gain further understanding of course content, a broader appreciation of the discipline, and an enhanced sense of personal values and civic responsibility'' (p. 127). Thus, service learning has three critically important components: service to the community, learning connected to the course content, and reflection.

Service Learning and Civic Learning

For many years, the literature on service learning focused on content learning—that is, engaging with the community as a way of learning the content of the course while simultaneously benefiting the community. More recently, however, many argue that service learning courses should emphasize civic learning. (See, for example, Battistoni, Gelmon, Saltmarsh, Wergin, & Zlotkowski, 2003; Saltmarsh, 2002.) Some go a step further and argue that service learning courses should emphasize social change, social justice, and civic agency. (For a discussion of these issues, see, for example, Boyte, 2008; Chambers, 2009; Morton, 1995; and Welch, 2009.) Service learning is an effective pedagogy in many regards. Whether it should emphasize civic learning can lead to interesting and fruitful campus conversations, but in the end the individual faculty member is probably the one who will decide whether the course goals will or will not include civic learning, social change, social justice, or civic agency.

Service Learning and Values

In designing a service learning course, one needs to consider the issue of values, particularly if the course emphasizes social change or social justice. For example, what is the message conveyed to students when a service learning opportunity is at an agency that promotes legalizing euthanasia or one that supports gay marriage? Similarly, what is the message if a service learning opportunity involves developing a public relations campaign to ensure that euthanasia remains illegal or gay marriage is outlawed? Although these are somewhat extreme examples, it is not uncommon for service learning assignments to trigger values issues, and the more the service learning experience involves controversial political issues, the more the issue of values must be considered. ''Some faculty worry about whether efforts to promote political development might, even if only inadvertently, bias students in favor of or against particular perspectives or ideologies. And some believe that steering clear of all political issues is the only way to avoid being suspected or accused of political bias" (Colby, Beaumont, Ehrlich, & Corngold, 2007, p. 5). However, avoiding political issues is not always possible or desirable.

The question of values is a complex one, and there is likely to be intense reactions on all sides. Stanley Fish, Dean Emeritus at the University of Illinois, Chicago, argues against teaching values: "Neither the university as a collective nor its faculty as individuals should advocate personal, political, moral, or any other kind of views except academic views" (Fish, 2008, p. 19). Fish also states: "You know that you are being (or trying to be) something [other than an academic] when the descriptions you put forward are really stepping stones to an ideological conclusion (even one so apparently innocuous as 'we should respect the voices of others'). The academic enterprise excludes no topic from its purview, but it regards any and every topic as a basis for analysis rather than as a stimulus to some moral, political, or existential commitment" (p. 169). Eric Bain-Selbo (2010), in contrast, argues against Fish's view, asking rhetorically: "Given the failure of too many other institutions to inculcate the values of citizenship and social justice, is it appropriate for higher education—an institution through which an increasing number of our citizens pass—to simply ignore the situation and assume our values crisis will just work itself out?" He talks about the loss of social connectedness and the importance of social equality to the welfare of society, citing evidence from Robert Putnam, author of *Bowling Alone*, and Richard Wilkinson and Kate Pickett, who documented that social inequality negatively influences a host of social and personal issues. Bain-Selbo concludes: "The commitment [implicit in his university's mission statement] means educating our students to be effective citizens in our democracy, and this necessarily entails the inculcating of democratic values."

This section has merely touched on the topic of values as they relate to higher education in general and service learning in particular, but the topic is one with which faculty must grapple. There are strong competing views in the literature, and there are likely to be equally strong views among the faculty. Service learning is often tied to the idea of civic education, a topic that is inherently value-laden. Faculty must decide if or how to approach the issue of values. In general, making conscious decisions about dealing with students' values and one's own values is preferable to avoiding the issue.

It seems that, at the very least, faculty should help students find their own moral compass based on knowledge, experience, and critical thinking. Faculty might also identify some fundamental moral principles that they agree ought to be taught, such as fairness, respect for other persons and other viewpoints, and a commitment to the principles on which our democracy rests.

COMMUNITY-BASED RESEARCH

By definition, CBR involves the institution with the community in a reciprocal relationship to address a local problem or issue. Much of what has been discussed in other chapters of this book relates to CBR, which, at its best, involves students. The array of CBR projects is basically limitless. Generally, faculty work with students to complete CBR projects, but in some cases the work is largely the responsibility of the students, and faculty serve only in a supervisory capacity. When the department has a strong graduate program, a special effort must be made to include undergraduates, especially because the services that undergraduates can contribute and their ability to work independently are more limited than that of graduate students. One way to ensure that all students have a CBR experience is to require it as part of a capstone course, which is the case at some institutions. For example, Portland State University requires that each student (except honors and liberal arts majors) complete a CBR-based capstone course that is multidisciplinary, problem-focused, and community-based. As stated on its website (http://www.pdx.edu/unst/senior-capstone), "Capstone courses are designed . . . to build cooperative learning communities by taking students out of the classroom and into the field. . . . Students bring together the knowledge, skills, and interests developed . . . through all aspects of their education, to work on a community project. Students from a variety of majors and backgrounds work as a team, pooling resources, and collaborating with faculty and community leaders to understand and find solutions for issues that are important to them as literate and engaged citizens." Reflection, a critical element of service learning and an explicit component of the definition of scholarship, ought to be required of all students engaged in CBR.

CURRICULAR ISSUES

Some curricular issues relating to students' public engagement can be decided by individual faculty members while others must be decided at a programmatic or institutional level. Individual faculty can decide whether they want service learning to be a significant or relatively minor component of their course and whether it will be optional or required. Some find it preferable to require service learning because it sends a message that service learning is an important aspect of the course. Furthermore, research has shown that students experience greater personal transformation when service learning is required rather than optional (Holland & Gelmon, 1998).

CBR, in contrast to service learning, is generally the sole focus of a course or at least a very significant part of it. CBR is integrated into research methods or capstone courses, as at Portland State, or individual students may enroll for special courses in order to work one-on-one with a faculty member on a CBR project. These special courses carry such titles as independent study or directed research.

Service learning work should be rigorously evaluated, and students should be given credit for their learning, not simply their time investment. The evaluation is generally factored into the course grade along with all other course requirements. It can also be evaluated as a separate, add-on credit—that is, with some courses, students who elect the service learning option earn an additional course credit, which is assigned a grade. "Some instructors view this [additional credit option] as a useful way of making service learning available across the curriculum. However, others see it as reducing community service to an afterthought, a signal to students that the work that really matters still lies in the traditional classroom" (Zlotkowski, 1999, p. 106).

Some curricular policies can promote students' public engagement. For example, the institution should establish specific criteria and an approval process for identifying courses that incorporate service learning. This ensures that there are minimum standards for service learning and promotes quality experiences for all participating students. Identifying the designated service learning courses in the list of course options from which students choose their classes leads to several benefits: students can select a course section because it includes service learning; they can enroll in service learning courses only during those semesters when they have the available time to invest; and they can avoid taking more than one service learning course in a given semester. To promote and support service learning, institutions ought to transcript the experience, which is simplified when the institution has an official process for identifying service learning courses.

A final, but very important, issue concerns locating service learning in the curriculum. Many institutions overlook this issue, letting individual faculty determine if and when they want to include service learning in a course. When individual faculty adopt service learning—without a departmental, college, or institutionwide commitment—the influence on students is limited. It is greater when service learning is systematically woven throughout the curriculum. Consider a business major who takes a general education course that involves service learning. If the student never encounters public engagement in courses in her major, she is left to conclude that public engagement is irrelevant in the business world. If, in contrast, the student repeatedly encounters public engagement as she moves through her academic program, the message is clear: public engagement is important for everyone, including those going into business careers (Schneider, 2005). In order to weave service learning throughout the curriculum, it can be required of all students, incorporated into the general education program, or integrated into every major and every capstone experience.

EFFECTIVE SERVICE LEARNING PROGRAMS

Although this chapter talks about both CBR and service learning, the latter is given more attention because it is the most prevalent form of student' public engagement and dominates the professional literature. For example, entering *service learning* as a search term in Google Scholar produces about 2.3 million hits. Searching for service learning books and articles in *World Cat*, a database of the collections of thousands of libraries, yields more than 74,000 references. Of course, these sources cover more than higher education; nevertheless, the numbers document the extensive attention given to the topic.

PLANNING

Effective service learning programs do not just happen; they are carefully planned. The planning should begin by specifying clear goals including student learning outcomes. The service learning experience should be designed to achieve those goals. Placements must be carefully selected to ensure there is on-site supervision of students from qualified persons willing to provide feedback to faculty on student performance. The site should be eager to have students, offer an experience that matches well with course content, and provide a safe environment for students. To ensure mutual benefit, planning for service learning should be done jointly with the community agency where students will be placed. The expectations of the agency and the faculty member should be congruent.

ORIENTATION

Students need to be oriented to service learning. They need to learn the goals of service learning, the expectations of them, and the benefits they will derive. They also need to learn the purpose and form of the reflection assignment, and they are likely initially to need help with the reflection process. Students also need to be oriented to the facility where they will be placed. They need to understand the "historical, racial, economic, and social factors" (Dunlap & Webster, 2009, p. 141) of the community in general and the place where they will be doing their service. They need to understand the culture and expectations of the agency: the dress code, acceptable language, prevailing policies and practices, management style, and so forth. They need to understand the importance of their role, both in relation to their service and as a representative of the university. Basic responsibilities should be discussed, such as showing up on scheduled days, arriving on time, avoiding agency politics, and not exceeding their assigned role. Students need to be firmly grounded in professional ethics as they apply to the setting in which they will be working. They need to know how to respond if they encounter situations in which they find the treatment of agency clients to be objectionable. Without a comprehensive orientation, students are unlikely to get maximum benefit from the experience, and there is a significant risk that they could damage university-community relations.

Agency management, staff, and volunteers should also be oriented to the program so they know what to expect from students, what services the students are competent to provide, what supervision they will require, and how they are to be evaluated. Agency personnel should know the extent to which faculty will be involved and how to reach faculty if problems arise.

REFLECTION

Reflection is defined as the "intentional consideration of an experience in light of particular learning objectives" (Hatcher & Bringle, 1997, p. 153). As Eyler and Giles (1999) reported: "The quantity and quality of [student] reflection was most consistently associated with academic learning outcomes: deeper understanding and better application of subject matter and increased knowledge of social agencies, increased complexity of problem and solution analysis, and greater use of subject matter knowledge in analyzing a problem" (p. 173). Students have many options for expressing the results of their reflections: journals, reflection papers, portfolios, artwork, oral presentations with or without Power Point, and many others described in the service learning literature.

GETTING STARTED

Organizations, books, and journals provide extensive help for starting a service learning program or developing a service learning course. One excellent resource is Campus Compact, an organization of more than 1,100 college and university presidents that "provides resources and training for faculty seeking to integrate civic and community-based learning into the curriculum" (http://www.compact.org/). The group's website offers a wealth of information about service learning, as do the websites of some of the 35 statewide Campus Compact organizations. The Indiana Campus Compact website is particularly helpful (http://www.indianacampuscompact.org/). The website of *Learn and Serve America* (http://www.servicelearning.org/), a program of the Corporation for National and Community Service, is an exceptionally rich resource for service learning. A valuable print resource is the 21-volume set of books titled *Service-Learning in the Disciplines* (Zlotkowski, multiple dates). Each volume addresses how service learning can be handled in a different discipline, such as accounting, archaeology, architecture, and so forth. A relevant journal is the *Michigan Journal of Community Service Learning*, which publishes articles on "research, theory, pedagogy, and other issues related to academic (curriculum-based) service-learning in higher education" (http://www.umich.edu/~mjcsl/ index.html). Past issues are available online (http://quod.lib .umich.edu/m/mjcsl/browse.html). In addition to web-based and written resources, much can be gained by talking with and observing those who have already adopted service learning.

INSTITUTIONAL SUPPORT

Institutions should expect to provide support if they are to have effective service learning programs systematically embedded in the curriculum. A service learning office, such as that discussed in Chapter 5, can help immensely with the myriad details associated with implementing service learning and provide professional development that matches the skill and experience level of the faculty. Reassigned time is very valuable for faculty who want to incorporate service learning into an existing course or develop a new service learning course. An advisory committee composed of faculty and community members can aid in the expansion of service learning.

ASSESSMENT

There are several aspects to the assessment of service learning. In order to assign grades, the faculty member must evaluate the extent to which students meet the student learning outcomes for the program. These assessments are most often based on both the student's reflection materials and inputs from the community agency where the student was placed. Grades should be based on learning, however, not on service (Bringle & Hatcher, 1995). Setting goals for the service learning experience, as previously recommended, provides the criteria against which student performance can be compared.

A second aspect of assessment goes beyond looking at whether student learning outcomes are achieved and looks at issues such as students' self-perceptions, likelihood of volunteering in the future, and commitment to active citizenship. This aspect of assessment considers both intended and unintended consequences, as well as short- and long-term impacts. Chapter 9 provides more information on assessment and evaluation.

A third aspect of assessment involves the community agency. Are agency personnel satisfied with the service learning program? Are they deriving the benefits they anticipated? Are they providing the appropriate supervision? Does the site continue to be a good placement for students? Information for this aspect of assessment should integrate perceptions from both the students and the community personnel with whom they worked. It might also include inputs from the agency's clientele.

EFFECTIVE COMMUNITY-BASED RESEARCH

Four undergraduate students, each of whom had extensive experience in CBR and each of whom attended a different institution, identified five conditions that are necessary for CBR to be successful (Willis, Peresie, Waldref, & Stockmann, 2003). First, in collaboration with the community partner, the faculty member should set clear goals for the research project. Second, she should help students be realistic about what can be accomplished and in what time frame. As Jason Willis and his colleagues pointed out, students often embark on CBR with unrealistically high expectations that can lead them to become disillusioned. In addition, both students and faculty need to be realistic about the time frame: it is common for a research project to require more than a single semester and to extend beyond the anticipated end date.

Third, the students need support and supervision at least from the faculty, and preferably from the community as well. Fourth, the faculty must be realistic about the students' skill levels and ensure they have the knowledge and skills to carry out the tasks expected of them. Students need to be familiar with the content area as well as the required research methods. Fifth, students need help to become personally invested in the project. The commitment should be greater than the attainment of a good grade, because it is the personal commitment that will sustain the students when things fail to unfold as planned.

Potential Issues: Student-Related

Faculty cannot assume that students will be eager to engage in service learning or CBR. There will be resisters. Some simply find it an alien way to learn: they expect the teacher, the textbook, and the classroom to constitute their entire learning platform. They may lack confidence in their ability to work in the community. In some instances, they simply lack the motivation or the maturity needed for service learning or CBR.

Those students who, for whatever reason, fail to fulfill all of their service learning or CBR responsibilities are unlikely to derive the full benefit of the experience. They may also prevent the target clientele from obtaining needed services in a timely fashion, and they may damage the reputation of the institution as well as relationships between the institution and the community. It is therefore important to understand and address the various challenges that make it difficult for students to fulfill their obligations. Probably the most significant challenge is lack of time. Many students today work long hours at outside jobs, and some have families and other outside responsibilities. For some, a scholarship can eliminate or reduce their need for outside employment. At institutions with large commuter populations, students often come to campus only for their classes, leaving immediately afterward, which means they have difficulty meeting with their fellow students, often a necessary part of CBR. At residential campuses, some students lack transportation to off-campus sites, making it important that at least some of the placements are within walking distance. Each institution must identify the major obstacles for their students.

Service learning and CBR are valuable pedagogies for use with graduate students as well as undergraduates. With their advanced knowledge and greater maturity, graduate students have the potential to contribute even more to the community than do undergraduates (Stanton, 2008). They can assume more responsibility at service learning sites, assist with the supervision of undergraduates working on a project, be involved in CBR at a deeper level and with less oversight, and have greater potential to produce scholarly output.

When academic advisors have a thorough understanding of public and civic engagement, they can help prevent some student-related challenges and increase the number of students who take advantage of these valuable learning opportunities. Academic advisors can promote engaged learning experiences by communicating to students the benefits they will derive, encouraging students to enroll in the classes, and ensuring that students fully understand the commitment involved in a service learning or CBR experience. Advisors can help students understand the seriousness of failing to fulfill their obligations to the community and encourage students to enroll in these course-related experiences during a semester when they have sufficient time to fulfill the necessary commitment. Students may lack the confidence to enroll in a course that will put them in direct contact with the community—often a community that is unfamiliar to them—or fail to recognize their own potential to make a positive impact on the community. Before students become involved in service learning or CBR, advisors can help them explore these issues and become comfortable with the idea of working in the community.

POTENTIAL ISSUES: FACULTY-RELATED

A significant part of aligning for student engagement is faculty development. Faculty will need to learn how to implement service learning and CBR effectively, but first they will need to be convinced of their value. Their concerns can be addressed by sharing the professional literature that shows that service learning and CBR enhance rather than diminish students' education. For example, Alexander Astin (1999) pointed out that service learning incorporates many effective practices whose value has been documented through research, including "student involvement, collaborative learning...reflection and self-knowledge, active learning...and laboratory or field experience" (p. 46). Extensive research has looked at both the short- and long-term impact of service learning in terms of content learning, personal growth, acquisition of civic skills, and relevant behaviors after college. The results have been largely, although not exclusively, positive. Similarly, student involvement in CBR increases student learning. There are several good compilations of the impact of service learning and the impact of CBR. (See, for example, Antonio, Astin, & Cress, 2000; Astin, Vogelgesang, Ikeda, & Yee, 2000; Eyler & Giles, 1999; Eyler, Giles, Stenson, & Gray, 2001; Pascarella & Terenzini, 2005; Strand, Marullo, Cutforth, Stoecker, & Donohue, 2003a; and Willis, Peresie, Waldref, & Stockmann, 2003.) Some of the benefits are also discussed in Chapter 1 of this book, in the section headed "Student Benefits."

Recognizing that service learning and CBR demand more faculty time than delivering a lecture three times a week, faculty are concerned about having enough time to devote to these pedagogical approaches. They are also concerned that adopting these pedagogies will reduce the course content they can cover and their productivity in other areas. Their concerns will be partially addressed if they know that there is support to minimize their administrative burden.

Potential Issues: Community-Related

Both service learning and CBR should be mutually beneficial—beneficial to the students and to the community—but this is not necessarily the case. For example, agencies may find it difficult to adapt to having students in some semesters but not in others, or losing students during campus vacations. When students participate in a one-semester service learning experience, the benefits to the student may outweigh the benefits to the agency where the student is placed. The student gets an opportunity to see how the agency functions and gains valuable experience, but the agency loses the student at the point when he or she is likely to contribute more than is required in supervision. In fact, the benefits of service learning are often tipped to benefit the students, and a concerted effort is required to be sure that the benefits are truly mutual. Of course, the long-range benefits of a citizenry educated in part through service learning should not be discounted.

When developing a service learning placement or establishing a CBR project, it is important to consult with the management of the partnering organizations to identify and address their concerns. How would they like to set up the program? What is important to their organization? Do they feel the benefits to the organization will compensate for the time they will invest supervising students? In advance of such consultation, it is useful to be familiar with the issues raised in Randy Stoecker and Elizabeth Tryon's (2009) *The Unheard Voices: Community Organizations and Service Learning*, which looks at service learning through the eyes and voices of community organizations and discusses the concerns that partnering agencies are likely to have.

Chapter 11 discusses the qualities associated with a successful partnership. When these qualities exist in a CBR or service learning partnership, it is likely that most of the issues and concerns of the community will be addressed.

RECOGNIZING THE WORK

Many universities provide individual awards and hold celebrations that honor students and share information about their contributions to the community. For example, California State University at Fresno gives a *Volunteer of the Year Award* to a student who has made a major contribution to the community; the University of Nebraska at Omaha gives the *Service Learning Award* to a student who "demonstrates a thorough understanding of reflective practice techniques in coursework, provides service for a community agency in an outstanding manner, establishes and maintains an excellent relationship with the community agency, and embraces the philosophy of service-learning and community service" (http://www.unomaha.edu/aandsaffairs/insidepages/honorsstudent.php); and Indiana State University gives the *President's Award for Civic and Community Leadership*. This annual award is given "to an undergraduate student at Indiana University who has made community and civic engagement integral to her/his

college experience" (http://www.indstate.edu/publicservice/
Presidents_Award_Civic_Community_Leadership.htm).

CONCLUDING COMMENTS

In aligning the institution to support public engagement, it is
important to align student engagement and the related curricular
issues. Student engagement should never lower academic standards or reduce learning; to the contrary, it should increase and
deepen learning by tying it to the real world.

It should be noted that student affairs staff can play a significant role in ensuring that students integrate their academic
experiences and their public engagement. They can encourage
students to enroll in service learning or CBR courses. They can
advocate, along with academic affairs, to have these experiences
transcripted. They can use their community contacts to create
additional linkages between the campus and community. Even on
the academic side of students' public engagement, student affairs
may have a valuable role.

Although significant benefits accrue from service learning
and CBR, the work makes many demands on the faculty. Before
sending students into the community, the faculty need to learn
how to effectively incorporate these teaching techniques into
their classes. This, in itself, is time-consuming. In addition, they
will need to meet with their community partners to determine
the ground rules for the partnership and develop an appropriate course syllabus with clear goals both for student learning
and community benefit. Furthermore, these pedagogies are not
without risk. The risk is greater when the work has political implications or the students are not fully oriented and prepared before
going into the community. Despite the additional workload and
added risk, the pedagogies are strongly recommended because
they greatly enrich and advance students' education, significantly
expand human resources to support the institution's engagement,
and benefit the community.

CHAPTER NINE

ALIGNING ACCOUNTABILITY AND REPORTING SYSTEMS

It is often said that we measure what we value, and we value what we measure. Universities regularly measure and report enrollment data, graduation rates, and research dollars, yet for most, nothing they routinely measure sheds light on the extent and impact of their involvement with the broader community. If colleges and universities truly value public engagement, then this must change: they must measure and report not only the quantity of the work but also its quality.

Where does one begin? There are so many questions to consider: Who at the university should be responsible for the assessment and evaluation of public engagement? What are the assessment and evaluation goals? What should be measured? How, when, and by whom should measurement be done? How should the reporting be handled? To whom should the results be reported and how should they be used? In addressing these questions, one must also be careful to ensure that the process of measurement and the use of the results do not deter faculty and staff from undertaking public engagement activities. As one NKU faculty member said: "We have to be careful not to take the fun and joy out of engagement by measuring it to death." If reporting requirements become burdensome, faculty may be less inclined to undertake public engagement, and if results are used punitively, faculty will be less inclined to cooperate in measurement activities or may even forgo public engagement altogether.

This chapter focuses on three important aspects of reporting about public engagement: (1) accountability for institutional performance; (2) assessment of its impact on students, faculty, the curriculum, and the community, and assessment of the engagement process itself; and (3) evaluation of specific projects and programs.

ACCOUNTABILITY FOR INSTITUTIONAL PERFORMANCE

Institutional accountability encompasses three questions: (1) Does the campus support engagement? (2) To what extent are the academic units appropriately and sufficiently engaged? (3) Are the faculty and staff engaged? These three questions parallel the organizational levels in the alignment grid: the first question relates to the university, the second to the colleges and departments, and the third to individual faculty and staff.

DOES THE CAMPUS SUPPORT ENGAGEMENT?

An obvious option for institutional self-assessment is the alignment grid described in Chapter 2. By asking some administrators and faculty to assign ratings to the 16 organizational dimensions, one can track the extent of campus engagement over time and look at the consistency in perceptions across raters.

Another approach is to apply either of the two following measures developed specifically for the purpose of institutional self-assessment:

- Campus Compact's *Indicators of Engagement* (http://www .compact.org/indicators-of-engagement-project-categories-page/) includes 13 categories (for example: "Academic and Administrative Leadership") with two to six items in each category (for example: "The president, the chief academic officer, and the trustees visibly support campus civic engagement, in both their words and their actions").
- Gelmon and her colleagues (2005) developed a tool for institutional self-assessment that contains six general dimensions (for example: "Definition and Vision of Community Engagement"), each including 3 to 12 specific items (for example: "Promotion of Community Engagement

through the Mission"). For each item, the measure describes four levels of the extent to which the institution observes best practices. For example, the lowest level associated with the "Promotion of Community Engagement through the Mission" is "Reference to the concept of community engagement is not included in the institution's mission," and the highest level is "The community engagement aspect of the institution's mission is openly valued and is explicitly used and promoted by leaders" (p. 3).

A third approach is to evaluate a campus based on lists of important characteristics associated with successful service learning or public engagement. Examples of such lists can be found in Bringle, Games, and Malloy (1999); Burkhardt and Lewis (2005); Furco and Holland (2004); and Ramaley (2005).

ARE THE ACADEMIC DEPARTMENTS ENGAGED?

Portland State University has developed a rubric to assess the extent to which engagement is institutionalized at the departmental level. This measure, which builds on the work of other researchers, includes six dimensions (for example, "Mission and Culture Supporting Community Engagement") with three to seven components that help clarify each dimension. A faculty team, working first independently and then collectively, rates each dimension as falling into one of four stages: "awareness building," "critical mass building," "quality building," and "institutionalization." The rubric and instructions on its use are available at http://www.pdx.edu/cae/engaged-department-rubric.

Program review provides the perfect opportunity for determining whether departments are appropriately and sufficiently engaged. As a self-study process, program review allows a department to assess itself, determine whether it is satisfied with the quantity and quality of its public engagement, use the findings for self-improvement, and report to the administration. When an external reviewer is used, as is often the case, the department gets the benefit of an objective perspective from someone outside the university. Including public engagement in the program review process sends a powerful message that public engagement is on a par with research and teaching. Program review is mandatory at most colleges and universities; the review of faculty and student engagement should be a required component.

Are the Faculty and Staff Engaged?

One aspect of institutional performance is the extent to which faculty and staff are publicly engaged—that is, how much public engagement is taking place? NKU determined that it needed a process for answering the question, but to no one's surprise, it found that counting and inventorying public engagement is by no means a simple matter.

Because NKU wanted to summarize (cumulate) the data, prepare useable reports for internal and external audiences, and develop a searchable database, it could not simply collect anecdotal stories from faculty and staff about what they were doing. To obtain a strong response rate, the university wanted a measure (a) with fixed responses, (b) that could be self-administered, and (c) was relatively easy to complete. NKU spent nearly two years developing its measure.

Survey Development

In 2002–03, the university conducted an open-ended, paper-and-pencil pilot test, and gave the data to Dr. Joan Ferrante, a sociology professor, who involved her research methods class in a survey development project the following year. The students interviewed about 25 publicly engaged faculty and staff, combined what they learned from the interviews with the pilot data from 2002–03, and drafted a survey with fixed-response options for many items. The students then tested the survey using a modified cognitive interviewing approach with 40 faculty and staff. Using the interview responses, the students, with significant oversight from Professor Ferrante, developed the first online survey. Each year it was refined based on what was learned from the prior year's data collection.

Survey Description

The survey collects basic contact information and then covers five areas: (1) membership on boards, committees, and commissions; (2) individual engagement activities, defined as those not significantly supported by a university department, college, center, or institute, where the faculty or staff member assumes ownership and responsibility for the activity, or the initiative is not dependent on NKU resources; (3) institutional engagement activities, defined as those sponsored or supported, with dedicated resources, by a university department, college, center, or institute; (4) publications, conference presentations, and written reports that relate to public engagement activities; and (5) service learning courses.

Survey instructions direct faculty and staff to report only those activities that relate to their disciplinary expertise or role at the university. For example, if an accounting professor serves as a soccer coach in the community, it is not to be included, but if that accounting professor handled the accounting function for a nonprofit child care center, then the activity should be included.

Exhibit 9.1 shows the survey items and response options—though not the formatting—used in NKU's data collection procedure.

Exhibit 9.1. Survey Items and Response Options

Boards, Committees, and Commissions

1. Name of agency/organization:
2. Name of board/committee/commission:
3. Role or position on the board:
   (a) Officer
   (b) Member
   (c) Judge/juror
   (d) Advisor to board, committee, commission
   (e) Other (please specify)
4. Length of time on the board, committee, or commission:
   (a) Less than one year
   (b) 1–2 years
   (c) 3–4 years
   (d) 5–6 years
   (e) More than 6 years
   (f) Other (please specify)
5. Strategic area that best characterizes this board, committee, or commission's activities:
   (a) Birth up to, but not including, preschool
   (b) P–12 education

  (c) Economic development
  (d) Government
  (e) Health care
  (f) Environment
  (g) Art
  (h) Public knowledge
  (i) Professional development
  (j) Social services
  (k) Other nonprofits
  (l) Other (please specify)

6. Optional: list a second strategic area using the options above
7. Geographic reach of this board, committee, or commission's activities (check all that apply):
  (a) Northern Kentucky only
  (b) Metro-region (KY, OH, IN)
  (c) Other Kentucky counties or regions
  (d) State-Kentucky only
  (e) State-Ohio only
  (f) Other states
  (g) National
  (h) International/global
  (i) Other (please specify)

Individual Activities

1. Name of activity:
2. Name(s) of associated external (non-NKU) organization/ agency (if applicable):
3. Your role and brief description (30 words or less):
4. Length of involvement:
  (a) Less than a month
  (b) 1–5 months
  (c) 6–11 months
  (d) 1–2 years
  (e) 2–3 years
  (f) More than 3 years
  (g) Other (please specify)
5. Estimated number of hours per year you spent on activities associated with this project:
  (a) 1–5 hours
  (b) 6–10 hours

    (c) 11–20 hours

    (d) 21–50 hours

    (e) 51–75 hours

    (f) 76–100 hours

    (g) Other (please specify)

6. Number of NKU students participating (enter 0 if none):

7. Number of teachers outside the university served or participating:

8. Number of other adults outside the university served or participating:

9. Number of youth (birth through age 18) served or participating:

10. Strategic area that best characterizes this activity:

    (a) Birth up to, but not including, preschool

    (b) P–12

    (c) Economic development

    (d) Government

    (e) Health care

    (f) Environment

    (g) Art

    (h) Public knowledge

    (i) Professional development

    (j) Social services

    (k) Other nonprofits

    (l) Other (please specify)

11. Optional: list a second strategic area using the options above:

12. Geographic reach of this activity (check all that apply):

    (a) Northern Kentucky only

    (b) Metro-region (KY, OH, IN)

    (c) Other Kentucky counties or regions

    (d) State-Kentucky only

    (e) State-Ohio only

    (f) Other states

    (g) National

    (h) International/global

    (i) Other (please specify)

13. Public engagement/outreach type that best characterizes the focus of this activity:

    (a) Outreach instruction to children in grades K–12

    (b) Outreach instruction to teachers

    (c) Outreach instruction to community-based organiza-
        tions
    (d) Research/technical assistance/disciplinary expertise
    (e) Clinical service
    (f) General public events or information sessions
    (g) Targeted audience events or information sessions
    (h) Other (please specify)
14. Type of funding support:
    (a) None
    (b) External grant or contract
    (c) External gift
    (d) Internal grant
    (e) Department/college funding
    (f) Personal funds
    (g) Other (please specify)

Institutional Activities

The section on institutional activities matches the section on individual activities except that one additional question is included for institutional activities: "Name of sponsoring college, center, department, institute or other university unit." This item appears as the third item on the list, and all succeeding items are renumbered.

Publications and Other Reports

1. Type of publication:
    (a) Book
    (b) Book chapter
    (c) Refereed journal article
    (d) Nonrefereed article
    (e) Unpublished report or manual
    (f) Other (please specify)
2. Title of contribution (for book chapter, include title of book):
3. Name(s) of coauthors (if any):
4. Status of contribution:
    (a) Submitted
    (b) Accepted for publication
    (c) In press
    (d) Unpublished report submitted
    (e) Other (please specify)

5. Date or expected date of publication, or for unpublished work, submission date:
6. Answer one of the three items below:
    (a) For journal article, specify name of journal, volume, issue, and pages, or provide other relevant information if not published in a conventional paper-based journal.
    (b) For book or book chapter, specify publisher.
    (c) For an unpublished report or manual, specify organization or person (with institutional affiliation and/or title) for whom it was written and describe the purpose of the report/manual.
7. Geographic reach of contribution:
    (a) Northern Kentucky only
    (b) Metro-region (KY, OH, IN)
    (c) Other Kentucky counties or regions
    (d) State-Kentucky only
    (e) State-Ohio only
    (f) Other states
    (g) National
    (h) International/global
    (i) Other (please specify)
8. Primary audience for contribution:
    (a) Academics
    (b) Practitioners
    (c) General public
    (d) Students
    (e) Other (please specify)
9. Secondary audience (if applicable) (options as above):

Conference Presentations
1. Title of presentation:
2. Name of conference/meeting:
3. Sponsoring organization for conference:
4. Location of conference (city and state):
5. Conference date:
6. Name(s) of coauthors or copresenters (if any):
7. Geographic reach of conference (check all that apply):
    (a) Northern Kentucky only
    (b) Metro-region (KY, OH, IN)

(c) Other Kentucky counties or regions
(d) State-Kentucky only
(e) State-Ohio only
(f) Other states
(g) National
(h) International/global
(i) Other (please specify)
8. Audience type (check all that apply):
   (a) Academics
   (b) Practitioners
   (c) Government body or officials
   (d) Members of a community group
   (e) General public
   (f) Other (please specify)

Service Learning

1. Term and year:
2. Course title:
3. Course prefix and number:
4. Section number:
5. Name(s) of community partner(s):
6. Type of community partner(s) (check all that apply):
   (a) Birth up to, but not including, preschool
   (b) P–12
   (c) Economic development
   (d) Government
   (e) Health care
   (f) Environment
   (g) Art
   (h) Public knowledge
   (i) Professional development
   (j) Social services
   (k) Other nonprofits
   (l) Other (please specify)
7. Number of NKU students enrolled in course:
8. Number of NKU students involved in service learning in the course:
9. Geographic reach of student activities (check all that apply):
   (a) Northern Kentucky only
   (b) Metro-region (KY, OH, IN)

(c) Other Kentucky counties or regions
(d) State-Kentucky only
(e) State-Ohio only
(f) Other states
(g) National
(h) International/global
(i) Other (please specify)

10. Estimated number of hours the students *collectively* contributed to each agency/organization involved:

11. Type of funding support for the course or its related service activities:
(a) None
(b) External grant or contract
(c) External gift
(d) Internal grant
(e) Department/college funding
(f) Personal funds
(g) Other (please specify)

So that all faculty and staff respond from a common understanding of what is being asked, NKU's survey includes explanations and definitions for many terms, including each of the response options related to: (a) strategic area, (b) geographic reach, and (c) outreach type, as well as each of the categories of activities: (a) boards, committees, and commissions; (b) individual activities; (c) institutional activities; (d) publications, conference presentations, written reports; and (e) service learning. These definitions are critically important to the process because they increase the likelihood that public engagement activities are correctly reported and consistently classified.

Maximizing Response Rates

To maximize response rates, NKU designed its survey so that it was relatively easy to complete and made it available online. The university recognized that those who had been most active might feel a disproportionate burden compared to their less engaged colleagues, because if they were involved in, for example, 10 public engagement activities, they would have to answer 10 sets of questions. As a result, those faculty and staff were allowed to submit their information in any form that was convenient for them, and the information was entered into the database on their behalf.

Faculty and staff received at least five e-mail reminders to complete the survey. Because these reminders were sent by a faculty colleague—the professor who developed the survey—they did not engender the negative reactions that they might have if they had come from an administrator. When repeated reminders failed to elicit responses, names of nonrespondents were given to department chairs via their deans. Chairs were asked to impress upon the nonrespondents the importance of completing the survey. A general e-mail reminder—not targeting any individuals—was sent out from the CAO. Initially the survey was available online for only a few months, and data for an entire year's worth of activities were collected from faculty and staff only during those months. This method was later changed to a 24/7 data gathering system that enabled people to enter data whenever they wished throughout the year. The reminder system was adjusted accordingly.

A highly effective aspect of increasing response rates was the *honor roll*. Each year, in its annual report of outreach and public engagement, NKU published an honor roll that listed each person—in alphabetical order by unit—who reported public engagement activities for the year. Informal conversations with department chairs, faculty, and staff confirmed that the first thing they did when getting the annual report was to see who was listed on the honor roll.

To underscore that public engagement is important across the breadth of the institution, special efforts were made to ensure that the president, CAO, other vice presidents, and deans always submitted completed surveys. Because most were involved in public engagement activities, most were listed on the honor roll and served as excellent role models for faculty and staff.

As a result of applying the various approaches described here, NKU was able to achieve a response rate of 75 to 85 percent.

Scrubbing the Data

NKU found it beneficial to "scrub the data." Dr. Ferrante, who developed the survey, reviewed all responses, corrected misclassifications, and eliminated activities that were actually service to

the university or the profession, activities that were unrelated
to the respondent's discipline, and duplicate activities (resulting
from two or more faculty reporting the same activity). This was
enormously time-intensive but resulted in a much more accurate
report of activities.

Adapting the Survey for Local Use

Universities adapting this survey for their campuses will need to
adjust the fixed-response options to accommodate the work their
university is doing. For example, engineering and agriculture are
likely to be strategic areas on many campuses, but they are not
relevant at NKU and thus were not listed as response options. The
geographic reach listing is clearly tailored to Kentucky and needs
to be modified for other campuses.

The following advice is offered to those adapting the survey
for local use:

- Consider how the responses will be used so that all necessary
  data elements are included on the survey. For example, NKU
  does not ask the city or county name where the work is done,
  but the university has received requests to report the data
  for specific cities. It is currently impossible to honor those
  requests.
- Avoid adding too many items; if the survey is excessively long,
  there is greater resistance to completing it.
- Avoid many open-ended questions because they require
  considerable person power to analyze and summarize. In
  addition, NKU found that too many open-ended questions adds
  to the time required to complete the survey and hence reduces
  the overall response rate and the quality of the answers.
- Conduct pilot testing with any fixed-response items to be sure
  the most common responses are included in the list of options.
- Include an "other" category for every item to accommodate
  those doing work that cannot be captured by the fixed-response
  options.
- Include definitions of terms, especially for terms used in the
  response options, unless they are absolutely unambiguous;
  the best way to make that determination is through cognitive
  interviewing and pilot testing.

Survey-Related Decisions

A variety of decisions have to be made in developing and administering a survey.

- *Who will be asked to complete the survey?* For example, who on the faculty will be given the survey: all faculty, including temporary and part-time faculty; only full-time faculty; only full-time, tenured, and tenure-track faculty? NKU elected to include only full-time faculty because the university could not assume that the public engagement of part-time faculty was associated exclusively with NKU or was under NKU's control.
- *Should activities for which the faculty or staff member is paid be included or should only unpaid work be reported?* NKU opted to include all work, regardless of whether one was paid, because payment is irrelevant to the impact on the community.
- Should faculty and staff report all public engagement activities or only a fixed number that they perceive to be most significant? NKU opted to collect information on all activities in order to have a full assessment of the potential impact on the communities served and to track trends over time. Collecting and reporting information about a subset of activities is equivalent to reporting enrollments for only a subset of classes. It paints a very incomplete picture.
- Should data be collected for an entire year at one time as NKU initially did, or should there be a 24/7 data reporting process? NKU moved to the 24/7 approach because the university believed that the data reported would be more accurate. That is, when faculty and staff are asked to report something they did 10 or 11 months ago, they are unlikely to remember the details, especially such things as the number of participants or the amount of time invested. However, there are also drawbacks to the 24/7 approach. Specifically, faculty and staff are likely to forget to enter ongoing activities. For example, if Professor Jones is working with the local school district to develop a new science curriculum and the project lasts three years, Professor Jones may not think to report the activity each year unless she is specifically asked: "What did you do this year?" This problem can be avoided by carefully crafting reminders that will spur faculty and

staff to report all of their public engagement for an agreed-upon time period.

• *How is the data collection period defined?* Will it be the calendar year, the fiscal year, or the academic year? NKU initially used the calendar year because it coincided with the period used for annual performance reviews. After moving to a 24/7 data collection period, data were collected continuously and this became a non-issue. One can extract information from the 24/7 database for any time period one chooses.

• *How will faculty and staff be "trained" to complete the survey?* It is probably unrealistic to expect faculty and staff to take time from their busy schedules to attend a workshop that prepares them to complete a survey. Instead, NKU used three approaches to assist faculty and staff in completing the survey: (a) the survey itself included definitions of all key terms via hyperlinks that opened temporary windows, so the definitions did not clutter the survey itself; (b) examples were provided; and (c) faculty and staff could submit questions via e-mail or telephone.

• *Should "individual" and "institutional" activities be differentiated?* NKU found the distinction to be valuable, particularly because the two types of activities tend to be quite different in scope, duration, and sustainability. However, requiring this distinction adds complexity to the survey that could be eliminated by combining the activities.

• *In what order should the survey sections be listed?* When NKU collected data only once a year, it listed "boards, committees, and commissions" first, because respondents found this the easiest section to complete. "Individual activities" were listed before "institutional activities" because many respondents put all of their work under "institutional activities" unless they first saw the "individual" option. With the 24/7 reporting system, faculty can now click on whichever section they need for reporting a particular activity. They no longer complete the sections in a set order.

Remaining Challenges

Although NKU has been collecting these data for many years, significant challenges remain. One is data accuracy. To improve accuracy, the survey includes definitions of all key terms, but many people fail to read the definitions, leading them to misclassify and under- or overreport their work. Accuracy is also a problem when respondents rely on estimates, as they often do when reporting the number of participants served or the amount of time they spent on various activities.

A sensitive issue arose when the survey was expanded to include a question asking whether the engagement work was paid or unpaid. Apparently some faculty omitted activities for which they were privately paid because they feared raising concerns about the extent of their outside work. The question was dropped from the survey.

Collecting data once a year produced some challenges that are largely overcome by the 24/7 reporting system. When faculty and staff are entering their data for the entire year, those who are involved in a large number of public engagement activities feel the survey is punitive. They omit some of their activities simply because it takes too long to enter all of the information. Also, the number of questions that can be asked is limited because of the data entry burden on faculty and staff. These problems are lessened with the 24/7 data collection, which spreads the data collection process across the year. In moving to the 24/7 system, NKU made another change that increased faculty motivation to report all of their work: faculty can now print what they enter and submit it as part of their annual performance review and their materials for RPT decisions.

Finally, a significant, remaining challenge will not be alleviated until large numbers of colleges and universities use the same definitions and the same data-gathering procedures. As it currently stands, NKU can look at its data over time and compare itself with a few Kentucky universities that ask similar questions on their engagement surveys, but the university's ability to compare cross-institutionally is severely limited.

ASSESSMENT OF IMPACT

Universities undertake public engagement on the assumption that it has a positive impact, but assumptions cannot take the place of evidence. Universities need evidence to determine if, when, and under what circumstances the impact is positive. Are there also negative impacts? How do the programs and projects affect students, faculty, and the community? Has the curriculum been altered as a result of the commitment to public engagement, and if so, are the changes seen as positive or negative by faculty and students? How is the partnership proceeding? Assessing impact is not easy, but it is important and can lead to unanticipated benefits: "Serendipitous outcomes of the student survey included improvement of teaching approaches, increased collaboration with community partners, recruiting of more service-learning faculty, and supporting the institutionalization of service-learning" (Henderson, Fair, Sather, & Dewey, 2008, p. 129).

IMPACT ON STUDENTS AND FACULTY

When looking at the impact on students it is important to assess cognitive, affective, and behavioral effects. The cognitive impact might include understanding of course content as well as ability to integrate and apply the learning to new situations. Affective impacts might include attitudes toward the population with which the student was working and tolerance for others. Behavioral impacts might relate to volunteering or voting or community activism. The impact on faculty might include changes in the way they teach their courses or the content they emphasize, a new focus or a new perspective on their research, acceptance of additional responsibilities in the community, satisfaction with public engagement, and likelihood of expanding public engagement in the future. For both students and faculty, it is important to assess both short- and long-term impact, though it is clearly more difficult and far more costly to look at the long term. In addition, the possibility of a "spillover effect," either positive or negative, on faculty and students not directly involved should be considered.

In *Assessing Service-Learning and Civic Engagement*, Gelmon and her colleagues (2001) provided an excellent, practical, and very thorough guide for assessing the impact of service learning and civic engagement on students, the faculty, the community, and the institution. Much of what they described can be applied to other forms of public engagement as well. They discussed the entire assessment process, from start to finish, and provided detailed information, as well as samples of the most commonly used instruments:

- Surveys (self-administered or administered by another person)
- Interviews (in person or telephone)
- Focus groups
- Document reviews
- Observations
- Journals
- Critical incident reports [p. 12]

The literature contains many other examples of measures and approaches to assessing impact. For example, the California Critical Thinking Skills Test (http://www.insightassessment.com/test-cctst.html) can be used to determine whether public engagement impacts students' critical thinking skills. AASCU spent two years developing a survey to be administered to freshmen and seniors, to measure three constructs, one of which is "preparation for civic engagement." The survey, which was field-tested with more than 3,000 students, is available on AASCU's website (http://www.aascu.org/accountability/survey/?u=1). Richard Meister and Charles Strain (2004) listed the measures DePaul University used to determine "the contribution of each service-learning course to five of the ten university learning goals" (p. 113). The Center for Information and Research on Civic Learning and Engagement (CIRCLE) provides several relevant measures on its website (http://www.civicyouth.org/) including, for example, indicators of political participation, volunteering, and community engagement. Once the measurement goals are clearly defined, a literature search should uncover additional assessment tools.

Impact on the Community

Impact on the community refers to the community at large as well as specific community agencies that are partnering with the university on projects or hosting service learning students. Has the university helped the community define problems, identify best practices, and otherwise be a partner in addressing community issues? Is there general satisfaction with the engagement work of the university? Is the community satisfied with the arrangements for students who are working in the community? Is the work of the students meeting the needs of the community? How do agencies with service learning students feel about the various components of the program? Although one can read about best practices in service learning, civic engagement, and public engagement, each institution needs to assess its own community's reactions to discover which practices are really best for its community. The publication by Gelmon and her colleagues (2001), described in the prior section, is helpful for developing measures of community impact.

Impact on the Curriculum

Curriculum committees at all levels—department, college, and university—can report how public engagement has affected the curriculum. Over time, they can track the number of courses that include service learning, the number of students enrolled in service learning courses, the number of courses that involve students in CBR—including independent study and directed research courses—and the number of students involved in CBR. They can look at whether specific academic programs require that students fulfill a public engagement requirement, whether service learning classes appear in the program's courses at different levels (that is, freshman, sophomore, junior, senior), and whether there is a mandatory capstone experience that involves the students with the community. A group—such as the alignment analysis committee described in Chapter 2—can look at whether the curricular changes—or lack thereof—are congruent with the institution's goals. Surveys or focus groups can address whether faculty and students react positively or negatively to any relevant curricular changes.

Assessment of Process

The engagement process can be assessed both formally and informally. From an informal perspective, one can use the idea of periodic *check-ins,* where the participants get together and discuss how things are proceeding. Are relationships developing well? Are the partners—university and community—satisfied with how the various roles and responsibilities have been apportioned and how they are being fulfilled? Are there any frustrations or minor concerns that need to be addressed before they escalate? It is vital that all significant players attend these check-in meetings, and it may prove helpful to retain a written record of the meeting. The check-in schedule should be established when a partnership is initially created, and it should be followed faithfully.

The relevant literature describes more formal approaches that can be used to assess process. For example, Bruce Frey, Jill Lohmeier, Stephen Lee, and Nona Tollefson (2006) developed the *Levels of Collaboration Survey* that can be used to assess the degree of collaboration between the university and a partnering organization. The scale is based on five levels of working together, each showing increasing collaboration: networking, cooperation, coordination, coalition, and collaboration (p. 387). The survey uses four phrases to define each of the five levels. At the start of a partnership, the partners should agree on the desired level of collaboration, because the highest level is not always most desirable.

In another example, Jim Scheibel, Erin Bowley, and Steven Jones (2005), building on Campus Compact's work as reported in *Benchmarks for Campus/Community Partnerships* (Torres, 2000), developed an assessment approach that looks at three overlapping stages (designing the partnership, building a collaborative relationship, and sustaining the partnership) and three facets of partnerships (values, organization, and processes).

EVALUATION OF PROJECTS AND PROGRAMS

Both formative and summative evaluations are important in drawing conclusions about specific projects or programs. The former considers whether a project is on target to achieve its goals and allows for improving the process before it is too late. The latter considers whether the project actually achieved its goals; it is conducted when the project is complete. The evaluation should be designed before the project is started to ensure that all necessary data are collected, including baseline data. Partners should work together to determine the purpose of the evaluation, articulate the goals of the project, determine the metrics that will be used, agree on the timing of data collection, and determine how the results will be used and with whom they will be shared.

There are significant challenges associated with evaluating a project. One is the longtime horizon associated with many projects. For example, a project designed to increase the college-going rate in the region might focus on working with middle school students. It would take at least four years to begin to know whether there was any impact, and during those years, many intervening variables will affect the results. Ethical issues can also be an obstacle in program evaluation. If a project involves clients or patients in the community, there may be privacy issues that prevent collecting data that would be most useful in evaluating the project.

Evaluation is complex and expensive and requires special skills that project directors often lack. External evaluators can provide the missing expertise and lend credibility to the findings because they are objective. However, they also add significant cost. Except for grant-funded projects, public engagement usually operates with very limited funding, all of which is generally consumed by project implementation with little or nothing available for project evaluation.

The specifics on how to conduct a quality evaluation are beyond the scope of this book. However, there are many good resources for learning about evaluation. (See, for example, McDavid & Hawthorn, 2006; Royse, Thyer, & Padgett, 2010; and Worthen, Sanders, & Fitzpatrick, 2004.)

USES OF THE INFORMATION

The value of information is in its use. Once collected and analyzed, the information acquired from the processes described in the preceding paragraphs can be used both internally and externally.

INTERNAL USE OF INFORMATION

The institutional accountability data and impact assessment data are particularly useful for determining the extent to which the university is fulfilling its engagement mission and living up to its obligations to the community. The data enable the campus to track trends over time and determine which sectors are benefiting most from the engagement work. Conversely, the campus can tell whether there are sectors that should be given more attention and campus units that should be more involved. The data can be used in planning and goal setting with specific targets set by sector or by academic unit.

Universities benefit significantly when they can compare their performance with that of similar institutions. This, of course, requires that the same measurement tools be used at different institutions. If groups of colleges and universities voluntarily agree to the same measures, or if legislators or statewide governing boards mandate the use of particular measures, then these inter-institutional comparisons will be possible.

Project evaluation data can also be used internally. Formative evaluation will indicate whether corrective action is needed in order to achieve the ultimate goals of a particular project, and summative evaluation will reveal whether the project achieved those goals. The university will learn which projects are worth replicating with other groups and which need to be modified before being implemented elsewhere.

External Use of Information

Before information is shared with an outside group, such as the media, project evaluation data and conclusions should be shared with the partnering organizations. Problems with information sharing can be avoided if, at the time the partners are jointly planning the evaluation, they also jointly determine how and where to share the findings.

There are many groups to which the university is accountable and with whom the accountability, assessment, and evaluation findings should be shared. This includes the general public, the campus community, current and prospective students and their parents, alumni, legislators, donors, higher education boards, and accrediting bodies. The process of sharing these data enhances the institution's image in the community: it is good public relations to show how the campus is benefiting the community. Many fascinating stories can be extracted from the data. These stories are useful for recruiting students to attend the institution and recruiting current students to service learning and CBR. They also add to the university's public relations efforts and motivate more public engagement activities. How NKU shared its data is discussed in Chapter 10.

Although not mandatory, sharing the accountability, assessment, and evaluation results through traditional academic outlets—journal articles and conference presentations—is an important part of engaged scholarship. The benefits accrue to those who author the materials, those who read or hear the papers, and the reputation of the college or university where the work was done.

Concluding Comments

Institutional accountability, impact assessment, and project evaluation are not easy, though of the three, institutional accountability is the easiest because it looks at inputs. Measuring impact and results is much more difficult. It is important to measure unintended as well as intended outcomes and short-term as well as long-term results.

This chapter has suggested many measurement approaches, but as Jim Scheibel, Erin Bowley, and Steven Jones (2005) pointed out: "You will need to adapt any assessment tool to reflect your specific situation" (p. 75). Furthermore, it is often difficult—perhaps even impossible—to do a comprehensive assessment or evaluation. In that case, the institution should do the best it can and accept that, for many public engagement activities, it is very difficult to measure success. The absence of evidence of success does not imply failure. What is most important is to gather and analyze the most appropriate data that are available and accurately report the results.

CHAPTER TEN

ALIGNING COMMUNICATION

Institutions need a strategic plan for communicating about public engagement. The plan should be developed and implemented jointly by the institutional unit responsible for external communications and the academic unit that represents public engagement, and it should be integrated, or at least compatible, with the institution's overall communication plan. Because the communications unit has many priorities, only one of which is to promote public engagement, the academic unit should expect to assume major responsibility for ensuring that a strong plan is developed and implemented. A good strategy for enlisting support from the communications unit is to include the unit's director on the advisory committee for public engagement. As a result of listening to the discussions and participating in planning, the communications director is likely to develop a greater interest in, and commitment to, public engagement.

Those developing the strategic plan need to address several questions: Who are the target audiences? What are the key messages? What are the most effective methods for communicating?

THE AUDIENCE

The institution should expect to communicate with diverse audiences. Internal audiences will include current students, faculty and staff, administrators, and members of the institution's governing board. External audiences will likely include system office personnel; the general public; specific subsets of the public such as business leaders, K–12 educators, government officials, and nonprofit agencies; legislators; community partners; donors; alumni; prospective students; and parents of current and prospective students. Advisory board members, another important audience, may be internal or external or a combination of both.

THE MESSAGE

The message will vary depending on the intended audience and the institution's goals relative to that audience. Among the institution's communication goals might be the following:

ENHANCE THE INSTITUTION'S PUBLIC IMAGE

With college costs rising and state support declining, it becomes increasingly important for the public to understand the institution's contribution to the public good. Institutions must communicate both what they do and the impact that it has on the community. Although one usually thinks of public relations as targeting an external audience, a high-quality public relations campaign will also influence the thinking of governing boards, administrators, faculty, and staff. Influencing their perceptions will help achieve many other alignment goals.

MOTIVATE PARTICIPATION IN, OR OTHERWISE SUPPORT, PUBLIC ENGAGEMENT

Some faculty, staff, students, and community agencies are drawn to this work with little encouragement. They will see the value in it, and they will get involved. However, many need encouragement. They need to hear about the opportunities, needs, and benefits, and they need to learn how to become involved. If faculty and staff are to support the public engagement mission of the university, they need to know the forces that are driving the administration's commitment to it; they need to know what the university plans to do and how it is going to measure its success. Students need to know its impact on their general education and their postgraduation job search.

ENCOURAGE AND FACILITATE DISCUSSIONS ABOUT PUBLIC ENGAGEMENT

It is important for others in addition to faculty and staff to engage in conversations about public engagement, as was emphasized in Chapter 6; administrators and students should have their own conversations about the benefits and challenges of public engagement, and members of the external community should discuss how best to partner with the campus. To facilitate discussions, campus leaders should create opportunities for discussions and strongly urge attendance; share definitions so everyone starts from a common understanding of what is being explored; ensure that discussants understand the institution's public engagement goals and the benefits to be derived; and share information about the public engagement efforts currently under way.

DOCUMENT THE EXTENT TO WHICH THE INSTITUTION IS ACHIEVING PUBLIC ENGAGEMENT GOALS

In higher education today, accountability is critically important. Institutions must gather and interpret the data to document what they are doing and how effectively they are doing it. They must communicate the information in different ways to different audiences. For example, what is shared with an academic audience may be different from what is shared with legislators, but both groups should be educated about the breadth of public engagement and its impact. Sharing information with partners is particularly important because they need to be kept apprised of the progress of the partnership. This requires sharing formative as well as summative information. For most other audiences, summative information is sufficient.

RECRUIT MORE STUDENTS TO ENROLL AT THE INSTITUTION

Although this is not a primary goal of public engagement, strong service learning and CBR programs can positively influence student interest in the institution, especially if the institution communicates how these experiences benefit students. Some prospective students—and some parents—will be attracted to an institution because it encourages students to make a positive difference in their communities, provides them with real-world experience, and develops civic skills that prepare them to be active, contributing citizens.

FACILITATE TWO-WAY COMMUNICATION ABOUT PUBLIC ENGAGEMENT

Faculty and staff need a mechanism for sharing their views with the administration, raising questions, and reporting barriers and challenges that limit their participation or effectiveness; community members need a vehicle for connecting with the university to seek partners, obtain help with existing partners, or provide feedback, positive and negative, on the progress of an initiative; and students need to be able to ask questions about opportunities and report problems they encounter in the community. Open forums, focus groups, e-mail, discussion boards, feedback cards distributed at events, and telephone access to public engagement offices are among the various options for two-way communication.

THE MEDIUM

The method of communication will be a function of the intended audience and the goals of the communication. A variety of options are possible:

- *Oral communication* includes campus conversations as well as formal and informal presentations to large and small audiences. Public engagement might be a minor part of the message or the focal point. There are numerous opportunities for talking to internal audiences, including, for example, new faculty and staff orientations, convocations, building dedications, department and college meetings, campus senate meetings, commencement, and forums focused on public engagement. Similarly, there are numerous opportunities to reach off-campus audiences, including addresses to service organizations such as Rotary or Lions Club, talks to business groups such as the chamber of commerce, keynote addresses at gatherings of local leaders, and presentations to legislators and legislative committees. In any of these examples, the communication may come from the president, CAO, or other institutional voice including faculty. Oral presentations by students can be particularly persuasive with some audiences; similarly, presentations by community partners can be effective with some.

- *Internally prepared, print communication* can be very powerful and encompasses a large variety of options, such as brochures, alumni magazines, annual reports focused solely on public engagement, broadly focused institutional annual reports, internal newsletters, undergraduate and graduate catalogs, recruitment materials, and other marketing materials. Whether to distribute the materials in hard copy or electronically depends on both the intended audience and the goals associated with the communication.

- *Media coverage* can be extremely powerful, at least in part because there is greater credibility when the communication emanates from an external source. Several strategies encourage positive coverage by the local media: invite representatives of mainstream, minority, and targeted media, such as business-oriented newspapers, to campus to visit a service learning class; facilitate connections between the media and faculty and staff who are involved in successful public engagement; ensure that the media is invited to attend campus events that relate to public engagement; hold press conferences to launch significant partnerships or to share results from highly successful partnerships; arrange for the institution's president to meet periodically with the newspaper's editorial board to talk about public engagement and share specific examples of projects that have benefited the community; include someone from the media on the advisory committee for public engagement; provide the local media with news stories about successful partnerships; and provide students' hometown papers with success stories that involve their local students. If the communications office lacks staff to prepare the news stories, press releases can be written by those who are committed to public engagement, and the communications office can simply distribute them. Finally, student-run media can help promote student involvement and institutional pride in public engagement.

- *The institution's website* communicates much about its public engagement commitment, even if the institution does not intend the web to fill that role. This means institutions should be proactive and establish a web presence that represents their public engagement in a positive, easily accessible manner. Just as there is a link for students and one for faculty on the home page of most colleges and universities, there should be a link for the community. It should enable potential partners to locate a starting point, an office where they can make their first contact. Those interested in learning about the institution's public engagement should be able to read descriptions of various projects and link to various campus units that are heavily involved in public engagement. Examples of public engagement links on a university's home page can be found at NKU, where the link is called *Community Focus* (http://www.nku.edu/); the University of Minnesota, where the link is *Community Engagement* (http://www1.umn.edu/twincities/index.php); Emory University, where the link is called simply *Community* (http://www.emory.edu/home/index.html); and Widener University, where it is called *Civic Mission* (http://www.widener.edu/).

- *Electronic copies of printed materials* that promote public engagement should be available on the website. To ensure that the website is user-friendly, it should be tested by community members who know little about the institution: Can they locate what they need without much difficulty?

- *Radio and television broadcasts* can reach large audiences, which make them potentially very valuable. Stations owned by the institution as well as local cable and public broadcasting stations are possible venues for promoting public engagement. As an example, faculty, students, and community partners can discuss their partnership work on a university-based or cable-based interview show. Because radio, and especially television, can easily become very expensive, their use has to be carefully planned.

- *Special events* such as award celebrations, student research exhibits, and community open houses provide an opportunity to promote the institution's public engagement. For example, the university can host an annual event to honor all completed CBR projects, inviting the students, faculty, community partners, community at large, and the media to attend and celebrate. Cookies and punch add to the festive atmosphere. If there are too few CBR projects to warrant a separate event, the event can be combined with a celebration of all student research, or there might be a small gathering to celebrate a single project. Community members can be invited to an open house in which a variety of academic departments provide information about the public engagement potential of their department.

• *E-mail and social media* such as Facebook and Twitter are useful for targeted communications, but to be effective they must be skillfully used. Because people receive so much spam, they often overlook mass e-mails. Students often report that they ignore e-mail altogether, and many faculty do as well. It is difficult to know which external audiences pay significant attention to electronic communication. However, social media may be useful with selected audiences. For example, it might be very effective for reaching students but less successful with donors. Furthermore, the social media that is most effective at one point in time may be totally passé two years later.

CREATING THE STRATEGIC COMMUNICATION PLAN

Those creating the strategic communication plan need to carefully match the audience with the right messages delivered through the most appropriate medium. What does each audience already know? What do they want or need to know? What do you want them to know? How can you most effectively reach them? The strategic planning group must also take account of budgetary constraints and consider how the communication plan for public engagement will interface with the institution's overall communication plan. Are there places where multiple goals can be achieved through a single effort, thereby saving money? Through careful planning, the group can ensure the best return on the institution's investment of time and money. Finally, "who" delivers a message can be as important as the content of the message. On most campuses, messages delivered by the president have greater impact than messages delivered by a dean. For faculty, a message from the CAO is generally quite influential, but it may be possible to delegate this authority to the chief public engagement officer if it is clear she is speaking on behalf of the CAO.

Table 10.1 can be used to facilitate the development of a strategic communication plan that identifies the appropriate medium—that is, the communication tool—for each combination of audience and message. The columns list the various messages to be communicated; in this example, they are the six messages described earlier in the chapter. The rows list the various audiences with whom the university wishes to communicate; in this example, there are 14 different audiences. Each institution will need to identify its own set of messages and audiences to address the needs and realities of the institution. The cells are used for describing the medium that will be used with the specific audience to deliver the desired message. Several examples from NKU follow.

Each year, NKU prepares *Engaging with Our Region*, a four-color, glossy, 8.5 x 11 inch magazine documenting selected public engagement projects. To communicate the centrality of public engagement to the institution's mission, a letter from the university president is included on the inside front cover. The magazine tells the story of each selected project and includes many photographs as well as quotations from the faculty, their community partners, and the beneficiaries of the project. The magazine also features information about, and photographs of, faculty who won awards for their public engagement. The publication is distributed to the system office; local governing board members; administrators including deans, directors, and chairs; full-time faculty; all university, college, and department external advisory board members; legislators; selected community partners; K–12 principals in the region; selected government officials; and selected donors. In Table 10.1, NKU would list *Engaging with Our Region* as reaching nine audience groups (all except students, prospective students, the general public, alumni, and parents of current and prospective students) and satisfying three communication goals: enhancing public relations, motivating and supporting participation or commitment, and documenting effectiveness.

TABLE 10.1. STRATEGIC COMMUNICATION PLAN

COMMUNICATION GOAL

		Enhancing Public Relations	Motivating and Supporting Participation or Commitment	Facilitating Discussions	Documenting Effectiveness	Enabling Two-Way Communication	Recruiting Students
	Current students						
	Faculty and staff						
	Administrators						
A	Governing board						
U	System office						
D	Advisory boards						
I	General public						
E	Specific publics						
N	Legislators						
C	Community partners						
E	Donors						
	Alumni						
	Prospective students						
	Parents of current and prospective students						

Consider another example: NKU prepares an annual report of its public engagement activity. It includes three sections: a narrative describing the major public engagement accomplishments of the year, including one page per college for listing college accomplishments; a report on the extent of public engagement activity based on the data collection procedure described in Chapter 9; and the honor roll of faculty and staff who were involved in public engagement during the year. The honor roll was described in Chapter 9. Because this publication is intended for internal audiences, it is neither four-color nor glossy. It is still a bound publication but it is printed at a fraction of the cost of the magazine. It is distributed to all faculty and administrators and shared with the governing board. In Table 10.1, this publication would be listed under documenting effectiveness for each of four audiences: system office, governing board, administrators, and faculty and staff.

Here is a third example: NKU created a unit called Community Connections for the express purpose of serving as the university's "front door" for anyone wishing to access services other than the university's traditional teaching-learning function. Community Connections maintains a website and a telephone line and issues two different catalogs of events and activities that serve the external community: one for the general public, the other for K–12 educators. In Table 10.1, Community Connections would be listed as meeting three communication goals: enhancing public relations, motivating and supporting participation or commitment, and enabling two-way communication. It targets three audience groups: the general public, specific publics, and alumni.

These are examples of several communication efforts that have proven effective at one institution. It is important for each institution to look at what opportunities it has and to be creative in identifying how best to meet its communication goals. For example, if sporting events are significant on the campus, the institution could highlight public engagement during a half-time show or in the printed program; an institution that offers a degree in broadcasting could have students prepare a service learning "documentary" for viewing on the local cable channel; and a university with an agriculture school could have a booth at the state fair to highlight its public engagement.

Concluding Comments

The development and implementation of a strong communication plan is an important part of alignment. Communication motivates, keeps people informed, and strengthens and protects the institution's image. It is highly unlikely that all public engagement will be successful or that all community members will be satisfied with the institution's public engagement. At the very least, some will be disappointed because the school's capacity falls short of the community's needs. Through effective communication, the institution can ensure that its positive work will get more attention and recognition than complaints or disappointments voiced by a few people in the community. The value of the institution to the community will be well-known to the external community, and the value of public engagement to the institution, its students, and faculty will be well-known to the internal community.

Universities must be careful that their external communication does not create unrealistic expectations in the community. Given the breadth of a community's needs, its members hope to hear that the university can solve their problems. However, the university alone cannot own or solve a community's problems. The university can work with a community to address its issues, but communities should be realistic about what the institution can accomplish, how much capacity it has, how long it will take to address specific issues, and what resources are required. For example, several colleges and universities in Cincinnati and Northern Kentucky are working jointly with three inner-city school districts and a variety of community agencies to improve the college-going rate of students in those districts. This is an ambitious collaboration, but it will not show results in six months or a year. On the contrary, it will take many years before the full impact of the undertaking will be felt.

In designing the communication plan, the university needs to consider what its audiences want to know and what they will understand. For example, data alone, although very interesting to academics, is likely to be of limited interest to external audiences, especially if accompanied by complex statistical analyses. They find the stories of how projects affect the community to be much more compelling. Likewise, significant financial gifts in support of public engagement are of considerable interest in the short run, but in the long run most audiences want to know about the work that was supported with the gift and how the work affected the internal and external communities.

Finally, universities should be creative in designing communication strategies, especially in finding low-cost, high-impact ways to communicate. However, they cannot assume that what they do is effective. They need to follow up to learn whether the intended message was accurately received and understood.

CHAPTER ELEVEN

ALIGNING WITH THE COMMUNITY

In today's world, partnerships can be an integral element in institution building. Through partnerships, a campus can leverage its human and financial capacity, build strong public support, strengthen public advocacy, generate increased donor support, and reinforce its status as an indispensable contributor to advancing the public interest. Aligning with the community means aligning the elements that enable the campus to work effectively in partnership with the community.

AN INTRODUCTION TO PARTNERSHIPS

A partnership is defined as "a relationship between individuals or groups that is characterized by mutual cooperation and responsibility, for the achievement of a specified goal" (www.dictionary.com). Although partnerships are generally less efficient than working alone, the partnership adds value because it is able to achieve what none of the partners could achieve alone.

TYPES OF PARTNERSHIPS

As Beere (2009) concluded from reviewing the 2006 submissions for Carnegie's elective Community Engagement Classification (http://classifications.carnegiefoundation.org/descriptions/

community_engagement.php), campus-community partnerships vary in almost every dimension imaginable:

- Size, ranging from two people—one faculty member working with one individual in one community agency—to hundreds of people—large numbers of faculty and staff from multiple universities working with multiple community agencies or groups on a single project
- Focus, which may be in any area, such as economic development, agriculture, nonprofit capacity building, K–12 education, health, environment, arts and culture, criminal justice, government improvement, and so forth
- Partners, such as elementary and secondary schools; hospitals and health clinics; social service agencies; small businesses and large corporations; environmental advocacy groups; governmental agencies; economic development groups and chambers of commerce; community development organizations; nonprofit corporations; arts and literary groups; loose alliances of individuals; and the list goes on and on
- Duration, ranging from less than a single semester to many decades
- Complexity, ranging from a single, very circumscribed project to a community-wide, transformative initiative
- Length of time to produce results, ranging from results occurring immediately at the end of the project to results that are not apparent for at least a decade
- Formality, ranging from casual, informal working arrangements to highly structured arrangements involving formalized agreements that have been officially approved by various governing boards

Not surprisingly, partnerships involving large numbers of people, lasting a long time, and tackling complex problems produce far more challenges and require far more advance planning than simpler projects.

The Challenges of Collaboration

Campus-community partnerships, by definition, require collaboration with an external partner, often involve internal partners, and sometimes include other colleges and universities. These collaborations can be challenging for faculty who are used to working autonomously. The more partners there are, the more challenges and complications. But more partners are likely to mean more resources and expertise to focus on goals, and more partners attract more attention.

Although it may be relatively easy to obtain a commitment to collaborate at the upper echelons of an organization, that does not guarantee strong collaboration among those responsible to implement the project. For example, a college president and a local school superintendent might enthusiastically agree to partner on improving mathematics achievement among sixth graders, but this in no way guarantees that those implementing the project will work well together. Peter Robertson (1998) identified four prerequisites for people to collaborate effectively: "incentive, willingness, ability, and capacity" (p. 70). He provided more information, based on the professional literature, about each of these prerequisites. Chapter 6 listed some specific challenges encountered in university-community collaborations, including the need for great patience; the need to share decision making and control; the time demands associated with process issues and establishing trust and rapport; the challenges of community politics; and the mismatch between community and university calendars.

LAYING THE FOUNDATION FOR COMMUNITY PARTNERSHIPS

Although jumping into a partnership may periodically be effective, success is more likely if partnering is approached systematically. The first step is to identify the community.

IDENTIFY THE COMMUNITY

Chapter 1 discussed the various ways in which community can be defined: by geography such as a neighborhood or city or even a country located halfway around the world; by persons' identity or status, such as women or Muslims; by belief systems or interest areas, such as liberals, conservatives, or chess players; by age or occupation, such as preschoolers or mine workers; and by online connections, such as a Facebook community or a group of distance learners. Chapter 3 talked about the importance of planning, and it is the institution's strategic planning process that should identify the community for the purpose of creating partnerships. When the plan fails to identify the community, it must be identified by some other process. The selected community will be a function of the institution's history, culture, mission, and environment. Moreover, there are likely to be numerous different communities with which an institution will partner. Not surprisingly, the larger the defined community or the farther away it is located, the greater the challenges to a successful partnership.

VIEW THE COMMUNITY AS A PARTNER

The community should be viewed as a potential partner, not something to be studied or acted upon. Residents of low-income communities, in particular, are tired of being studied and treated like objects.

As Votruba (2004) stated: Our communities "want us to treat them as partners, not supplicants. They want us to seek first to understand and then be understood. They want us to recognize that they have the capacity to teach us as well as learn from us. And they want us to appreciate that our future as well as theirs is dependent on our work together" (p. 5).

The community should be viewed in terms of its assets: the strengths, wisdom, knowledge, and experience that it offers to the partnership. Faculty are one source of knowledge, but they are not the sole source. As pointed out in *Benchmarks for Campus/Community Partnerships* (Torres, 2000), community members know the community, its history, its resources, and its problems. They have contacts in the community, know what has been tried previously, and may have access to resources unavailable to the campus. Community members can mitigate language or cultural barriers and may have credibility the campus lacks. Colleges and universities must understand what it means to act *with* the community rather than act *on* the community (Pew Partnership for Civic Change, 2004).

Get to Know the Community

Those who will be partnering with the community—or those arranging the partnership—should be very familiar with it. They need to understand the community's history as well as the history of its relations with the campus; its different subcultures; its needs and priorities; the sources of power and influence within it; and its politics. Regional strategic plans can be very helpful in this regard. If the community is divided internally, those partnering should understand the origins of differences and proceed with caution in order to avoid being pulled into ongoing conflicts. The community is often a complex, heterogeneous entity that includes many subgroups with different priorities. If the campus plans to work with a loose alliance of community people, the campus needs to know how to reach them: Are they heavy computer users, or is putting flyers on telephone poles a better way to reach them? Is there a community center where they congregate?

When initially seeking to collaborate, the potential partners should spend time getting to know each other. They should engage in informal conversations, read each other's publications, explore each other's websites, exchange data with each other, and talk with people who bridge the institution and the community. The time spent getting to know each other is likely to pay off in the form of stronger, more productive partnerships. It is also important that the partners know themselves well and are realistic about their own capacity, commitment, and potential contribution.

When the community is involved in the institution's planning efforts and vice versa, it is easier for the two to get to know each other well. Chapter 3 explained the *Vision, Values, and Voices* strategic planning process, which is how NKU involves the community in university planning, and Chapter 4 described a regional planning process involving both the community and the university.

Repair Negative Relations

There are a variety of reasons why a community may see the campus through a negative lens. As Holland (2005) pointed out: "Academic institutions . . . take property off local tax rolls, raise property values, consume nearby land and neighborhoods, generate traffic and parking problems, and occasionally release large numbers of party-minded students into once quiet residential areas" (p. 11). The community may remember a time when faculty used the community to secure grants but then excluded them from any further involvement. Or they may remember times when the community served as a laboratory for faculty research without consideration for the feelings of the community members and without sharing the results in any way that would benefit the community. In communities where there has been very little interaction between the campus and community leaders, there may be considerable suspicion on the part of community leaders, who wonder why the institution is suddenly interested in partnering.

The community's negative attitudes cannot be ignored. If the community members are simply suspicious or mildly critical, the university might counter that by demonstrating through action that it is trustworthy and has much to offer. This can be accomplished by developing a partnership with a single, trusted, well-respected agency in the community and then faithfully fulfilling the institution's commitments to this partnership. When the institution as a whole lacks good relations with the community, it is still possible that individual departments have developed strong partnerships with agencies that have accepted campus interns or practicum students. These connections may provide the foundation for new partnerships.

When town-gown relations have been particularly acrimonious, it will take considerable time to repair them. The institutional leadership will need to listen to the community, understand their concerns, and acknowledge past problems before trying to move forward. Initially, a campus or community leader may need to work with each group separately to help them understand the other's perspective. An outside facilitator may help improve communication.

UNDERSTAND CAMPUS-COMMUNITY DIFFERENCES

Colleges and universities are likely to differ significantly from community partners, and a particular institution will differ from a particular community organization as well. There may be differences in daily schedules, the definition of year, time constraints, degree of diversity, size, complexity, size of resource base, access to resources, degree of independent decision making, approach to decision making and problem solving, flexibility or autonomy in controlling one's own time, use of acronyms, tolerance for long meetings, organizational structure, accountability requirements, self-concept, and reward systems. All relevant differences should be uncovered and explored during the get-acquainted stage. The implications of the differences should be discussed, and to the extent possible, there should be a plan for addressing those that will affect the partnership. If they are ignored, differences may jeopardize the future of a partnership.

Sometimes the differences are so great, or the tolerance for the differences so limited, that there is little chance for a successful partnership. When discussing the idea of partnering with a university, the executive vice president of a large, multinational corporation said:

> If I have a choice between partnering with a competitor, a serial entrepreneur, or a university, the university is my *last* choice. Faculty are in a parallel universe. They are unaware of the realities of the business world; businesses can't wait. When you deal with a professor, there is a middleman. They have to check with the department chair or dean or others in the administration. It isn't clear who has the authority to enter into agreements. The review process can take forever. Universities want overhead, and we aren't going to pay that. Why should we? It seems that the faculty are focused on getting their next grant, and we don't care about that. When something new is developed, the university wants a 50 percent split on royalties, but they don't have the resources to contribute to the marketing. [personal conversation with one of the authors, September 2008]

There are many ways to counter these criticisms, and there are countless examples of productive, mutually beneficial university-business partnerships. The point is that there are times when the differences between the university and a potential partner are, or are believed to be, too great to overcome. If the university wished to have a partnership with this multinational corporation, the first step would be to understand this individual's perspective. In all likelihood, it would require many hours of discussion and a clearly laid-out, mutually agreeable plan before he would change his views. Furthermore, his views, if unchanged, would likely antagonize potential faculty partners.

CREATE EASY ACCESS TO THE UNIVERSITY

Community organizations are frequently unaware of how to access potential campus partners. "To the non-academic, the university is a near-inscrutable entity governed by its own mysterious sense of itself. It's difficult to get a grip on this institution, understand its points of leverage, and find a way through the academic maze" (Kellogg Commission on the Future of State and Land-Grant Universities, 1999, p. 20). This is especially true for low-income people, who may be intimidated by the campus.

An institution that is aligned to support public engagement will have taken steps to make it easy for the community to connect. One option is to include a link for "the community" on the institution's website, as described in Chapter 10; this is an audience page analogous to the ones for students and faculty. The web pages can facilitate the creation of partnerships by telling potential partners about the university; its values, mission, and goals; and how to access potential partners in the university. This link can take people to an annotated listing of university units available to partner with community agencies and businesses. As stated in Chapter 10, those wishing to partner with the university need to find a starting point, an office that functions as a front door to the university. As mentioned earlier, NKU created *Community Connections,* a unit that provides the community with easy access to other university units, services, and resources. It is accessible by telephone, e-mail, and web.

CREATE LINKS WITH THE COMMUNITY

The specific approaches for linking campus to community will be a function of the campus, the community, and their shared history, whether it is positive, negative, or nonexistent. The campus could, for example:

- Invite the community to participate in campus planning initiatives or join with the community in regional planning efforts.
- Include community members on advisory boards for the campus's various public engagement units.
- Use its public relations or public affairs office to help identify and connect with potential partners or to communicate the institution's interest in partnering with the community.
- Hold special campus events, such as a community agency fair, that bring potential community partners together with the units that are seeking partners; use the opportunity to educate the community about the campus.
- Encourage faculty and staff to serve on community boards where they will develop relationships with potential partners.
- Ask neighboring colleges and universities to include the campus in some of their partnerships.

BEGINNING TO PARTNER

Although selecting "the right project" and "the right partner" are discussed separately here, they are deeply intertwined. Both must be addressed, and they generally come as a pair. Furthermore, the selections do not arise in a vacuum. Rather, they evolve from existing relationships, internal conversations about campus strengths and intended focus, and community opportunities. The university may approach a potential partner with a particular idea, or the university might be approached by a community group that wants to partner.

THE RIGHT PROJECT

The university's strategic plan should drive campus decisions about the projects to undertake. Where does the campus want to focus its efforts: K–12 education, health care, economic development, or somewhere else? Where is its strength? Where is it most likely to make a significant impact? Where does it want to expand its capacity? Institutions should limit themselves to projects that are compatible with their strategic goals, capacity, and areas of expertise. The campus should only commit to a project if it has—or is willing to hire—persons with the necessary expertise and commitment to undertake the project. Community needs and priorities should play a significant role in the selection of projects.

THE RIGHT PARTNER

The institution needs to consider the type of partner it is seeking. Does the campus want to partner with a nonprofit agency, a government group, a corporation, or a neighborhood group? Is there an ideal partner size? How much capacity for contributing resources will the partner need? To what extent will the partner be expected to contribute resources? It is much easier to partner with an existing, structured organization than it is with a loose confederation of individuals, but the potential for impact consistent with university goals might require a loose confederation to be the partner. The campus should think beyond the obvious. For example, a faculty member in art, looking for a service learning project for her students, might look at local arts organizations, but an alternative would be to partner with a community center to help at-risk youth create murals on the center's walls.

Campus representatives should talk with various potential partners—those they approach as well as those who approach the institution. They should learn about the mission and priorities of potential partners and determine whether the partnership will have the support of the partner's leaders and workers alike. The campus needs to know a potential partner sufficiently well to determine if it will be compatible, which is more likely when the agency's culture and values are similar to those of the campus. The more the partner differs from those they will be working with on campus, the greater the number of challenges that will arise; challenging partnerships are probably best reserved for those who are experienced with partnering.

A campus unit that lacks partnership experience is advised to begin with organizations or entities with which the institution already has a positive, productive relationship. If no such

relationships exist, the campus can consider the earlier sugges-
tion to work with neighboring colleges or universities that already
have partnerships the institution could join.

THE RIGHT COMMITMENT

Before making a commitment, the university needs to evaluate
both the partnership and the project. The following questions
should be considered:

- Is the problem to be addressed significant?
- Is the project compatible with the institution's mission, goals,
  and priorities?
- Are the partner and the campus compatible with each other?
- Is the partner prepared to make a tangible commitment to the
  partnership?
- Does the campus have the expertise or is it willing to hire the
  expertise necessary to address the problem?
- Are the human and financial resources allocated to the project
  sufficient for the campus to fulfill its commitment?
- Is success defined in such a way that there is a reasonable
  likelihood of success?
- Is the time line realistic and consistent with the partners'
  commitment?
- Does the project put the institution at too great a risk for legal,
  financial, political, or public relations issues? For example,
  there may be some topics that are so explosive in the
  community that the campus is best served by avoiding them.

The questions—and what constitutes acceptable answers—
will be slightly different if the project under consideration will be
addressed by an individual class of students in a single semester,
by an ongoing service learning program, or through a broad,
institutional initiative.

TIME TO DEVELOP THE PARTNERSHIP

It takes time to develop relationships with the community, forge
partnerships, and nurture them. Failure is likely if one approaches

a potential partner only weeks before the project is slated to begin, and failure can have implications for any future partnerships.

Partnerships between unlike cultures take even more time: the more divergent the two cultures, the more time it takes to develop trust and establish good working relationships. Likewise, the more complex the project and the more partners involved, the greater the required time investment. As Judith Ramaley (2003), former president of the University of Vermont and Portland State University and current president of Winona State University, explained: "It takes time, much more time than you might expect, to build trust and to open up genuine communication across differences in social status, education, culture, and experience. It is often best to bring people together first and build an agenda later through dialogue and exploration" (p. 22).

The initial stages of a partnership set the tone for the partnership. If the early meetings go poorly, the partnership is unlikely to work. A positive beginning does not guarantee that things will continue to go well, but it is a good start. Given their importance, the early stages should not be rushed.

WRITTEN AGREEMENT

The importance of a signed partnership agreement cannot be stressed too strongly. A signed agreement leads to a more focused and productive partnership than would otherwise exist. It ensures that the partners have a shared understanding of the significant issues before they begin work. Both the process of reaching agreement and the final document itself are important. During the negotiating process, partners get to know each other better, identify areas of agreement and potential disagreement, resolve whatever differences exist, determine what resources each partner will contribute, and clarify their understanding of goals, processes, and lines of authority and responsibility. The written agreement is a road map for the partnership and the project. It should be developed with as much care and attention to detail as a proposal for a large federal grant. If problems later arise, the written agreement provides the "rules" for resolving differences.

The agreement must be negotiated by those who have the requisite knowledge and the authority to commit their institution or organization. Although specific elements of the agreement will vary as a function of the partnership and the projects, the following are likely to be included:

- Start and end dates for the partnership or specific project
- Participants, including involved institutions, units, and individuals
- An "official" contact person and spokesperson for each partner
- Mission and objectives of the partnership
- Goals of the project
- Scope of the project
- Project plan
- Project governance (oversight)
- Project management (implementation)
- Roles and responsibilities of each partner (who will do what)
- Detailed description of the resources to be contributed by each partner
- Statement of anticipated outcomes
- Evaluation plans, both formative and summative
- Identification of committees and subcommittees (if needed)
- Plan for internal communication, including a plan for regular meetings
- Plan for external communication, including public relations and dissemination of results
- Allowable use of data or resulting products
- Control of other intellectual property (if applicable)
- Exit plans for successful termination of the project as well as conditions and procedures for early termination
- Detailed project time line
- Detailed project budget

Qualities of Strong Partnerships

Partnerships do not emerge fully developed. Rather they evolve over time and are frequently described as occurring in three stages: the first is analogous to a courtship in which the partners are getting to know each other and enthusiasm tends to run high; the second is when things really get serious, conflicts are more likely to surface, obstacles to success become more obvious, issues from the first stage must be revisited, and the partnership begins to be tested; finally, if the partnership survives the second stage, the third stage is one of productivity, success, and either sustainability or termination when the goals are achieved (Cauley, 2000; Scheibel, Bowley, & Jones, 2005; Torres, 2000).

A partnership that thrives is likely to evolve and deepen over time as the partnership matures. The qualities discussed in the following paragraphs are based on the experiences of the authors combined with the itemized lists of characteristics of successful partnerships contained in books and articles by Holland, 2005; Judd & Adams, 2008; Scheibel, Bowley, & Jones, 2005; Strand, Marullo, Cutforth, Stoecker, & Donohue, 2003b; and Torres, 2000.

Mutual Benefit

Successful partnerships are mutually beneficial. The partners are unlikely to derive the same benefits, but they must derive benefits they feel are of comparable value. Ensuring mutual benefit requires a conversation at the outset: What important benefits is each partner seeking? Is it realistic that these benefits will occur? How will matters be handled if one of the partners perceives a lack of mutuality?

Shared Vision and Goals

Before moving forward with a partnership, partners should discuss their respective vision and goals to learn whether they are congruent. Some differences are understandable; for example, the faculty will be interested in working with and helping the community, but at the same time they want to enhance the education of their students and advance their own scholarship. The community, in contrast, may be interested only in responding to a community need or challenge. These and other differences should be acknowledged, discussed, and resolved or they may fester and cause problems in the future.

Respect and Trust

Respect and trust go hand in hand and can only be achieved when the partners spend time together and get to know each other. The partners must set aside their own biases and learn to understand their partner from the partner's perspective. In his study of what community partners expect from universities, Sean Creighton (2006) found: "Participants felt disrespected by higher education partners, expressing the opinion that higher education had an elitist attitude. The feeling of inferiority was a core finding" (p. 143). Academics need to realize that the knowledge they bring to the table, while very valuable, is not the sole source of knowledge; community members bring their own knowledge, a wealth of experience, and a valuable perspective that enriches the partnership and informs the project.

Realistic Expectations

Partners need to be realistic about what can be accomplished in a particular project, how long it will take, and what it will cost. If the partners are not realistic at the outset, they are likely to become discouraged and disappointed later on. A project to test the pollution level in a local stream might be completed in a relatively short period of time, at a relatively low cost, and the resulting report will constitute the successful completion of the project. Reducing teenage smoking, in contrast, is a much more ambitious project that will require significantly more resources and take far longer to show results; in fact, the project may fail.

Equality

Ideally, there should be equality in all aspects of the partnership but this is not always possible or even desirable, because the skills, knowledge, and resources of the partners are likely to differ (Strand, Marullo, Cutforth, Stoecker, & Donohue, 2003b). Thus, it is more reasonable to strive for equity—fairness—rather than equality (Sandmann, 2008). For example, the partners may bring different and unequal resources to the partnership, but each must contribute something tangible. Equality should be a goal in those areas where it is realistic, such as setting the agenda for the partnership, establishing specific project goals, establishing the rules by which the partnership will function, determining who will represent the project to the media, deciding what constitutes success and how it will be celebrated, and determining how problems will be resolved when things go awry.

JOINT PLANNING

Joint planning is a critical element of a successful partnership. Planning should be as broad yet as detailed as possible, and it should ensure equity (fairness) and mutual benefit. Planning should focus on all the elements to be included in the written agreement. The planning process should include all partners as well as target populations. For example, in developing a program to teach English to immigrants, the planning process should include representatives from the immigrant population, not just from the church where the classes will be held or the community organization whose mission is to help immigrants. Although detailed planning and the development of a written agreement may delay starting a project, these activities are likely to avoid, or at least minimize, future problems.

FLEXIBILITY

Participants in a partnership need to be flexible. Regardless of how carefully a project is planned and how detailed the written agreement, there will be surprises. The more complex the partnership, the more surprises there will be. Circumstances may change, unanticipated roadblocks may be encountered, and personnel may be shifted. To survive, the partnership must adapt.

EVALUATION

Both the process and the outcomes of a partnership must be periodically evaluated. The evaluation serves a dual purpose: it provides the data needed for the partners to take corrective action to strengthen the partnership and ensure it stays on course, and it satisfies the need for accountability to various governing boards, funders, and other interested groups. An evaluation plan should delineate how the process and product will be evaluated: Who will do the evaluation? At what points in the partnership will it be done? What data collection methods and instruments will be used? From whom will data be collected? The plan should also indicate how and with whom the findings will be shared.

COMMUNICATION

There are two aspects to partnership communication: internal, meaning within the partnership, and external, meaning with other audiences. It is important to have regular internal communication that is respectful, open, and transcends differences in communication styles and language usage. There must be formal communication channels, such as scheduled meetings, e-mail alerts, or newsletters, as well as provisions for informal communication. Before beginning the project, partners should agree on the rules for communications: Who has the authority to speak publicly on behalf of the project? When will such communication need approval? Who has the authority to give the approval? If the project is likely to attract considerable public interest, there should be a plan for the timing and method of external communications, including the publication of periodic formal reports.

CELEBRATION

Strong partnerships celebrate their success. These celebrations may occur in conjunction with the inauguration of the partnership, the successful completion of some phase of the project, or the conclusion of the project. They may also occur simply as a form of self-congratulation because the partnership is proceeding well.

EXIT STRATEGY

There are at least four reasons for ending a partnership: (a) its purpose is satisfied; (b) it is not working; (c) there is no longer funding available to support the project; or (d) one side no longer wishes to participate. The first reason reflects a positive conclusion, a happy ending. The challenge occurs when one of the other reasons leads to termination. There should be a means of exiting that does not damage the overall relationship between the campus and community. Although there is no guarantee that one can avoid bitterness when a partnership terminates without a successful conclusion, it is more likely if provisions for exiting are written out in the partnership agreement. This is particularly important when the university intends to start a project in partnership with the community, but once it begins flourishing, plans to turn it over to the community. That must be made clear in the original written agreement or the community may expect the university's involvement to continue indefinitely. Without a disengagement strategy at the outset, there is significant risk that the community will be unprepared to assume total responsibility for the project or perhaps even be angry when the institution says it is time to leave.

CHALLENGES

The recommendations contained in this chapter can help address many of the challenges that campus-community partnerships bring, but implementing all of them is not easy.

OVERCOMING CHALLENGES

Finding sufficient time and funding can be enormous challenges. Overcoming differences between campuses and their communities can be a significant problem. Collaboration, a necessary element of a partnership, is difficult and requires cooperation and compromise that are not always forthcoming. Partnering across racial and class lines presents its own set of special challenges, and before embarking on such a partnership, one ought to be familiar with the relevant literature that shows how to approach such partnerships. See, for example, Vivian Chávez's (2005) "Silence Speaks: The Language of Internalized Oppression and Privilege in Community-Based Research."

SUSTAINABILITY

Sustainability is not an issue for short-term, circumscribed projects, but it can be a significant challenge for long-term, broadly focused projects. In order for some partnership projects to have any real impact, they may have to be sustained for long periods of time: decades or longer. Two challenges commonly surface for long-term partnerships: funding and personnel.

Public engagement projects tend to be cost centers for the university. Even when there are significant funds at the start of a project—perhaps from grants or gifts—external funding is likely to end at some point. This is a significant challenge for projects with a long time horizon (for example, increasing the college-going rate of students in the inner-city schools) and for ongoing projects (for example, a health clinic serving low-income community residents).

As for personnel, it is not unusual for those who begin a long-term partnership to move on to other projects or even to leave the university or the community partner. If the project is to continue, there has to be a way to bring new people in, and these new people must demonstrate the same level of competence and commitment as the original collaborators did. If not handled well, changing project personnel may threaten the partnership's survival.

A different challenge arises when a project should not be sustained: "Enduring partnerships may be a symptom of an unhealthy partnership that persists because of increasing or chronic dependency of one party or another (Strube, 1988). That is, a partnership can be maintained because it prevents one of the parties from developing the capacity to be self-sufficient and maintains power differences" (Bringle & Hatcher, 2002, p. 511). The goal of the university should be to build community capacity, not to assume a never-ending responsibility in the community. Setting the terms of engagement and disengagement at the beginning of the partnership, as suggested earlier, can help avoid long-term damage to the relationship when partnerships cannot or should not be sustained.

CONCLUDING COMMENTS

Campus-community partnerships are powerful collaborations that can bring enormous benefit to both partners. As John Hitt (2009), president of the University of Central Florida, pointed out in his address to the presidents of AASCU institutions: "No single individual or organization acting alone has the resources to solve the significant problems we face. Thus, if we want our institutions to offer meaningful societal benefits that compel support, we need to find partners for our efforts" (p. 5). At the same time, partnerships are not easy: they are time-consuming and pose risks and challenges that must be faced. Short-lived, narrowly focused partnership projects carry less risk and pose fewer challenges than complex, far-reaching, multi-organizational partnerships, but the latter are likely to have greater impact.

Many universities give awards to community partners or university-community partnerships as a way to recognize their contribution to the university and the community. See, for example, Indiana State's *Outstanding Community Partner Award* (http://www.indstate.edu/news/news.php?newsid=2218); Virginia Commonwealth's *Currents of Change Award* that recognizes university-community partnerships that have had a significant impact on the life of the Richmond community (http://www.40th.vcu.edu/caring/currents.html); and California State University Monterey Bay's *Marian Penn Partnership Award,* which "recognizes community partners and faculty who have demonstrated exceptional commitment, communication and success in strengthening communities through service learning programs" (http://service.csumb.edu/site/x9750.xml).

Regardless of the size or type of partnership, the community and campus should remember that colleges and universities create, preserve, transmit, and apply knowledge. They can often provide knowledge to help communities solve their own problems, and they can even provide person power in the form of faculty and students, but they cannot assume responsibility for community problems. Doing so violates the university's mission and is likely to lead to deep disappointment on the part of everyone involved.

Campus-community partnerships are complex, and space limitations here do not allow an in-depth look at all factors to be considered. The following resources are recommended for those who wish to learn more about partnering: *Benchmarks for Campus/Community Partnerships* (Torres, 2000); *The Promise of Partnerships: Tapping into the College as a Community Asset* (Scheibel, Bowley, & Jones, 2005) and *Partnership Perspectives*, Volume 1, Issue 2 (Connors & Seifer, 2000), which provides an in-depth discussion of nine principles of good partnerships; these principles were slightly revised in 2006 (http://depts.washington .edu/ccph/principles.html). An excellent source for more information about partnering specifically for CBR is *Principles of Best Practice for Community-Based Research* (Strand, Marullo, Cutforth, Stoecker, & Donohue, 2003b).

CHAPTER TWELVE

ALIGNING PUBLIC POLICY

Internal alignment is not the only alignment needed to support public engagement. Also required is strong public policy alignment that incentivizes and supports public engagement as a core institutional mission. Indeed, one can argue that strong public policy can drive internal campus alignment, and without the support of strong public policy, internal alignment becomes more challenging.

Throughout the history of American higher education, public policy has been a key driver of institutional behavior, as was discussed in Chapter 1. To reiterate, at the federal level, public policy in the early 1900s created the Cooperative Extension Service, the most ambitious and successful example of university outreach in the nation's history. The extension service, located in each of the fifty states, is supported by a combination of federal, state, and local funding and was created to enhance agricultural production and promote rural quality of life. As successful as this model was in demonstrating how universities can use their knowledge to advance a public agenda, the model has not been replicated on behalf of a broader array of public priorities.

After World War II, the federal government established massive resource streams to support federal research priorities through a variety of federal agencies, including the National Institutes of Health, the National Science Foundation, the Department of Commerce, and the Department of Defense. These agencies provided not only direct support for research projects but also indirect support for the university itself. The result was that both individual faculty members and the institution had an incentive to pursue federal research funding. Rhodes (2001), former president of Cornell University, made the point: "The pattern of federal support for research has been critical to the success of the American research university" (p. 15).

At the state level, higher education policy has generally been directed at ensuring both student access and affordability through enrollment-driven funding formulas, capital construction, and student financial aid. The result has been that public colleges and universities have had an incentive both to grow and to serve those who could not otherwise afford the full cost of their education.

Although research and student enrollment have had robust public policy support, outreach and public engagement have not. Indeed, there are few examples of either federal or state public policy initiatives that support partnerships on behalf of advancing important public priorities such as economic development or K–12 education. In most cases, the public engagement undertaken by postsecondary institutions represents a cost center, not a revenue center. Until public policy is available to support this work, it is challenging to make it a major campus priority, particularly in times of financial stress.

Campus leaders who are committed to public engagement would be wise to focus their attention not only on internal alignment but also on the alignment of public policy with an emphasis on creating funding streams to support public engagement. Although federal policy can be enormously important, campus and system leaders have a far greater chance of influencing state policy.

BUILDING A STATE POLICY INITIATIVE

It is often said that all politics are local, and so it is with much of the public engagement work pursued by colleges and universities. Campuses frequently form partnerships with local entities around community priorities. The question becomes: To what extent does a state want to encourage and support these partnerships in order to advance a larger public agenda?

In general, higher education is a state responsibility. Dennis Jones (2005), president of the National Center for Higher Education Management Systems, makes the point that it is at the state level that college and university missions are established, substantial amounts of funds are allocated, accountability mechanisms are determined, and governance structures are decided.

Jones (2005) lays out five elements that are needed in a state policy. First, a statement of priorities and desired outcomes should be formulated. What does the state want from its colleges and universities? The response must be clear, focused, and measurable. These goals should focus primarily on the needs of the state and its citizens, and only secondarily on the needs of the higher education institutions. The more clearly and comprehensively defined the public agenda is, the easier for higher education leaders and public policymakers to respond. The public agenda must be statewide in its perspective, yet allow for local and regional variation and adaptation. Business, civic, education, and political leaders should be involved in developing the public agenda, and it should be driven, or at least informed, by data and information on state performance in key priority areas. For example, a state may set as a goal to meet or exceed the national average in the percentage of high school graduates going on to college. The greater the consensus among key stakeholders, the more likely the public agenda will be sustained over time.

Second, a finance and resource allocation policy should be created. Spending levels and incentives for action, rather than constraints or sanctions, should be established. It is worth noting that this is not just about the amount of funds that states allocate to their colleges and universities; it is to clarify the purpose for which the allocations are made and with what level of accountability. Jones (2005) wrote: "Ensuring that the incentives embedded in the resource allocation mechanism lead to pursuit of stated objectives is a critical feature of sound state policy making" (p. 15).

Accountability mechanisms are the third necessary element to develop. Historically, little effort has been made to assess the contributions that colleges and universities make to advancing public priorities. Accountability requires a clear statement of goals and agreement on the ways in which progress will be demonstrated. It also requires an annual "report card" that assesses progress toward the achievement of the state's priorities. Using the preceding example, there would likely be expectations for college and university partnerships with area high schools in order to strengthen college readiness, along with a process for monitoring both statewide and individual institutional progress toward the goal.

Fourth, rules, regulations, and procedures are needed to define how mandates are to be carried out. The danger here is that the requirements will become so burdensome and inflexible that they will actually inhibit performance. To the extent possible, state policy should set outcome objectives and allow the colleges and universities flexibility in achieving them, with the understanding that each campus will be accountable for its performance.

The final element is governance structures and policy leadership. Which state entities will be responsible for defining the public agenda and holding institutions accountable? In states with a higher education governing or coordinating board, it is the board that will define state priorities and accompanying accountability measures. However, there must be ample opportunity for state government leaders, as well as campus leadership, to influence these strategic decisions, and there must be sufficient flexibility to tailor institutional responses to local and regional conditions.

These policy elements have been presented as discreet dimensions, but in reality they must be treated as seamless and interdependent. If any one of them is out of alignment, it can serve to undermine the ultimate goal of encouraging colleges and universities to focus on the public agenda rather than exclusively on their own institutional agenda.

THE KENTUCKY REGIONAL STEWARDSHIP PROGRAM

The experience of Kentucky provides some useful insight into how the preceding policy dimensions play out in support of public engagement. In 1997, the Commonwealth of Kentucky embarked on one of the most ambitious postsecondary reform agendas in the nation. Landmark legislation established a new set of expectations for the state's colleges and universities. Close on the heels of this legislation, the Kentucky Council on Postsecondary Education (CPE), the state coordinating board, developed a postsecondary education public agenda expressed as five questions that each institution was asked to address:

1. Are more Kentuckians ready for postsecondary education?
2. Is Kentucky postsecondary education affordable for its citizens?
3. Do more Kentuckians have certificates and degrees?
4. Are college graduates prepared for life and work in Kentucky?
5. Are Kentucky's people, communities, and economy benefiting?
   [Kentucky Council on Postsecondary Education, n.d.]

These questions, each offered with detailed expectations and measurable outcomes, provided the basis for organizing institutional efforts on behalf of Kentucky's future. Once in place, the state's colleges and universities began immediately to organize their work to demonstrate their contribution to improvement around the five questions. At the same time, policymakers used the five areas of intended progress to shape funding strategies.

Early in 2005, the presidents of several comprehensive universities in Kentucky met with the CPE president and began to make the case for a public resource stream to support their public engagement role. The presidents pointed out that their institutions were deeply embedded in their respective regions and had the capacity to be anchor institutions for advancing regional progress in such areas as K–12 education, college readiness, economic competitiveness, local government decision making, improved health, and a host of other initiatives important to specific regions. The presidents also pointed out that, absent state funding, this work was likely to be limited and conducted at the institutional margin.

At the same time conversations were occurring with the CPE, several of the presidents were beginning to meet with the governor and key leaders in the Kentucky General Assembly to make the case for funding support. Both the governor and the general assembly leadership were intrigued and asked for more details. An initial challenge was explaining exactly what the work involved and how the colleges and universities could bring significant and measurable value-added. Examples were helpful, as were community leaders who could speak to the impact of the work in local settings. For example, NKU was able to document that elementary student performance on state-administered science and reading tests improved significantly at both the local and state levels as a result of a program in which NKU faculty modeled new teaching techniques for elementary school teachers.

Once the governor and general assembly leadership were convinced, campus and CPE leaders began to make the case with other members of the General Assembly. It was not a difficult case to make because the legislation held out the promise of significant and measurable progress in their specific districts.

As a result of this concerted effort, in 2006 the Commonwealth of Kentucky became the first state in the nation to create a public policy initiative designed to support the involvement of the state's six comprehensive universities in local and regional public engagement initiatives. The legislation vested governance, accountability, and policy leadership in the CPE. The CPE, in turn, established three streams of funding to support institutional public engagement efforts. The first was a recurring allocation to each institution to help build the infrastructure to support the work. The second was recurring funding to each institution to support specific initiatives. The third was nonrecurring funding, available on a competitive basis each year to support new initiatives. In order to minimize early battles between the individual universities over their share of the allocation, it was agreed that each institution would receive an equal share of the first two funding streams.

The CPE also formulated policies for the program, including accountability requirements and guidelines for the distribution of funds. Each campus had to form a regional advisory committee made up of local government and community leaders, business and industry representatives, education leaders, and citizens from across the university's area of geographic responsibility. This committee was designed to help ensure that what the university was proposing was, in fact, consistent with the region's priorities.

Once the advisory committee was formed, the university was required to develop a plan for aligning institutional priorities, resources, and infrastructure to support public engagement initiatives; identify key indicators of regional vitality; engage in environmental scanning to pinpoint priorities; produce a planning document that highlights regional needs; establish partnerships with local and regional entities that are key to advancing a specific regional agenda; encourage faculty members to generate proposals around the regional priorities; and provide professional development for faculty related to public engagement, including how best to integrate this work with both teaching and research. Each university received its money after meeting the CPE criteria and submitting a specific proposal approved by the CPE. Once funded, each university also had to provide an annual report to the CPE that addressed, with supporting data, program outcomes and the relationship of those outcomes to the state's public agenda.

The impact of this funding program can be understood at several different levels. First, the funding provided much-needed infrastructure and programmatic support for public engagement efforts. Second, it required the universities to take the lead in establishing a strategic plan for their region, a process that was suggested earlier in this book. Third, it mandated that the universities formalize the public's voice in their strategic planning process and form community partnerships on behalf of desired goals, practices that were also recommended earlier in the book. Fourth, it required the universities to begin institutionalizing public engagement as a core institutional mission, including addressing many of the alignment issues described in this book. Finally, it made clear that public engagement was not simply the preference of a particular president or CAO but was now established as a state priority for the comprehensive universities. For many of the universities, public engagement was a new institutional priority. This legislation sent a powerful message to both campus and community audiences that this work was here to stay. Presidents and provosts might come and go but the work will continue to be a public policy priority.

Public engagement has much to make it attractive to state policymakers: the work focuses on priorities that the public has defined as important; much of the work is local or statewide, which appeals to legislators; and the work has the potential to further leverage one of the state's largest investments on behalf of local and state progress.

A Note to Campus Leaders

The Kentucky experience demonstrates that a few presidents and provosts working together with the state coordinating board can catalyze public policy in support of the public engagement mission. To do so requires campus leaders to undertake several tasks that may not be part of the prevailing culture and approach to state government.

The advancement of state public policy in support of public engagement involves campus leadership at every level. First, presidents, provosts, and other campus leaders must work across institutional lines—not in competition with each other but collaboratively on behalf of the public policy agenda. This is often easier said than done, particularly when resources are limited. In Kentucky, it would have been understandable if each campus had chosen to make the case for a disproportionate share of the regional stewardship funding. Institutions from more affluent regions could have argued from the perspective of return on investment while institutions from poorer regions could have argued that the funding should go to the regions with greatest need. Success in advancing the policy depended on getting beyond these wedge arguments. Otherwise, opponents of the policy could have used the lack of institutional agreement to undermine the policy's merits.

Second, campus leaders need to be willing to spend large amounts of time explaining the initiative to legislators and executive staff, many of whom may have trouble understanding the concept and potential of public engagement. Here, it is important to have key faculty members, chairs, and deans provide clear examples of how public engagement has advanced important public priorities in significant and measurable ways.

Third, leaders need to make clear to their campuses why this work is important not only for the state but also for the institution. U.S. higher education has historically received enormous public support because it was seen as inextricably linked to larger public priorities, including bringing science to agriculture, supporting intergenerational mobility, providing the workforce for industrial expansion, strengthening national defense, and pushing back the frontiers of knowledge in every dimension of our lives. To be seen as strongly engaged in advancing public priorities helps position the institution to make the case for public support across the full breadth of its mission. Public engagement also provides an opportunity to enrich both the teaching and research missions of the campus.

A NOTE TO POLICYMAKERS

Harnessing the capacity of the state's postsecondary institutions to help advance an important public agenda requires that policymakers do their homework and become familiar with the nature of public engagement. It is not simply about providing more money to campuses to do this work. It is about providing funds in a form that prompts certain types of institutional behavior. In this era of accountability, it would be tempting to load the legislation with so many requirements that it becomes a burden for campuses to comply. There needs to be sufficient oversight to ensure that the work gets done and is evaluated. However, it is important to avoid overloading the funding requirement with so much bureaucracy and reporting that it collapses under its own weight or lacks sufficient flexibility for institutions to adapt their work to their local setting.

Votruba (2005) suggests five key questions for policymakers who want to promote campus public engagement:

1. Does the state have a "public agenda" focused on the needs of its population? For example, are there priorities for economic development, education, health, and crime prevention?
2. Are colleges and universities held accountable for addressing the public agenda through their teaching, research, and public engagement efforts?
3. Have we articulated the importance of public engagement in both rhetorical and financial terms?
4. Have we developed criteria that allow us to measure the quantity and quality of campus public engagement activity?
5. Have we created resource streams to support higher education's engagement of our most important public priorities? [p. 260]

It can be demonstrated, at both the state and local levels, that colleges and universities have enormous capacity to advance priorities important to the public. If we invest in postsecondary institutions to support public engagement, it will reap significant public returns.

CONCLUDING COMMENTS

State and federal policies have influenced the work of U.S. colleges and universities for much of their history. Today, there continues to be significant federal funding for research, and although recent years have seen dramatic declines in state funding for higher education, states have historically provided significant support for both capital construction and enrollment growth. What has been missing at both state and federal levels is significant financial support for the extension and application of knowledge in order to advance the public agenda. This gap in state and federal policy prevents colleges and universities from expanding their public engagement at a time when that work is critically needed. Campus and system leaders need to collaborate with local and state business, civic, and political leaders to establish public policy that supports the public engagement function. Without policy support, this work is unlikely to occur at the level required to advance an ambitious public agenda.

This chapter has focused on policy leadership at the state level, but it is important not to overlook federal initiatives that, although more difficult to achieve, have the potential to create a major national shift in support of campus public engagement initiatives. To be successful, such policy initiatives need the support of the national higher education associations, several of which have recently advocated for a more aggressive federal role in the public engagement domain.

CHAPTER THIRTEEN

MOVING FORWARD

Institutional change is inevitable, but colleges and universities have a choice: they can allow change to happen to them—they can be the victims of change—or they can elect to direct change in ways that benefit them, their students, and their faculty. Former University of Michigan President James Duderstadt (2000) noted: "Most institutions continue to approach change by reacting to the necessities and opportunities of the moment rather than adopting a more strategic approach to their future" (p. 36). The premise of this book is that the alignment process, properly done, is an effective, powerful, strategic approach for facilitating institutional change.

The authors of this book know only too well that administrators spend much of their time in reactive mode, responding to immediate challenges and problems. It is often difficult to make time to look at the big picture, to determine how to facilitate change. Moreover, change on a campus will not be successful without buy-in from the various campus constituencies. The alignment process addresses both of these issues. It delegates to a committee of carefully selected representatives from different constituent groups the task of looking at the big picture by studying the organizational dimensions that the picture comprises, and it provides a road map for creating the desired change.

There is tremendous variability across colleges and universities: they are large and small; two-year and four-year; public and private; research-centered and teaching-centered; and so forth. The communities and regions in which they operate are also different from each other. How a campus implements public engagement is a function of its own history, culture, mission, and size, as well as the history, culture, and needs of the community and the past relationships between campus and community. The power of the alignment process comes, in part, from its versatility, its usefulness for all types of institutions located in all sorts of communities. Furthermore, this powerful tool can be used to work with other campus priorities; for example, NKU used it to look at improving retention and graduation rates. Regardless of the characteristics of the institution or the priority that is being considered, the alignment process ensures that the institution's highest priorities are approached from an analytic as well as a systems perspective.

The alignment analysis, conducted by a carefully selected committee, considers various organizational dimensions to determine, first, what evidence is needed to document that the organization is aligned for public engagement, and second, whether that evidence is apparent on the campus. For example, if the institution is aligned for public engagement regarding "individual incentives and rewards," then public engagement would be recognized in the institution's RPT guidelines; there would be awards for outstanding public engagement; those involved would be recognized in university publications; and so forth. The final report of the alignment analysis includes a road map showing how to align dimensions that are not adequately aligned.

Although each campus can modify the list of organizational dimensions to accommodate its circumstances, this book has considered 16 important organizational dimensions:

- Vision, mission, and values
- Planning and goal setting
- Internal and external resources
- Facilities and environment
- Internal policies and procedures
- Leadership selection, evaluation, and development
- Organizational structure
- Faculty and staff recruitment, selection, orientation, and professional development
- Individual incentives and rewards
- Unit-level incentives and rewards
- Rituals, awards, and ceremonies
- Curriculum and student educational opportunities

- Information and reporting systems
- Evaluation and accountability
- Communication
- Public policy

Each organizational dimension is considered at four levels: university; college; department or academic unit; and faculty and staff.

The alignment process is time-consuming, but having used this approach, the authors can attest that it is worth the investment. It is a proven strategy for embedding public engagement—or any other campus priority—deep in the fabric of the institution where it is no longer so dependent on the support of specific individuals. The alignment analysis will help ensure that the importance of public engagement will not decline once those promoting the work leave the institution. At the same time, one must keep in mind that alignment is not easy. It is an ongoing, iterative process that must be monitored, nurtured, and supported until public engagement—or the priority for which alignment is sought—is as deeply embedded in the institution as are teaching and research.

Throughout this book, the authors have provided very specific advice and cautions regarding the institutionalization and expansion of public engagement. Some of the most important ones are reviewed here.

ADVICE

- *Align the vision, mission, and values before striving to align elsewhere.* These are foundational statements that undergird the institution. To justify making public engagement an institutional priority, it must be reflected in these documents.
- *Use the institution's strategic agenda to set a limited number of priorities for public engagement.* Although individual faculty may continue to do good work in other areas that interest them, the strategic agenda should identify where the institution will invest its resources. This will enable the institution to have a strong impact in a limited number of areas, which is generally preferable to having a minimal impact in many areas. Furthermore, the university will have a clear, understandable, and acceptable

rationale for declining a suggested partnership or project that falls outside these priorities.

- *Communicate, communicate, communicate—both on-campus and off-campus.* Effective communication requires that one listen as much as one speaks. Effective communication also requires that people have a common understanding of terms. Keep in mind Holland's (2001) warning: "The lack of a sufficiently common language . . . makes it easier for opponents of engagement as academic work to question its rigor and legitimacy" (p. 28). Moreover, spending time arguing about terms wastes time that could be spent in more productive discussions to advance public engagement.

- *Relate public engagement to what faculty members value.* Although this may vary somewhat from campus to campus, faculty generally value what is good for their students, what enhances their own scholarly productivity, and what adheres to high standards of academic rigor. Help faculty explore the intellectual foundations for this work and its potential to benefit the institution, its students, and the community.

- *"Get the right people on the bus AND the wrong people off the bus"* (Collins, 2001, p. 199), an admonition pointed out in Chapter 5. Hire people who already have a commitment to public engagement and mentor those who do not, so they develop the commitment. Recognize that some who continue to resist public engagement might focus on other university priorities, and some might be a better fit elsewhere.

- *Remember that departments and their chairs are absolutely essential in the alignment process.* Cultivate the support of department chairs and attend to their professional development.

- *Recognize that faculty are often more focused on their discipline than on their institution.* Take advantage of support from various disciplinary associations that are actively promoting public engagement.

- *Use "pull" strategies, designed to entice people to want to be publicly engaged, rather than "push" strategies, which try to force people to be publicly engaged.* Modifying the RPT guidelines to recognize and reward public engagement is one of the most important and effective pull strategies.

- *Support the work.* This requires providing the necessary tangible support, such as a chief public engagement officer, a service learning office, and financial support. It also requires intangible support such as celebrating successful partnerships, recognizing faculty who excel at the work, and assuring that public engagement is prominent in campus speeches.

- *Set high standards and hold people accountable for public engagement.* As pointed out in Chapter 9, "we measure what we value, and we value what we measure." It is not sufficient to do public engagement; the institution and the community must know whether the work is having the desired effect. When the results are used strategically, measuring public engagement and its impact has powerful benefits both inside and outside the institution.

- *Be discerning in dealing with the external community.* This means dealing with the community as a full and equal partner. Require a tangible commitment, such as financial or human resources, from each of the partners. Before the work begins, develop a written agreement so that everyone involved understands the goals and terms of the partnership. Be sure it includes a plan for eventual disengagement, unless a permanent partnership is anticipated. Clarify what happens when the partnership ends.

- *Be patient.* Lasting change does not occur quickly. Colleges and universities are complex institutions, generally resistant to change. However, those who persevere will be richly rewarded by a transformed campus in which public engagement is institutionalized.

CAUTIONS

- *Do not contribute to a silo mentality in which public engagement is pitted against other mission dimensions.* It is not public engagement *versus* teaching or *versus* research. The entire system functions most effectively when the work of the faculty integrates the various mission dimensions. For example, when faculty in a college of education work with their students to design and implement a program to reduce the high school dropout rate, the project can contribute to teaching, scholarship, and service.

- *Do not overpromise.* It is impossible for the institution to be all things to all people, to honor all community requests or meet all community needs. Avoid rhetoric that leads the community to think otherwise. It is best to realistically assess the institution's capacity, and based on that capacity, communicate what the campus can do. Spreading the institution too thin is a prescription for failure. Focusing on a few areas where the university has the expertise and the capacity is the route to success.

- *Do not be surprised to discover that the more the university does, the more the community expects.* Set realistic limits. Faculty need to know that the administration will protect the campus from unreasonable community expectations.

- *Avoid taking sole ownership of a community problem.* Many communities may be eager to hand their problems over to their local college or university, and many faculty, with their hearts in the right place, may be willing to take ownership for a community problem. But it will not work! It creates expectations that the institution cannot possibly meet. The problems a community is willing to hand over are often ones that are deeply rooted, systemic, and complex, such as poverty, urban blight, and underperforming schools. Assuming sole ownership of those problems sets the institution up for failure. Academic institutions are first and foremost promoters of learning. In the engagement arena, higher education's most powerful contribution is to provide the learning that allows communities to resolve their own problems.

- *Do not expect a partnership to eliminate the problems of the type just mentioned.* It is important for partnerships to have clear, focused, achievable goals. Success must be defined in such a way that it is possible for the partnership to succeed.

- *Avoid getting caught in political conflicts.* This is not always easy to do. Faculty may wander into political territory by becoming involved in controversial issues such as abortion rights, racism, or even the high school biology curriculum. As an institution committed to learning, the focus should be on the data: let the data speak for itself.

- *Do not expect every faculty member to be publicly engaged.* Not all have the talent or skill set for working in partnership with the community. Be sure that those going into the community are properly prepared and realistic about what they will encounter.

• *Do not respond to budget reductions by disproportionately cutting public engagement.* This sends a message to the campus that the work is not really important. Likewise, public engagement cannot take a disproportionate share of the resources, either. Public engagement is an important mission dimension and an important institutional priority; it deserves its fair share of funds when institutional resources are plentiful and when they are scarce.

• *Do not expect all projects to unfold as planned.* There will be unexpected bumps along the way. A written agreement reflecting careful planning coupled with flexibility and a sense of humor can help move a partnership over those bumps to a successful conclusion.

• *Do not expect legislators or community leaders initially to understand this work.* Public engagement must be explained to them in ways they can understand accompanied by examples, especially ones that show how their communities are benefiting.

• *Do not let perfect be the enemy of good.* Waiting until everything appears to be in place is likely to result in inaction. Accept that partnerships will not be perfect, projects will not be perfect, assessment will not be perfect, and alignment will not be perfect. However, making a solid, albeit imperfect, contribution to the community will provide the benefits described in this book.

CONCLUDING COMMENTS

Postsecondary institutions have important roles to play in advancing state, regional, and local progress. The public needs its local colleges and universities to produce well-educated graduates and cutting-edge research, but it needs more. Colleges and universities possess enormous intellectual capacity that, if harnessed in support of public progress, can make a significant contribution. In partnership with local leaders, colleges and universities can engage in applied research to help better understand the nature of the problem to be addressed. They can research best practices, create demonstration projects, provide technical assistance, and analyze policy approaches to the problem at hand.

Regardless of the community's wealth and demographics, it can accomplish more in partnership with the university than it can possibly accomplish alone.

Certainly public engagement enriches and enhances the community, but the campus is at least an equal beneficiary. Public engagement significantly enhances the education of the students and invigorates faculty scholarship. It adds cost, but it also can provide financial benefits, and for public institutions it can provide political benefits. Donors are more likely to contribute to a university that is working in partnership with the local community. The local press is more likely to feature positive stories highlighting the institution's public engagement. Community leaders are more likely to stand with the campus in advocating with the legislature if the campus is seen as standing with the community in addressing its challenges. Legislators who have seen their communities benefit from their local college or university's public engagement will be more supportive of the institution and more willing to protect its funding. These are not simply presumed benefits; they have been repeatedly experienced by a broad range of universities that are heavily engaged in their communities.

Now is the time for colleges and universities across the country to become even more indispensable to their communities and to the country as a whole. They must produce the highest-quality graduates, generate cutting-edge research, and apply their vast knowledge resources to strengthen their communities. Through this, they will be serving their institutional self-interest while serving the public good.

REFERENCES

Abes, E. S., Jackson, G., & Jones, S. R. (2002). Factors that motivate and deter faculty use of service-learning. *Michigan Journal of Community Service Learning, 9*(1), 5–17.

Alter, T. R., & Book, P. A. (2001). The engaged university: Reorganizing to serve the public good. *Metropolitan Universities: An International Forum, 12*(3), 30–40.

American Association of State Colleges and Universities. (2002). *Stepping forward as stewards of place: A guide for leading public engagement at state colleges and universities.* Washington, DC: Author.

Anderson, N. (2006, November 27). *Experts rate Wikipedia's accuracy higher than non-experts.* Retrieved June 23, 2010, from http://arstechnica.com/old/content/2006/11/8296.ars

Antonio, A. L., Astin, H. S., & Cress, C. M. (2000). Community service and higher education: A look at the nation's faculty. *Review of Higher Education, 23,* 373–398.

Astin, A. W. (1999). Promoting leadership, service, and democracy: What higher education can do. In R. G. Bringle, R. Games, & E. A. Malloy (Eds.), *Colleges and universities as citizens* (pp. 31–47). Boston: Allyn & Bacon.

Astin, A. W., Vogelgesang, L. J., Ikeda, E. K., & Yee, J. A. (2000). *How service learning affects students.* Los Angeles: Higher Education Research Institute, University of California.

Bain-Selbo, E. (2010, June). *Reclaiming the values discussion: Devising campus strategies.* Paper presented at the American Democracy Project National Meeting, Providence, RI.

Battistoni, R. M., Gelmon, S. B., Saltmarsh, J., Wergin, J., & Zlotkowski, E. (2003). *The engaged department toolkit.* Providence, RI: Campus Compact.

Beere, C. (2009). Understanding and enhancing the opportunities of community-campus partnerships. In L. R. Sandmann, C. H. Thornton, & A. J. Jaeger (Eds.), *New directions for higher education: Vol. 147. Institutionalizing community engagement in higher education: The first wave of Carnegie classified institutions* (pp. 55–63). San Francisco: Jossey-Bass.

Bentley, C., Dunfee, R., & Olsen, B. (2009). *Advancing a civic engagement agenda*. Washington, DC: American Association of State Colleges and Universities.

Bok, D. (1982). *Beyond the ivory tower: Social responsibilities of the modern university*. Cambridge, MA: Harvard University Press.

Boyer, E. L. (1990). *Scholarship reconsidered: Priorities of the professoriate*. Princeton, NJ: Carnegie Foundation for the Advancement of Teaching.

Boyer, E. L. (1996). The scholarship of engagement. *Journal of Public Service and Outreach, 1*(1), 11–20.

Boyte, H., & Hollander, E. (1999). *The Wingspread declaration on renewing the civic mission of the American research university*. Providence, RI: Campus Compact. Retrieved from http://www.compact.org/initiatives/civic-engagement-at-research-universities/wingspread-declaration-on-the-civic-responsibilities-of-research-universities/

Boyte, H. C. (2008). Against the current: Developing the civic agency of students. *Change: The Magazine of Higher Learning, 40*(3), 8–15.

Bringle, R. G., Games, R., & Malloy, E. A. (1999). Colleges and universities as citizens: Reflections. In R. G. Bringle, R. Games, & E. A. Malloy (Eds.), *Colleges and universities as citizens* (pp. 193–204). Boston: Allyn & Bacon.

Bringle, R. G., & Hatcher, J. A. (1995). A service-learning curriculum for faculty. *Michigan Journal of Community Service-Learning, 2*, 112–122.

Bringle, R. G., & Hatcher, J. A. (2002). Campus-community partnerships: The terms of engagement. *Journal of Social Issues, 58*, 503–516.

Bringle, R. G., & Hatcher, J. A. (2004). Indiana University-Purdue University Indianapolis: Advancing civic engagement through service-learning. In M. Langseth & W. M. Plater (Eds.), *Public work and the academy: An academic administrator's guide to civic engagement and service-learning* (pp. 125–145). Bolton, MA: Anker.

Brukardt, M. J., Holland, B., Percy, S. L., & Zimpher, N. (2004). *Calling the question: Is higher education ready to commit to community engagement?* Milwaukee: University of Wisconsin-Milwaukee. Retrieved from http://servicelearning.org/filemanager/download/215/calling_the_question.pdf

Burkhardt, J. C., & Lewis, R. (2005). Research universities working together to serve multiple communities: The committee on institutional cooperation engagement initiative. In P. A. Pasque, R. E. Smerek, B. Dwyer, N. Bowman, & B. L. Mallory (Eds.), *Higher education collaboratives for community engagement and improvement* (pp. 38–44). Ann Arbor: National Forum on Higher Education

for the Public Good. Retrieved from http://www.thenationalforum
.org/Docs/PDF/Wingspread_05_Final_Monograph.pdf

Cauley, K. (2000). Principle 1: Partners have agreed-upon mission, values, goals and measurable outcomes for the partnership. *Partnership Perspectives, 1*(2), 13–16. Retrieved from http://depts.washington .edu/ccph/pdf_files/summer1-f.pdf

Chambers, T. (2009). A continuum of approaches to service-learning within Canadian post-secondary education. *Canadian Journal of Higher Education, 39*(2), 77–100.

Chambers, T. C. (2005). The special role of higher education in society: As a public good for the public good. In A. J. Kezar, T. C. Chambers, & J. C. Burkhardt (Eds.), *Higher education for the public good: Emerging voices from a national movement* (pp. 3–22). San Francisco: Jossey-Bass.

Chávez, V. (2005). Silence speaks: The language of internalized oppression and privilege in community-based research. *Metropolitan Universities: An International Forum, 16*(1), 9–25.

Checkoway, B. (2001). Renewing the civic mission of the American research university. *Journal of Higher Education, 72*(2), 125–147.

Checkoway, B. (2003). Strategies for involving the faculty in civic renewal. *Higher Education Exchange*, 42–53. Retrieved from http://www.kettering.org/File Library/HEX/HEX2003.pdf

Clark, K. (2008, September 4). A failing financial aid system keeps students out of college. *U.S. News and World Report*. Retrieved May 27, 2009, from http://www.usnews.com/articles/education/2008/09/ 04/a-failing-financial-aid-system-keeps-students-out-of-college .html

Colby, A., Beaumont, E., Ehrlich, T., & Corngold, J. (2007). *Educating for democracy: Preparing undergraduates for responsible political engagement.* San Francisco: Jossey-Bass.

Collins, J. (2001). *Good to great: Why some companies make the leap... and others don't.* New York: HarperCollins.

Collins, J. C., & Porras, J. I. (1994). *Built to last: Successful habits of visionary companies.* New York: HarperBusiness.

Commager, H. S. (1960, September 17). Is ivy necessary? *Saturday Review, 43*, 69–70, 86–89.

Connors, K., & Seifer, S. D. (Eds.). (2000). Partnership perspectives. *Community-Campus Partnerships for Health, 1*(2). Retrieved from http://depts.washington.edu/ccph/pdf_files/summer1-f.pdf

Creighton, S. J. (2006). *Community partner indicators of engagement: An action research study on campus-community partnership.* (Doctoral dissertation, Antioch University). Retrieved from http://

www.ohiolink.edu/etd/send-pdf.cgi/Creighton%20Sean%20J.pdf?
antioch1158867184

Curry, B. K. (1992). *Instituting enduring innovations: Achieving continuity of change in higher education.* (ASHE-ERIC Higher Education Report no. 7). Washington, DC: George Washington University, School of Education and Human Development.

Davies, G. K. (2006, December). *Setting a public agenda for higher education in the states: Lessons learned from the national collaborative for higher education policy.* National Collaborative for Higher Education Policy. http://www.highereducation.org/reports/public_agenda/public_agenda.pdf

Diamond, R. M. (1999). *Aligning faculty rewards with institutional mission: Statements, policies, and guidelines.* Bolton, MA: Anker.

Diamond, R. M. (2004). *Preparing for promotion, tenure, and annual review: A faculty guide* (2nd ed.). Bolton, MA: Anker.

Diamond, R. M., & Adam, B. E. (Eds.). (2000). *The disciplines speak II: More statements on rewarding the scholarly, professional, and creative work of faculty.* Washington, DC: American Association for Higher Education.

Dominick, C. A. (1990). Revising the institutional mission. In D. W. Steeples (Ed.), *Managing change in higher education.* New Directions for Higher Education, Vol. 71 (pp. 29–36). San Francisco: Jossey-Bass.

Driscoll, A. (2008). Carnegie's community-engagement classification: Intentions and insights. *Change: The Magazine of Higher Learning, 40*(1), 38–41.

Driscoll, A. (2009). Carnegie's new community engagement classification: Affirming higher education's role in community. In L. R. Sandmann, C. H. Thornton, & A. J. Jaeger (Eds.), *Institutionalizing community engagement in higher education: The first wave of Carnegie classified institutions.* New Directions for Higher Education, Vol. 147 (pp. 5–12). San Francisco: Jossey-Bass.

Duderstadt, J. J. (2000). *A university for the 21st century.* Ann Arbor: University of Michigan Press.

Duderstadt, J. J. (2001, January 12). *Preparing future faculty for future universities.* Paper presented at the annual meeting of the Association of American Colleges and Universities, New Orleans. Retrieved on November 5, 2008, from http://milproj.ummu.umich.edu/publications/aacu_text/aacu_text.pdf

Duderstadt, J. J., & Womack, F. W. (2003). *The future of the public university in America: Beyond the crossroads.* Baltimore: Johns Hopkins University Press.

Dunlap, M. R., & Webster, N. (2009). Enhancing intercultural competence through civic engagement. In B. Jacoby (Ed.), *Civic engagement in higher education: Concepts and practices* (pp. 140–153). San Francisco: Jossey-Bass.

Eckel, P., Green, M., Hill, B., & Mallon, W. (1999). *On change III: Take charge of change: A primer for colleges and universities* (pp. 35–43). Washington, DC: American Council on Education. Retrieved from http://www.acenet.edu/bookstore/pdf/on-change/on-changeIII.pdf

Eckel, P., Hill, B., & Green, M. (1998). *On change: En route to transformation: Vol. 1.* Washington, DC: American Council on Education.

Edwards, R. (1999). The academic department: How does it fit into the university reform agenda? *Change: The Magazine of Higher Learning, 31*(5), 17–27.

Exley, R. J., & Young, J. B. (2004). Miami-Dade Community College: Past, present, and future of service-learning. In M. Langseth & W. M. Plater (Eds.), *Public work and the academy: An academic administrator's guide to civic engagement and service-learning* (pp. 179–195). Bolton, MA: Anker.

Eyler, J., & Giles, D. E., Jr. (1999). *Where's the learning in service-learning?* San Francisco: Jossey-Bass.

Eyler, J. S., Giles, D. E., Jr., Stenson, C. M., & Gray, C. J. (2001). *At a glance: What we know about the effects of service learning on college students, faculty, institutions and communities, 1993–2000* (3rd ed.). Nashville: Vanderbilt University. Retrieved from http://www.compact.org/resources/downloads/aag.pdf

Farmer, D. W. (1990). Strategies for change. In D. W. Steeples (Ed.), *Managing change in higher education.* New Directions for Higher Education, Vol. 71 (pp. 7–18). San Francisco: Jossey-Bass.

Farrell, C. (2009, May 21). The rise of higher education abroad. *Marketplace Money.* Retrieved May 27, 2009, from http://www.publicradio.org/columns/marketplace/farrell/2009/05/the_rise_of_higher_education_abroad.html

Fish, S. (2008). *Save the world on your own time.* New York: Oxford University Press.

Fisher, R., Fabricant, M., & Simmons, L. (2004). Understanding contemporary university-community connections: Context, practice, and challenges. In T. Soska & A.K.J. Butterfield (Eds.), *University-community partnerships: Universities in civic engagement* (pp. 13–34). Binghamton, NY: Hawthorne Social Work Practice Press.

Fogelman, E. (2002). Civic engagement at the University of Minnesota. *Journal of Public Affairs, 6* (Supplemental Issue 1: Civic Engagement and Higher Education), 103–118.

Frey, B. B., Lohmeier, J. H., Lee, S. W., & Tollefson, N. (2006). Measuring collaboration among grant partners. *American Journal of Evaluation*, *27*, 383–392.

Furco, A. (2001). Advancing service-learning at research universities. *New directions for higher education*, *114*, 67–78.

Furco, A., & Holland, B. A. (2004). Institutionalizing service-learning in higher education: Issues and strategies for chief academic officers. In M. Langseth & W. M. Plater (Eds.), *Public work and the academy: An academic administrator's guide to civic engagement and service-learning* (pp. 23–39). Bolton, MA: Anker.

Gamson, Z. F. (1997). Higher education and rebuilding civic life. *Change: The Magazine of Higher Learning*, *29*(1), 13.

Gelmon, S. B., & Agre-Kippenhan, S. (2002a). A developmental framework for supporting evolving faculty roles for community engagement. *Journal of Public Affairs*, *6* (Supplemental Issue 1: Civic Engagement and Higher Education), 161–182.

Gelmon, S. B., & Agre-Kippenhan, S. (2002b). Promotion, tenure, and the engaged scholar: Keeping the scholarship of engagement in the review process. *AAHE Bulletin*, *54*(5), 7–11.

Gelmon, S. B., Holland, B. A., Driscoll, A., Spring, A., & Kerrigan, S. (2001). *Assessing service-learning and civic engagement: Principles and techniques* (3rd ed.). Providence, RI: Campus Compact.

Gelmon, S. B., Seifer, S. D., Kauper-Brown, J., & Mikkelsen, M. (2005). *Building capacity for community engagement: Institutional self-assessment*. Seattle: Community-Campus Partnerships for Health. Retrieved from http://depts.washington.edu/ccph/pdf_files/self-assessment-copyright.pdf

Giles, J. (2005). Internet encyclopaedias go head to head. *Nature*, *438*(7070), 900–901.

Glassick, C. E., Huber, M. T., & Maeroff, G. I. (1997). *Scholarship assessed: Evaluation of the professoriate*. San Francisco: Jossey-Bass.

Golde, C. M., & Dore, T. M. (2004). The survey of doctoral education and career preparation: The importance of disciplinary contexts. In D. H. Wulff & A. E. Austin (Eds.), *Paths to the professoriate: Strategies for enriching the preparation of future faculty* (pp. 19–45). San Francisco: Jossey-Bass.

Goodnough, A. (2009, May 8). Slump revives town-gown divide across U.S. *New York Times*. Retrieved December 29, 2009 from http://www.nytimes.com/2009/05/09/education/09towngown.html?_r=1

Hartley, M., Harkavy, I., & Benson, L. (2005). Putting down roots in the groves of academe: The challenges of institutionalizing service-learning. In D. W. Butin (Ed.), *Service-learning in higher education:*

Critical issues and directions (pp. 205–222). New York: Palgrave Macmillan.

Hatcher, J. A., & Bringle, R. G. (1997). Reflections: Bridging the gap between service and learning. *College Teaching, 45*(4), 153–158.

Henderson, S., Fair, M., Sather, P., & Dewey, B. (2008). Service-learning research as a feedback loop for faculty development. In M. A. Bowdon, S. H. Billig, & B. A. Holland (Eds.), *Scholarship for sustaining service-learning and civic engagement* (pp. 113–137). Charlotte, NC: Information Age Publishing.

Higher Learning Commission. (2003). *Handbook of accreditation* (3rd ed.) (pp. 3.1–6). Chicago: Author. Retrieved on June 13, 2009, from http://www.ncahlc.org/download/Handbook03.pdf

Hillery, G. A., Jr. (1955). Definitions of community: Areas of agreement. *Rural Sociology, 20*(2), 111–123.

Hitt, J. C. (2009, November). *Discovering our futures: The power of partnerships*. President-to-Presidents Lecture at the Annual Meeting of the American Association of State Colleges and Universities, San Antonio, Texas.

Holland, B. A. (1999). From murky to meaningful: The role of mission in institutional change. In R. G. Bringle, R. Games, & E. A. Mally (Eds.), *Colleges and universities as citizens* (pp. 48–73). Boston: Allyn & Bacon.

Holland, B. A. (2001). Toward a definition and characterization of the engaged campus: Six cases. *Metropolitan Universities: An International Forum, 12*(3), 20–29.

Holland, B. A. (2005). Reflections on community-campus partnerships: What has been learned? What are the next challenges? In P. A. Pasque, R. E. Smerek, B. Dwyer, N. Bowman, & B. L. Mallory (Eds.), *Higher education collaboratives for community engagement and improvement* (pp. 10–17). Ann Arbor: National Forum on Higher Education for the Public Good. Retrieved from http://www.thenationalforum.org/Docs/PDF/Wingspread_05_Final_Monograph.pdf

Holland, B. A., & Gelmon, S. B. (1998). The state of the "engaged campus": What have we learned about building and sustaining university-community partnerships? *AAHE Bulletin, 51*(2), 3–6.

Howard, J.P.F. (1998). Academic service learning: A counternormative pedagogy. In R. Rhoads & J. Howard (Eds.), *New directions for teaching and learning: Vol. 73. Academic service learning: A pedagogy of action and reflection* (pp. 21–30). San Francisco: Jossey-Bass.

Jacoby, B. (Ed.). (2009). *Civic engagement in higher education: Concepts and practices*. San Francisco: Jossey-Bass.

Jones, D. P. (2005). Shaping state policy to encourage stewardship of place. *Metropolitan Universities: An International Forum, 16*(4), 11–27.

Judd, A. H., & Adams, M. S. (2008). Lessons learned from a decade in a university-community partnership: Keys to successful engagement and outreach. *Journal of Higher Education Outreach and Engagement, 12*(3), 117–127.

Kecskes, K. (Ed.). (2006). *Engaging departments: Moving faculty culture from private to public, individual to collective focus for the common good.* Bolton, MA: Anker.

Kecskes, K. J., Gelmon, S. B., & Spring, A. (2006). Creating engaged departments: A program for organizational and faculty development. In S. Chadwick-Blossey & D. R. Robertson (Eds.), *To improve the academy: Vol. 24. Resources for faculty, instructional and organizational development* (pp. 147–165). Bolton, MA: Anker.

Kellogg Commission on the Future of State and Land-Grant Universities. (1999). *Returning to our roots: The engaged institution.* Washington, DC: National Association of State Universities and Land-Grant Colleges. Retrieved on March 10, 2009, from http://www.aplu.org/NetCommunity/Document.Doc?id=183

Kellogg Commission on the Future of State and Land-Grant Universities. (2000). *Renewing the covenant: Learning, discovery, and engagement in a new age and different world.* Washington, DC: National Association of State Universities and Land-Grant Colleges. Retrieved from http://www.aplu.org/NetCommunity/Document.Doc?id=186

Kelshaw, T., Lazarus, F., Minier, J., & Associates. (2009). *Partnerships for service-learning: Impacts on communities and students.* San Francisco: Jossey-Bass.

Kentucky Council on Postsecondary Education. (n.d.). *Five questions of postsecondary reform.* Retrieved on July 30, 2009, from http://www.cpe.ky.gov/planning/5Qs/default.htm

Kerr, C. (1991). *The great transformation in higher education 1960–1980.* Albany: State University of New York Press.

Kezar, A. J., Chambers, T. C., & Burkhardt, J. C. (Eds.). (2005). *Higher education for the public good: Emerging voices from a national movement.* San Francisco: Jossey-Bass.

Klotsche, J. M. (1966). *The urban university and the future of our cities.* New York: Harper & Row.

Kotter, J. P. (1995, March-April). Leading change: Why transformation efforts fail. *Harvard Business Review, 73*(2), 59–67.

Kotter, J. P. (1996). *Leading change.* Boston, MA: Harvard Business School Press.

Kuh, G. D., Kinzie, J., Schuh, J. H., Whitt, E. J., & Associates. (2005). *Student success in college: Creating conditions that matter*. San Francisco: Jossey-Bass.

Leiderman, S., Furco, A., Zapf, J., & Goss, M. (2003). *Building partnerships with college campuses: Community perspectives*. Washington, DC: Council of Independent Colleges. (ERIC Document Reproduction Service No. ED 481879)

Levine, A. (1980). *Why innovation fails*. Albany: State University of New York Press.

Lynton, E. A. (1996). Reversing the telescope: Viewing individual activities within a collective context. *Metropolitan Universities: An International Forum, 7*(3), 41–55.

Lynton, E. A., & Elman, S. E. (1987). *New priorities for the university: Meeting society's needs for applied knowledge and competent individuals*. San Francisco: Jossey-Bass.

Marcelo, P. (2009, May 3). Providence seeks student tax at private colleges. *Providence Journal*. Retrieved on May 4, 2009, from http://www.projo.com/news/content/STUDENT_TAX_05–03–09_U5E75IG_v53.34233cd.html

McCormick, A. C. (2009, April 22). *Accountability and improvement: Don't let proving you're good interfere with getting better*. Paper presented at the NSSE User Workshop, Highland Heights, KY.

McDavid, J. C., & Hawthorn, L.R.L. (2006). *Program evaluation and performance measurement: An introduction to practice*. Thousand Oaks, CA: Sage.

Meister, R. J., & Strain, C. R. (2004). DePaul University: Strategic planning and service-learning. In M. Langseth & W. M. Plater (Eds.), *Public work and the academy: An academic administrator's guide to civic engagement and service-learning* (pp. 101–123). Bolton, MA: Anker.

Mikkelsen, M., Gelmon, S. B., Seifer, S. D., & Kauper-Brown, J. (2005). *Community-engaged scholarship for health collaborative: Review, tenure and promotion analysis protocol*. Seattle: Community-Campus Partnerships for Health. Retrieved on July 21, 2008, from http://depts.washington.edu/ccph/pdf_files/RPT%20Analysis%20Protocol.pdf

Moore, M. T. (2009, November 15). Pittsburgh eyes students' wallets. *USA Today*. Retrieved on January 6, 2009, from http://www.usatoday.com/news/education/2009–11–15-tuition-tax_N.htm

Morreale, S. P., & Applegate, J. L. (2006). Engaged disciplines: How national disciplinary societies support the scholarship of engagement. In K. Kecskes (Ed.), *Engaging departments: Moving faculty culture from private to public, individual to collective focus for the common good* (pp. 264–277). Bolton, MA: Anker.

Morton, K. (1995). The irony of service: Charity, project and social change in service-learning. *Michigan Journal of Community Service Learning, 2,* 19–32.

Morton, K. (1996). Issues related to integrating service-learning into the curriculum. In B. Jacoby (Ed.), *Service-learning in higher education: Concepts and practices* (pp. 276–296). San Francisco: Jossey-Bass.

National Science Foundation, Division of Science Resources Statistics. (2008). National patterns of R&D resources: 2007 data update. (NSF 08–318). Retrieved from http://www.nsf.gov/statistics/ nsf08318/

Northern Kentucky University. (n.d.). *Faculty policies and procedures handbook* (pp. 23–32). Retrieved on March 12, 2009, from http:// academicaffairs.nku.edu/docs/Working_Master_Facul.pdf

Northern Kentucky University. (2006). *Aligning for public engagement: Laying the foundation.* Retrieved from http://pod.nku.edu/ shapebook.pdf

Northern Kentucky University. (2009). *Undergraduate catalog, 2009–2010* (pp. 3–4). Retrieved on January 22, 2010, from http://access.nku.edu/Catalog/2010catalog/AboutNKU.htm

Novak, R., & Johnston, S. W. (2005). Trusteeship and the public good. In A. J. Kezar, T. C. Chambers, & J. C. Burkhardt (Eds.), *Higher education for the public good: Emerging voices from a national movement* (pp. 87–101). San Francisco: Jossey-Bass.

O'Meara, K. A. (2008). Motivation for faculty community engagement: Learning from exemplars. *Journal of Higher Education Outreach and Engagement, 12*(1), 7–29.

Pascarella, E. T., & Terenzini, P. T. (2005). *How college affects students: A third decade of research* (Vol. 2). San Francisco: Jossey-Bass.

Percy, S. L., Zimpher, N. L., & Brukhardt, M. J. (2006). *Creating a new kind of university: Institutionalizing community-university engagement.* Bolton, MA: Anker.

Pew Partnership for Civic Change. (2004). *New directions in civic engagement: University avenue meets main street.* Charlottesville, VA: Author. Retrieved from http://www.pew-partnership.org/ resources/newdirections.html

Plater, W. (2004). What recognitions and rewards should a campus create to promote civic engagement of students? In AASCU (Ed.), *Democracy and civic education: A guide for higher education* (pp. 75–81). Washington, DC: Authors.

Putnam, R. D. (2000). *Bowling alone: The collapse and revival of American Community.* New York: Simon & Schuster.

Ramaley, J. A. (1996). Large-scale institutional change to implement an urban university mission: Portland State University. *Journal of Urban Affairs, 18*(2), 139–151.

Ramaley, J. A. (2003). Seizing the moment: Creating a changed society and university through outreach. *Journal of Higher Education Outreach and Engagement, 8*(1), 13–27.

Ramaley, J. A. (2005). Scholarship for the public good: Living in Pasteur's Quadrant. In A. J. Kezar, T. C. Chambers, & J. C. Burkhardt (Eds.), *Higher education for the public good: Emerging voices from a national movement* (pp. 166–181). San Francisco: Jossey-Bass.

Redlawsk, D. P., Rice, T., & Associates. (2009). *Civic service: Service-learning with state and local government partners.* San Francisco: Jossey-Bass.

Rhodes, F.H.T. (2001). *The creation of the future: The role of the American university.* Ithaca, NY: Cornell University Press.

Rice, R. E. (2005a). The future of the scholarly work of faculty. In K. A. O'Meara, & R. E. Rice (Eds.), *Faculty priorities reconsidered: Rewarding multiple forms of scholarship* (pp. 303–312). San Francisco: Jossey-Bass.

Rice, R. E. (2005b). "Scholarship reconsidered": History and context. In K. A. O'Meara & R. E. Rice (Eds.), *Faculty priorities reconsidered: Rewarding multiple forms of scholarship* (pp. 17–31). San Francisco: Jossey-Bass.

Robertson, P. J. (1998). Interorganizational relationships: Key issues for integrated services. In J. McCroskey & S. D. Einbinder (Eds.), *Universities and communities: Remaking professional and interprofessional education for the next century* (pp. 67–87). Westport, CT: Praeger.

Rodin, J. (2007). *The university & urban revival: Out of the ivory tower and into the streets.* Philadelphia: University of Pennsylvania Press.

Rowley, D. J., Lujan, H. D., & Dolence, M. G. (1997). *Strategic change in colleges and universities: Planning to survive and prosper.* San Francisco: Jossey-Bass.

Royse, D., Thyer, B. A., & Padgett, D. K. (2010). *Program evaluation: An introduction* (5th ed.). Belmont, CA: Wadsworth Cengage Learning.

Russell, A. B. (1992). *Faculty workload: State and system perspectives.* Denver, CO: State Higher Education Executive Officers. (ERIC Document Reproduction Service No. ED 356728)

Saltmarsh, J. (2002). Introduction from the Guest Editor. *Journal of Public Affairs, 6* (Supplemental Issue 1: Civic Engagement and Higher Education), v–ix.

Sandmann, L. (2008, November). *Engaged scholarship in context*. Paper presented at the Third Annual Kentucky Engagement Conference, Lexington.

Scheibel, J., Bowley, E. M., & Jones, S. (2005). *The promise of partnerships: Tapping into the college as a community asset*. Providence, RI: Campus Compact.

Schneider, C. G. (2005). Liberal education and the civic engagement gap. In A. J. Kezar, T. C. Chambers, & J. C. Burkhardt (Eds.), *Higher education for the public good: Emerging voices from a national movement* (pp. 127–145). San Francisco: Jossey-Bass.

Schön, D. A. (1983). *The reflective practitioner: How professionals think in action*. New York: Basic Books.

Schön, D. A. (1995). Knowing-in-action: The new scholarship requires a new epistemology. *Change: The Magazine of Higher Learning, 27*(6), 26–34.

Seldin, P., & Miller, J. E. (2009). *The academic portfolio: A practical guide to documenting teaching, research, and service*. San Francisco: Jossey-Bass.

Shulman, L. S. (1997). Professing the liberal arts. In R. Orrill (Ed.), *Education and democracy: Re-imagining liberal learning in America* (pp. 151–173). New York: The College Entrance Examination Board.

Stanton, T. (2008). New times demand new scholarship. *Education, Citizenship and Social Justice, 3*(1), 19–42.

State Higher Education Executive Officers. (2008). *State higher education finance FY 2008*. Retrieved on December 29, 2009, from http://www.sheeo.org/finance/shef_fy08.pdf

Stoecker, R., & Tryon, E. A. (Eds.). (2009). *The unheard voices: Community organizations and service learning*. Philadelphia: Temple University Press.

Strand, K., Marullo, S., Cutforth, N., Stoecker, R., & Donohue, P. (2003a). *Community-based research and higher education: Principles and practices*. San Francisco: Jossey-Bass.

Strand, K., Marullo, S., Cutforth, N., Stoecker, R., & Donohue, P. (2003b). Principles of best practice for community-based research. *Michigan Journal of Community Service Learning, 9*(3), 5–15.

Surowiecki, J. (2004). *The wisdom of crowds: Why the many are smarter than the few and how collective wisdom shapes business, economies, societies, and nations*. New York: Doubleday.

Torres, J. (Ed.). (2000). *Benchmarks for campus/community partnerships*. Providence, RI: Campus Compact.

U.S. Census Bureau. (2009). *2009 statistical abstract.* Retrieved from http://www.census.gov/compendia/statab/cats/education/ higher_education_institutions_and_enrollment.html

Votruba, J. C. (1996). The university's social covenant: A vision for the future. *Adult Learning, 7*(3), 28–29.

Votruba, J. C. (2004). *Leading the engaged institution.* President-to-Presidents Lecture at the Annual Meeting of the American Association of State Colleges and Universities, Charleston, South Carolina.

Votruba, J. C. (2005). Leading the engaged institution. In A. J. Kezar, T. C. Chambers, & J. C. Burkhardt (Eds.), *Higher education for the public good: Emerging voices from a national movement* (pp. 263–271). San Francisco: Jossey-Bass.

Walshok, M. L. (1999). Strategies for building the infrastructure that supports the engaged campus. In R. G. Bringle, R. Games, & E. A. Malloy (Eds.), *Colleges and universities as citizens* (pp. 74–95). Boston, MA: Allyn & Bacon.

Weerts, D. J., & Sandmann, L. R. (2008). Building a two-way street: Challenges and opportunities for community engagement at research universities. *Review of Higher Education, 32*(1), 73–106.

Welch, M. (2009). Moving from service-learning to civic engagement. In B. Jacoby (Ed.), *Civic engagement in higher education: Concepts and practices* (pp. 175–195). San Francisco: Jossey-Bass.

Wergin, J. F. (2003). *Departments that work: Building and sustaining cultures of excellence in academic programs.* Boston: Anker.

Wilkinson, R. G., & Pickett, K. (2010). *The spirit level: Why greater equality makes societies stronger.* New York: Bloomsbury Press.

Willis, J., Peresie, J., Waldref, V., & Stockmann, D. (2003). The undergraduate perspective on community-based research. *Michigan Journal of Community Service Learning, 9*(3), 36–43.

Worthen, B. R., Sanders, J. R., & Fitzpatrick, J. L. (2004). *Program evaluation: Alternative approaches and practical guidelines* (3rd ed.). Boston: Allyn & Bacon.

Yett, J. R. (2006). Geology, children, and institutional change in southern California. In K. Kecskes (Ed.), *Engaging departments: Moving faculty culture from private to public, individual to collective focus for the common good* (pp. 76–88). San Francisco: Jossey-Bass.

Yudof, M. G. (2008, November). *Proving the value of higher education.* Speech at the meeting of the Commonwealth Club of California. Retrieved January 14, 2010, from http://www.universityofcalifornia .edu/president/speeches/yudof_commonwealthclubspeech.pdf

Zlotkowski, E. (Ed.). (multiple dates). *Service learning in the disciplines.* Sterling, VA: Stylus.

Zlotkowski, E. (Ed.). (1998). *Successful service-learning programs.* Bolton, MA: Anker.

Zlotkowski, E. (1999). Pedagogy and engagement. In R. G. Bringle, R. Games, & E. A. Malloy (Eds.), *College and universities as citizens* (pp. 96–120). Boston: Allyn & Bacon.

Zlotkowski, E. (2002a). September 11, 2001, as a teachable moment. In C. M. Wehlburg & S. Chadwick-Blossey (Eds.), *To improve the academy: Vol. 21. Resources for faculty, instructional, and organization development* (pp. 3–20). Bolton, MA: Anker.

Zlotkowski, E. (2002b). Social crises and the faculty response. *Journal of Public Affairs, 6* (Supplemental Issue 1: Civic Engagement and Higher Education), 1–18.

INDEX

243